WINCHESTER EXCAVATIONS

VOLUME II: 1949--1960

EXCAVATIONS IN THE SUBURBS

AND

THE WESTERN PART OF THE TOWN

BY

JOHN COLLIS, M.A., Ph. D., F.S.A.
University of Sheffield

WITH

K. J. BARTON AND OTHERS

CITY OF WINCHESTER
1978

The maps on pages 5, 12, 28, 41, 42, 62, 110, 142, 150, 163, 187, 198, 246, 264 are based upon the Ordnance Survey maps with the permission of the Controller of Her Majesty's Stationery Office. Crown Copyright Reserved.

ISBN: 0 86135 000 6
ISSN: 0140—7651

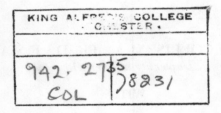
Printed in England by Stephen Austin and Sons Ltd, Hertford

To my parents

For years of muddy boots, and pots drying on the draining board

LIST OF CONTRIBUTORS

Gina D. Adams
Winchester Research Unit
13 Parchment Street
Winchester

Kenneth Barton, M.Phil., FMA, FSA
Hampshire County Museum Service
Chilcomb House
Bar End
Winchester

Mr C. E. Blunt
Ramsbury Hill
Ramsbury
Marlborough
Wiltshire

Miss Dorothy Charlesworth, M.A., FSA
Inspectorate of Ancient Monuments
Fortress House
Savile Row
London W1

Mr Graham S. Cowles
Sub-department of Ornithology
British Museum (Natural History)
Tring
Hertfordshire

Miss Jennie Coy
Faunal Remains Project
Department of Archaeology
University of Southampton
Southampton

Mr Geoffrey Brian Dannell, B.Sc.(Econ),
    FCA, FSA
42 Mymms Drive
Brookmans Park
Hatfield
Hertfordshire

Miss Brenda Dickinson, B.A.
Department of Archaeology
University of Leeds
Leeds

Nigel Fradgley
Winchester Research Unit
13 Parchment Street
Winchester

Ian H. Goodall
Royal Commission on Historical
    Monuments (England)
The White House
Clifton
York

v

Nick Griffiths
1 Oxford Road
Banbury
Oxfordshire

B. R. Hartley
Department of Archaeology
The University of Leeds
Leeds

John W. Hedges, B.Sc.(Hons), M.A.,
    FSA(Scot.)
North of Scotland Archaeological Services
South Ronaldsay
Orkney

David A. Hinton
Department of Archaeology
University of Southampton
Southampton

Professor Frank Hodson, Ph.D.
Department of Geology
University of Southampton
Southampton

Vivien Jones
Winchester Research Unit
13 Parchment Street
Winchester

Dr Derek Keene
Winchester Research Unit
13 Parchment Street
Winchester

Suzanne Keene, F.I.I.C.
Long Park
Crawley
Winchester

Miss Joan Liversidge, FSA
Cambridge University Museum of
    Archaeology and Ethnology
Cambridge

Dr W. H. Manning
Department of Archaeology
University College
Cardiff

Stuart May
102 Holly Road
Aldershot
Hampshire

Jennifer Price
Salisbury and South Wiltshire
    Museum
St Ann Street
Salisbury

Mrs Jacqueline G. Qualmann, B.A.
Office of the Winchester Rescue
    Archaeologist
Little Minster Street
Winchester

Kenneth E. Qualmann
Winchester Rescue Archaeologist
Little Minster Street
Winchester

Adrian B. Rance, B.A., AMA
Southampton City Museums
Southampton

Richard Reece, B.Sc., D.Phil., FSA
Institute of Archaeology
31-34 Gordon Square
London WC1

Pauline Sheppard
Winchester Research Unit
13 Parchment Street
Winchester

Josephine C. Turquet
9 Stanlake Villas
London W12

E. J. Wayman
4 Christina Terrace
Merchants Road
Bristol 8

-:-Calvin Wells
Castle Museum
Norwich

Mr Ian West, M.Sc.
Geology Department
Southampton University
Southampton

Mr Alwyne Wheeler
British Museum (Natural History)
Cromwell Road
London SW7

CONTENTS

LIST OF PLATES

LIST OF FIGURES

xii LIST OF FIGURES

LIST OF TABLES

PREFACE

The preparation of the first series of archaeological excavations in Winchester has proved both a sorrow and a pleasure. A sorrow, because much of what we did in the 1950s was hampered by lack of time, of knowledge, of money, and of trained personnel, and represents only the first stumblings towards the understanding of the complexities and techniques of urban excavations. Many of the excavations are an embarrassment to remember, but the information they produced is still worthy of record.

And yet a pleasure, at least for myself, who, as a young boy, could be left on shopping days looking into the excavations in Middle Brook Street, or later, simply abandoned during holidays and weekends to digging in the town. It was with little difficulty that I identified my first sherd of samian from the Westgate Car Park twenty years ago! But my continuous involvement during my school years up to 1961, and my sporadic connections supervising subsequent excavations for Martin Biddle, now lays on me the task of publishing this earlier work, as I am the only person with the facilities to do it, and the intimate knowledge of the sites necessary to carry it through.

I owe much to the various directors of excavations during those years: Dr Isobel Smith, who first accepted me as a volunteer; Miss Jean Cook and Mr Ian Cossar who gave me free rein to work on archaeological material; Mr Tony Ball, the only other volunteer continuously involved in the work; and finally—Mr Martin Biddle, who taught us all to think on a larger and more ambitious scale.

The uniting link throughout has been Mr Frank Cottrill, until recently the curator of the City Museums. It was he who initiated the scientific excavations in the city in 1949, soon after his arrival. By a policy of inviting young archaeologists to Winchester to direct excavations, he was able to organize the more substantial work in the 1950s, mainly rescue work in advance of the new road constructions in St George's Street. During this period he successfully established within the city a climate of opinion favourable to archaeology, so that it could readily accommodate the much more extensive researches of the 1960s. Yet during this time Mr Cottrill was meticulously recording chance finds revealed in service trenches, house foundations, and shop basements, a hotch-potch of information, which is nevertheless fundamental to our understanding of the city's development and which we can only now start to synthesize properly. Even though Mr Cottrill himself never found time to sort and publish his results, this series of publications is the direct outcome of his policy of encouragement towards schoolboys and students such as Barry Cunliffe and myself.

Since his retirement in 1973, his successor Miss Elizabeth Lewis has energetically supported the publication work and supervised the negotiations with the publishers. To Mr Adrian Rance I owe a special debt for his total re-organization of the Museum's collections. After the years of chaos when material was coming in too quickly to be adequately marked, boxed, let alone catalogued, he has ordered, reboxed, renumbered, and indexed the material. Without his periodic rediscovery of a vital plan or a lost bag of finds, our work would have been severely hampered.

Our relationships with the Winchester Research Unit have been particularly fruitful, and there has been a continuous interchange of ideas and information from which we have gained more than we have given. The director, Mr Martin Biddle, has not merely been a source of encouragement, but has arranged for the specialist reports on much of the material, and freely

opened his archives for our use. All of his staff have assisted our work in various ways: Mr
Fred Aldsworth gave considerable help in the preparation of the plans; Dr Derek Keene with
historical problems; Miss Katherine Barclay with pottery; and Mr Edward Harris with the
layer 'Matrix'. Martin Biddle, Derek Keene, and Adrian Rance have all given valuable
comments on the final text. I am also very grateful to Mr Kenneth Qualmann of the City
Archaeology Office who has discussed with me the results of his recent work in the city.

The finds have been resorted and boxed by means of a series of assaults usually of one or
two week's duration by a group of volunteers mainly working under Messrs John Reading,
David Whipp, and Stuart May, helped by the Museum staff. Stuart May also drew all the
plans, which involved much tedious work correlating notes and manuscript drawings. Due to
the problems of organizing the drawing of finds on a part-time basis over a number of years, it
has not proved possible to employ a single draughtsman. Various pots have been drawn by Mr
Eric Wayman and myself. However, we have relied heavily on Mr Nick Griffiths for many of
the pot drawings, and he is also responsible for all of the excellent small-finds illustrations. To
all those who have contributed specialist information and reports, I hope the appearance of
their names in the list of contributors will indicate my indebtedness. But especially I would
like to mention Mr Ken Barton, who, in preparing his contribution on the medieval pottery,
has systematically worked through all the bags of finds and whose comments are indistin-
guishably interwoven throughout the text.

Finally I would like to thank the various bodies who have provided the finance for this
work, especially the Winchester City Council through its Museums and Libraries Committee,
and since re-organization the Amenities Committee of the Winchester District Council. Two-
thirds of the publication cost of this volume has been supplied by the Department of the
Environment.

John Collis
Department of Prehistory and Archaeology
University of Sheffield

September 1976

ABBREVIATIONS

Ant. J.	*The Antiquaries Journal*
Camulodunum	Hawkes and Hull 1947
CK	Carson, Hill and Kent 1972, part II
Clausentum	Cotton and Gathercole 1958
HK	Carson, Hill and Kent 1972, part I
Orchard Street	K. J. Barton, in Down and Rule 1971: 153-164
PHFC	*Proceedings of the Hampshire Field Club*
RIC	Mattingly *et al.* (eds) 1923-1967

CHAPTER 1

INTRODUCTION

Contents

The original title given to the first volume is being retained for the series despite the inclusion of other material in this and subsequent volumes. With two separate series of volumes at present in production on excavations in Winchester, we hope this title will make it clear that the reports on the major excavations carried out between 1961 and 1971 by Mr Martin Biddle will be published in the other series, *Winchester Studies*. The main intention of *Winchester Excavations* is the publication of the excavations and rescue work carried out under the aegis of the City Museum. Though museum-sponsored excavation work in the city ceased in 1961, rescue observations by the museum staff have continued even after the establishment of the Winchester Research Unit, and only in 1972 was this task handed over to the City Rescue Archaeologist. Thus we shall be including a certain amount of material excavated after 1960.

A simple division of the work into 'Museum' sites and 'Research Unit' sites has, however, not proved possible. Some sites on which the Unit carried out excavations later yielded rescue material to the Museum, and some rescue work carried out by the Unit ties in better with the Museum sites. The decision on which site is included in which series is therefore sometimes based on criteria other than that of who actually did the work. Since 1972 the City Rescue Archaeologist, with the Winchester Archaeological Rescue Group, has been excavating in the city. *Winchester Excavations* will be continued for the majority of his reports, and where suitable some material will even be included alongside the earlier excavations, as for example the St Paul's Church report in this particular volume. Thus, between them, *Winchester Studies* and *Winchester Excavations* will contain all the major excavations in Winchester. In addition, some earlier discoveries, such as those from Highcliffe, warrant inclusion for the more complete picture they give in certain areas.

As they appear, each of the volumes will be sub-titled to give a better impression of the actual contents. Logically Volume II should have continued with the St George's Street excavations started in Volume I, but because of my closer personal involvement in some of the outlying sites, I had already written some of these reports before I agreed in 1972 to take over the remaining material. The documentation of St George's Street sites is more complex and has not always been readily available so it was therefore thought better to publish what was ready rather than stick strictly to sequence.

In this volume we shall not be attempting any synthesis of the finds, instead this will be left for a future volume which will not merely contain summaries of certain groups of finds, but also a general synthesis of the results. Some material will be better summarized with the results of all excavations in Winchester, and so items such as the samian and the Roman coins will be considered in detail in *Winchester Studies*. Finally, some groups of finds, often scattered throughout volumes in both series, may be treated in separate articles to be published in national journals (e.g. Biddle and Collis forthcoming, Collis and Kjølbye-Biddle forthcoming).

1

Lay-out

With a wide range of sites varying from large-scale excavations to a single sondage, from systematic collection to casual observation, and sometimes with both scientific excavation and rescue work on the same site, it has proved impossible to describe the sites on a period basis, and we have adhered rigidly to writing reports site by site, dealing with all periods. There is added difficulty in the great range of recording and find-marking systems that have been employed by various workers under differing conditions, ranging from bag numbers, trench and layer numbers, or simply information written out on labels or find bags. This problem was not tackled for Volume I, with the result that we have encountered considerable difficulty in locating and identifying the illustrated finds. In one or two cases where unmarked finds were removed for illustration, it is no longer possible to identify the original associations.

We have attempted to overcome these problems by imposing a single system on all the material. All the deposits have been assigned to one of two numerical sequences:

(1) Feature numbers for pits, walls, post-holes, floors, etc. These can be further sub-divided to distinguish between layers in pits, or between well or poorly stratified material (F1-2, F6-5, etc.).

(2) Layer numbers for deposits which are not incorporated into features, or for unstratified material (L2, L6, etc.). This annotation is used throughout this volume.

All the finds have been reboxed and renumbered, and fitted into the cataloguing system developed by Mr Adrian Rance for the whole of the Museum's collections. These numbers are also quoted in this report, thereby allowing direct access to the Museum's storage and cataloguing system. The correlation between our codes is as follows:

Collis	site code	feature number	(e.g. WCP55 F40-2)
	site code	layer number	(e.g. WLA58 L4)
Museum	site number.feature number/bag number		(e.g. 483.40.2/1)
accession number	site number.layer number/bag number		(e.g. 718.00.4/1)

Numbers preceded by C are Museum coin numbers (e.g. C 1723).

One problem with the system is that the markings on the pottery bear no relationship to our numbers, though cards with correlations are stored with our card-index system at the Museum. Also included in the card index are lists of all features, cross-referenced with certain categories of finds. These lists are gradually being incorporated into the Museum's system.

For this particular volume the sites are grouped into the four main suburbs, introduced by a short survey of the research and excavation that has taken place, and the pattern of development that is emerging from the archaeological and historical evidence for both the Roman and medieval periods. Where appropriate, each site is discussed in a series of sub-sections:

(1) The local topography, cause and course of the excavation, and acknowledgements.

(2) Summary of the archaeological and historical evidence.

(3) Details of the features and layers with their finds, listed in numerical order.

(4) Notes on special finds.

Where a subsection has been written by someone other than myself, the author's name is noted with the subtitle, as well as being included in the list of those who have contributed information.

The drawings of pottery have been arranged chronologically within each section. Therefore figures are sometimes not placed adjacent to the reference to them in the text.

Aims

We have been limited in our task both by the variable quality of the material and by lack of time, as the major authors have had only a few weeks available each year to work on Winchester's archaeology. With full-time work advancing in the Winchester Research Unit in collecting all previous information on the town, in the full publication of more extensive and better quality excavations, and in further rescue excavation, obviously our work must be seen as only an interim statement which will soon be outdated. I have, however, attempted some general description of how the suburbs developed, incorporating where possible the latest results.

Our aims must therefore be modest, preparatory to more sophisticated analysis. First, we are publishing contexts which can be quoted in all future work. This includes an impression of the range of finds in each feature or layer, the likely bias in its collection and recording, and contamination with later material. This is especially relevant, for instance, to the material in the Telephone Cable Trench, which has been used for dating the city defences (Cunliffe 1962). It is important to distinguish between finds which were securely stratified and others which were picked up on the dump, but which are likely to come from the Roman bank.

Our second aim is to provide a corpus of published finds, especially pottery. Obviously key deposits will have to be reworked when we know more about different fabrics and industries, but meanwhile we can at least make fellow-students aware of what is stored in the City Museums.

CHAPTER 2

THE SUBURBS

Almost from its very beginning, Winchester has been a defended position, lying on the gentle slope of chalk and gravel that runs down to the valley of the River Itchen (for map of sites see Fig. 1). To the east of the river the city is faced by the steeper slope of St Giles' Hill, which forms the sharp end of a long east—west ridge of chalk. This narrow point in the Itchen valley was the lowest point at which the river could be crossed with no wide expanse of alluvium to act as a barrier. Also it was up to this point that the river was from time to time navigable, at least for the lighter craft coming up from the various ports which preceded modern Southampton. With these initial assets Winchester rose to become the major market and administrative centre of the Hampshire Basin.

THE IRON AGE

Although there is a scatter of occupation belonging to the latest Bronze Age and Early Iron Age (defined in Collis 1977a), mainly on the upper gravel terrace of the Itchen, there is no evidence that it was at all intensive, and certainly there is no trace of a defensive earthwork. In the Middle Iron Age, however, the population increased rapidly, and an area of some 10—15 ha supported fairly dense settlement, again mainly on the gravel terrace, but extending up the hill on to the areas of chalk.

This settlement was defended by a massive earthwork enclosing up to 20 ha. The defended site, like its Roman and medieval successors, lay on the slope west of the Itchen, but it is further up the slope than the later town and only partially overlaps with it. The western defences on Oram's Arbour were to remain an important feature of the western suburb until well into the medieval period. The western and southern limits of the enclosure are well delimited by recent excavation (Biddle 1970, 5a Fig. 1) but the line of the eastern downhill limit is still a matter of conjecture. The lie of the land suggests it may have run a little to the east of Jewry Street, but Middle Iron Age pottery has turned up east of St Peter's Street, and the line of Parchment Street might be another possibility. But even taking the Jewry Street line, the enclosed defensive area demonstrates this to be one of the major defended sites of southern England, larger perhaps than either Maiden Castle or Hod Hill. True, not all the area was occupied, as excavations at Frederick Place demonstrate, but there were areas of intensive occupation at Tower Street, and this pattern of occupied and unoccupied areas is repeated at other hill-forts such as Danebury (Cunliffe 1974).

The occupation was short-lived. The later phases of the Early Iron Age (as defined in Collis 1977a) are virtually unrepresented, and equally the latest phase of the Middle Iron Age is not found in the occupied area, though it does occur at Winchester, notably in the

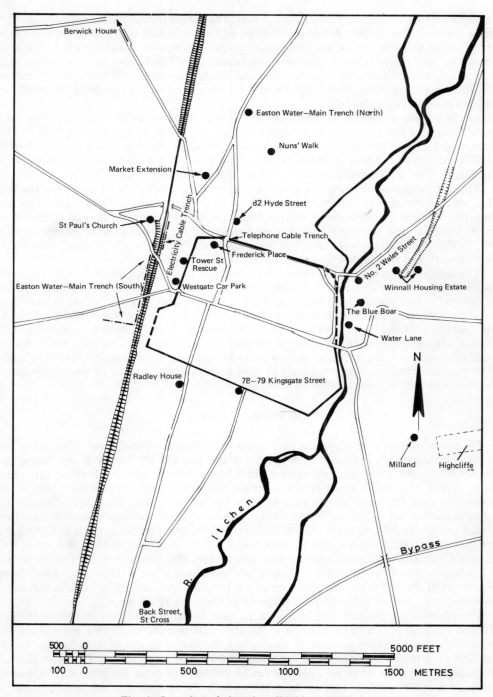

Fig. 1. Location of sites described in the volume.

ditch infill on the Assize Court site (Biddle 1969). The period of occupation may therefore only cover a century or so, *c.* 250/200 to *c.* 100 B.C. and the defences may belong only to the very end. Whether this site can be assigned urban status is a matter of definition. There is little evidence for industry or trade. The main subsistence of the inhabitants may have been largely agricultural, and this is true of other contemporary hill-forts in Wessex where extensive excavation has taken place. Personally I would not consider that the threshold of urbanization had been crossed (Collis 1974).

There is little evidence for occupation immediately outside the defences, but on the opposite bank of the river lay the relatively large hill-fort of St Catherine's Hill (Hawkes, Myres, and Stevens 1930) a defended site of some 9 ha. In size it is much smaller than Iron Age Winchester, but it had been intensively occupied from the Early Iron Age. It too, like Winchester, was abandoned before the end of the Middle Iron Age.

Though these two sites may not mark the beginnings of urban development in the Itchen valley, one aspect of the settlement pattern was being established at this time: the minor farming settlements which were to continue without break, often to the end of the Roman period. To the end of the Early Iron Age we can assign the settlements at Owslebury (Collis 1968, 1970), Worthy Down (Hooley 1929) and Berwick House, while Winnall and Twyford Down (Stuart and Birkbeck 1936) start in the Middle Iron Age.

The fate of the defended sites and their obviously large populations is still unknown. It would now seem that they had no Late Iron Age successors in central Hampshire, contrary to the views of a few years ago (Ordnance Survey 1962, Cunliffe 1964, 1974). There is only sporadic evidence for late Middle Iron Age finds (mainly from the Assize Court site) and Late Iron Age (from Radley House and the Easton Water-Main Trench), mainly on the western and southwestern periphery of the later town. Despite a single fragment of a coin mould from the Cathedral Green site, the coin evidence, or lack of it, tells the same story (Collis 1971), and the site of modern Winchester seems merely to have been occupied by one or two minor farming settlements at the time of the Roman conquest.

THE ROMAN PERIOD

Evidence is now accumulating to suggest that Roman Winchester, like many other Roman towns, owes its existence to military occupation. On the Lower Brook Street site a short length of ditch has been excavated which could belong to a pre-Flavian fort (Biddle 1975a, 1975b). The road which comes from the northwest from Cirencester heads straight towards this area. On the other hand the Bitterne-Silchester road bypasses it, but this could be related to another site in the southwest corner of the city where the later town defences form a peculiar salient, and where early chance finds include some Claudian samian and at least one item of military equipment. A pre-Flavian date for the Cirencester road is suggested by the results of K. Qualmann's excavation in the northern suburbs, while from 82 Hyde Street there is Claudian samian from the earliest surface of the Silchester road. This latter road dictated the position of the North and South Gates of the Roman town, although both in Roman and Saxon times the line of the road ran obliquely to the city's street grid.

Presumably the Roman fort formed a nucleus around which a *vicus* developed, but Claudian material is rare in the town, and the civil settlement is mainly a phenomenon of the late Neronian and Flavian periods. It was during the early Flavian period that the defences were first constructed (Biddle 1972), enclosing an area of some 55 ha. This was much less ambitious than the contemporary defences at Silchester, but more realistic, for the defensive circuit, once established, remained static throughout the Roman and medieval periods, and there was no contraction in the area planned for settlement such as occurred in many other *civitas* capitals (Wacher 1974). Thus from the Flavian period onwards the area of extra-mural settlement, which is our main concern in this volume, is well defined.

There is little that can be said of the activity in the first century in the areas immediately adjoining the defences. In the angle formed by the convergence of the Cirencester and Silchester roads, just outside the North Gate, a small cemetery was established in pre-Flavian times and continued to be used into the second century; but early Roman burials are notably absent from Winchester. Recently Don MacKreth and Martin Biddle have suggested that the siting of the forum in the eastern part of the town could imply that the main gateways of the town were not the North and South Gates, but a predecessor of the medieval Kingsgate to the south and a putative gate at the end of Middle Brook Street to the north. Recently an extra-mural road has been discovered at Hyde which seems to head from the Silchester road towards the end of Middle Brook Street, a hint of the existence of a gate at that point. If this is so, the main cemetery areas could lie along Park Avenue and Kingsgate Street, but in neither area has any excavation taken place. This earlier orientation could also explain why the western part of the town was much slower to develop.

The majority of settlement expansion in the first century took place within the defended area, though somewhat surprisingly K. Qualmann's excavation in Crowder Terrace in the western suburbs produced extensive debris from the manufacture of bone objects, filling a ditch datable to the first century. But other similar ditches in the western suburb (e.g. from the Easton Water-Main Trench) seem rather to belong in a farming context.

Rural settlements in the immediate vicinity of the city seem to have prospered. Winnall certainly continued, and Berwick House has also produced surface finds of early Roman pottery. But it is the burials which hint at the relative wealth of such settlements. Those from Milland, Highcliffe, and Winnall are all rich in samian vessels, while Grange Road produced bronze and glass vessels as well as other luxury items (Biddle 1967b). Generally these seem richer than those of more outlying sites such as Owslebury, where the richest grave only contained five samian vessels (Collis 1977b).

During the second century settlement expanded at least into the northern suburb. The recent excavations in Victoria Road and Hyde Street have produced evidence for rectangular structures lining the Cirencester road, and similar structures may have existed on the Silchester Road at 82 Hyde Street. In terms of lavish buildings, the construction of increasingly elaborate town houses makes the second and third centuries the wealthiest in Winchester. Outside the East Gate, on the far bank of the Itchen, there is also evidence for stone buildings, notably the plunge bath or tank on Water Lane. There were also stone buildings in the western suburb in the late third/early fourth century, when town life reached its height.

In the second half of the fourth century, however, there was a considerable change in the nature of the occupation. Town houses such as that in Middle Brook Street (Bennet-Clark 1954, Butcher 1955) were falling into disrepair and were demolished, and in this case over the remains of the house a corn-drying oven was constructed. Occupation in the suburbs contracted, and instead we have plentiful funerary evidence — in fact the vast majority of burials so far excavated in Winchester belong to this period. Of those published here, only that from the Telephone Cable Trench can definitely be assigned to the second century, while those from the Market Extension and Radley House could be third century, though perhaps later. Certainly in the second half of the fourth century massive cemeteries appeared in the northern suburb in Victoria Road, under the Cattle Market, and at Lankhills. Our evidence from the eastern suburb suggests another large cemetery coming into existence in the fourth century in the area of Water Lane and St John's Street. The Winnall farming settlement had thrived until the early fourth century, but after that it too may have contracted or disappeared.

Several late Roman graves have recently been excavated on the hill to the north of the medieval village adjacent to the railway cutting, and these may represent an extension of the urban cemeteries on to what must originally have been part of the farm's territory (Biddle 1975a). Burials, unfortunately undated, also occur in the western suburb in the area around Clifton Road and Crowder Terrace, and excavations in 1964 and 1975 in the Iron Age ditch adjacent to the railway station have also produced fourth century burials, though perhaps early rather than late in the century. Biased though this evidence obviously is, it seems to indicate a concentration of the population in the town, combined with a disappearance of the earlier wealth. The foreign origins of some of this population are implied by some of the grave goods from the cemetery at Lankhills, and by pottery finds within the city itself (Biddle 1969, 1970). There had clearly been a fundamental change in the economic and social structure of the town.

THE SAXON AND MEDIEVAL PERIODS

In the century and a half after A.D. 400, the town underwent further radical changes. First the population seems to have been greatly reduced, and settlement continued only sporadically within the walls. The street system fell out of use, and finally the collapsed buildings and streets were overlain by a homogeneous layer of dark, black soil containing abraded late Roman pottery and coins (e.g. on Frederick Place). This deposit already existed by the ninth century if not earlier, though how it formed is not yet clear. It may represent a cultivation soil, and fields have recently been identified in the southeast corner of the town under Wolvesey Palace (Biddle 1975a). The deposit occurs throughout the intra-mural area but has yet to be identified in any of the suburbs.

The implication of this evidence is that the settlement had lost its urban status, and that when urban settlement reappeared in Hampshire, it was the port site at Southampton which led the way. Winchester may have died as an urban settlement, but as an administrative and social centre it had not; by the mid seventh century at least, it was a royal residence for the kings of Wessex, and soon after replaced Dorchester-on-Thames as the episcopal centre for the region. Such occupation as existed seems to have been largely concentrated in the eastern part of the town adjacent to the river, and so some occupation might be expected in the eastern suburb. It is in this area that we have most evidence for sixth and seventh century activity, in the form of burials: the sporadic graves which have come to light on St Giles' Hill overlooking the city, and two cemeteries, one of sixth century, the other of seventh century date on the hill above Winnall Moor (Meaney and Hawkes 1970).

 These cemeteries, and that on West Hill in the southern suburb, presumably relate to independent extra-mural settlements, though one can only conjecture as to when the various small villages and hamlets came into existence around the city—Winnall, Hyde, Weeke, Sparkeford (St Cross), and others which may already have been incorporated into the city by the end of the Anglo-Saxon period. Evidence for these settlements and for the general development of the medieval suburbs relies more on documentary and topographical arguments which will be discussed more fully in *Winchester Studies,* Volumes 1 and 2.

The medieval access-routes into the town generally followed Roman lines. In the southern suburb the Kingsgate line may have remained in greater favour in the Saxon period, but later St Cross Road/Southgate Street formed the main route to Southampton. The recent excavation of the Roman South Gate showed that the gate had collapsed in the post-Roman period, but traffic continued to pass over the rubble. Later the gate was deliberately blocked, but was re-opened in the late Saxon period (Biddle 1975a). The physical constraints on the topography of the eastern suburb dictated that the route from the southeast (Portchester and Portsmouth) follow the Roman road, but it is not known if the major medieval route from the northeast along the river (Water Lane and Easton Lane) had a Roman predecessor. One that probably did is the road along St John's Street, towards Alresford and London, since it was referred to as *Portstret* in the tenth century. From the West Gate the Roman road to Old Sarum/Salisbury retained its importance at least until the twelfth century, but it was then superseded by the route which goes through Stockbridge and which enters the western suburb going up St Paul's Hill. Within the suburb itself the Sarum route was still important, as outside the suburb it was joined by the road to Romsey and the southwest.

It is in the northern suburbs that the most drastic changes took place. The main route from the north along the Itchen deviated from the Roman line as it neared the city and appears to have followed the line of Worthy Lane, Andover Road, and Sussex Street to enter the town at the West Gate. The gate or gates in the northern wall would appear to have gone out of use completely just as the South Gate had. The medieval North Gate presumably came into use in the late ninth century, for it is set symmetrically in relation to the medieval street grid within the walls. Immediately adjacent to it within the walls was an open space, perhaps a market. It was probably at this time that Hyde Street appeared as a link between Worthy Lane and the North Gate.

These changes may have been connected with the burghal organization under Alfred, when a grid-system of streets was laid out within the city. By this time streets in the suburbs were also beginning to appear. The 'twitchens', which ran round the outer perimeter of the later medieval City Ditch, seem to be a fundamental feature of the Saxon lay-out, and they survive in part in Swan Lane, Sussex Street, Canon Street, and College Street, although whether these roads were also surfaced like the internal streets has yet to be demonstrated. Urban expansion followed quickly on this official encouragement and during the tenth century the area within the town filled up rapidly, and proper suburban development was well under way by the eleventh. Finds of the ninth/tenth century 'Late Saxon Sandy Ware' (Biddle and Collis forthcoming) are virtually unknown in the suburbs; tenth/eleventh century 'Winchester-Ware' is not uncommon; twelfth century 'Tripod-Pitcher-Ware' and straw-marked pottery is ubiquitous.

At least two of the suburbs were enclosed by ditches. The western suburb already possessed the original Iron Age Enclosure. Part of the Iron Age defences was recut in the twelfth century, and the complex was extended to enclose the northern suburb on a line which also formed the boundary of the City Liberty. But there is documentary evidence for other ditched boundaries, and the eleventh century ditch found on 82 Hyde Street could mark the eastern limit of the northern suburb at the time.

The housing development was mainly confined to the frontage of the main streets running through the suburbs, and other than the 'twitchens' there was little in the way of subsidiary streets. There were fairly large open spaces, and certainly fields in the western suburb even at the period of its greatest prosperity. The western suburb boasted a market in the tenth century, and there was probably another just inside the North Gate at the same period. By the eleventh century the international fair of St Giles was held on the hill overlooking the eastern suburb. This was one of the great fairs of medieval England, and the only one of the first rank south of the Thames.

The economic decline, which followed the gradual removal of royal interest in the town, and the effects of the Black Death hit the suburbs to varying degrees (Biddle 1975b). By 1400 the formerly rich and extensive western suburb had all but disappeared, and much of the western part of the city within the walls was depopulated. The adjacent part of the southern suburb outside the South Gate was badly affected, although this suburb generally fared less badly due to the establishment of various religious houses and especially to the foundation of Winchester College which continued to expand while Winchester declined. However, with the

Dissolution the prop of the religious houses disappeared, and by the time of Speed's map of 1611, other than the cluster of houses around the College in College Street and Kingsgate Street, there was merely a handful of houses in the once prosperous extra-mural settlement.

In comparison, the northern suburb suffered little, even with the destruction of the great abbey at Hyde at the time of the Dissolution. The abbey had been founded in 1110 by the transference of the New Minster from the city centre, and its lands had restricted the growth of the suburb on its eastern side, so that the suburb had never consisted of much more than a line of houses along Hyde Street.

The eastern suburb over the Itchen may provide something of an exception. Being part of the Soke, and under the jurisdiction of the Bishop we do not have the benefit of the comprehensive picture derived from the surveys made of the City Liberty to chart its development; yet of all the suburbs in the sixteenth century, that outside the East Gate perhaps retained most of its earlier medieval prosperity.

By Elizabethan times the fortunes of the city seem to have settled down. Great areas within the town itself were derelict and not until the nineteenth century, in particular after the coming of the railway, did any notable expansion take place.

CHAPTER 3

THE SOUTHERN SUBURB

Little archaeological work or redevelopment has taken place in the southern suburb, and we must rely almost entirely on documentary evidence. Our knowledge of the Roman period is therefore very limited. Because of the siting of the forum, it has been suggested that the main axis from the south in the early Roman period was along the line of Kingsgate Street and a gate on or near the site of the medieval Kingsgate. However, the South Gate certainly belongs to the primary lay-out of the defences in the first century. Its earliest phase was a massive timber construction replaced later by one of stone. When this collapsed in post-Roman times traffic continued over the rubble, until access was blocked perhaps in Middle Saxon times. By the end of the ninth century the gate was again in use on a site slightly to the west.

The archaeological evidence from just outside the gate, on the Radley House site, demonstrates that there was occupation in this area at about the time of the Roman conquest, a hint of a settlement in the area of St James' Lane in the century between the disappearance of the large Middle Iron Age enclosure and the Roman settlement. Indeed the pottery from the Iron Age ditch on the Assize Court site seems typologically later than anything within the defended area, again indicative of a settlement outside the southern defences in this general area.

Little is known of the Roman cemeteries; the Radley House inhumations should date to the third century, but any earlier cemeteries may well have lain along Kingsgate Street. The change to domestic occupation, or perhaps only the dumping of rubbish on this earlier cemetery, is something of a contrast to the evidence from the eastern and northern suburbs. The odd scraps of fourth century pottery from Back Street, St Cross, hint that there may have been an area of settlement somewhere in the vicinity, and there was certainly a distinct settlement adjacent to the Roman road just south of St Cross. Here rich first century burials have been excavated at Grange Road (Biddle 1967b), and surface finds indicate occupation extending into late Roman times.

The medieval pattern of settlement in the southern suburb before the twelfth century is far from clear. An independent settlement existed at Sparkeford beneath the modern St Cross, but the weaving hut found in Back Street and the famous 'Winchester Ivory', found in the garden of 59 St Cross Road are the only tangible pieces of archaeological evidence for its existence. In *Winchester Studies 1,* Keene and Biddle have suggested that the church of St Faith may originally have served an independent hamlet, the fields of which would have lain within the later parish which extended out from, rather than into, the suburbs. In the twelfth century, however, the church of St Faith was probably included within the southern suburb, whose bounds Keene and Biddle have suggested were represented by Kingsgate Road and a cart-track running from the church of St Faith to that of St James on the west. The cart-track may have served as no more than a link between two parts of the Manor of Barton, avoiding the city and suburbs, but could have developed along the line of a physical boundary defining the suburban limits.

In the twelfth and thirteenth centuries the built up area extended well to the south of the walled area, along both the medieval Southgate Street (now St Cross Road) and Kingsgate Street. Palliards Twitchen, a street which survives as the modern Cannon Street and which lay just outside the medieval city, was densely built up and had probably originated as part of the late Saxon defensive lay-out. Further to the south there were other lanes on an east-west line.

In the later Middle Ages the presence of two friaries and eventually the new college founded by William of Wykeham appears to some extent to have counteracted the effects of the overall decline of the city on the southern suburb. After the Dissolution of the Monasteries, Kingsgate Street, which throughout the Middle Ages was the more populous of the two streets in the southern suburb, retained a degree of prosperity that was in part due to its proximity to the cathedral and the college. By contrast, Speed's map, published in 1611, shows no more than three or four houses outside the South Gate, a depressing picture confirmed by other documentary sources.

RADLEY HOUSE, ST CROSS ROAD
(RH 52, Site 716)

During the conversion of Radley House (now Wessex House) into a garage, an excavation 7·3 m north—south by 4·4 m, and 2·6 m deep was dug in the forecourt area to accommodate a 4,000 gallon petrol tank. The site is almost exactly 100 m south of the known site of the Roman South Gate and only 5 m from the present street frontage of St Cross Road (Fig. 2).

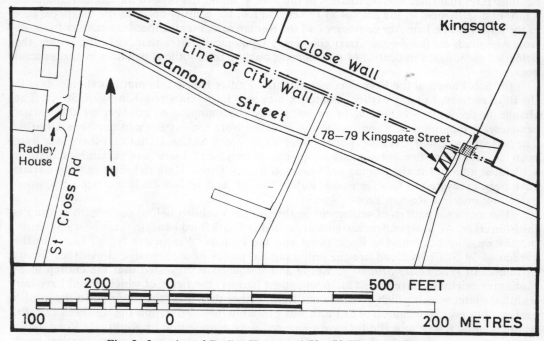

Fig. 2. Location of Radley House and 78—79 Kingsgate Street.

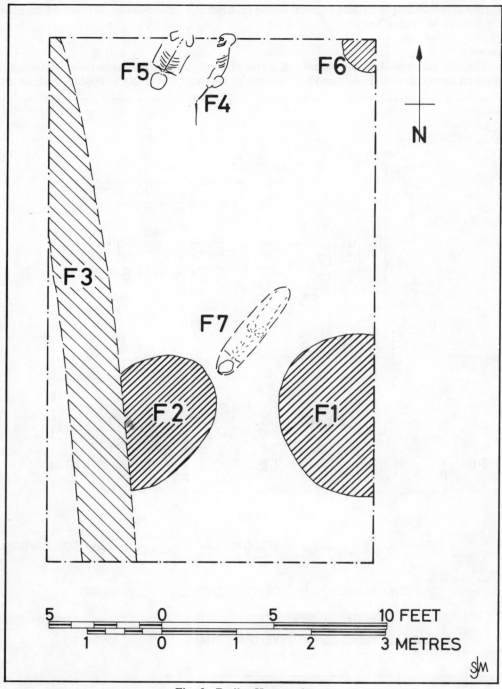

Fig. 3. Radley House: plan.

Permission to observe the site was given to Mr F. Cottrill by the owners, Wessex Motors, and the architect Mr Peter Sawyer.

Summary
The natural subsoil, encountered at a depth of about 2 m below the present surface, consisted of a brown gravel (Figs 3 and 4). The top of this was extremely irregular, with at least

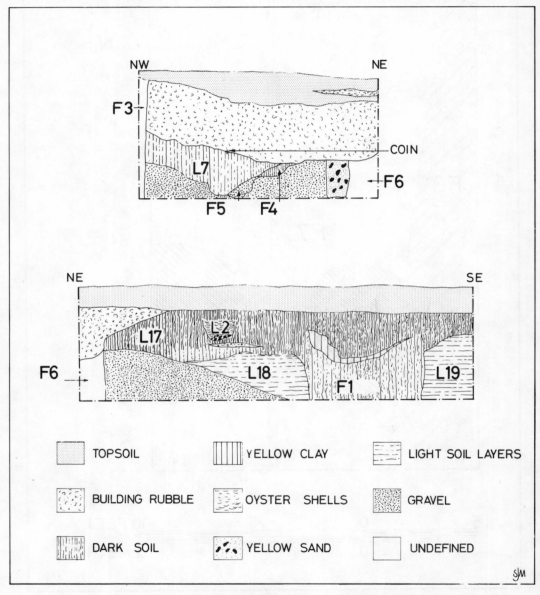

Fig. 4. Radley House: north (above) and east (below) sections.

two large hollows whose bottoms were not reached. One lay in the southeast corner, the other in the centre of the western side. Both were filled with light brown deposits, containing some late Roman pottery (L10, 18, 19). All the deposits lying directly on the natural brown gravel produced late Roman material. However, amongst the unstratified finds (L6, 15, 16, 17, 22), there are a number of early Roman sherds, including late first century bead-rim sherds. In L16 there is also a sherd of girth beaker (Fig. 5:20) and the sherds in L15 include some types which occur either side of the Roman conquest at Owslebury (Collis 1968, 1970), but which are virtually unrepresented among other finds from Winchester. It is possible that the depressions in the gravel could belong to the first century, and were left to silt up slowly.

Stratigraphically the next features are three burials, cut into the natural gravel. Burial 1 (F7) was removed by the workmen, but 2 (F4) and 3 (F5) were recorded *in situ,* and the graves appear in the north section. Burials 1 and 3 were orientated southwest—northeast, burial 2 northeast—southwest. None had any grave goods; there was no evidence for coffins; and burials 1 and 2 were both very casually laid out. Thus the burials are undated, but the brown earth or gravel filling of the graves was sealed by a dark deposit (L7, 9, 13, 14) that produced fourth-century pottery (folded beakers, red colour-coat, etc.) as well as two coins, one of Constans, the other of Valerian. Late Roman pottery was plentiful from the site as a whole, and implies it had been abandoned as a cemetery area by the fourth century.

Above the Roman deposits, especially in the southern part of the site, were layers of dark or black soil containing early medieval and later sherds (L12, L17). There is nothing which can be dated much earlier than the twelfth century. Two rubbish pits were encountered (F1 and F2) with scratch-ware, or sandy fabrics of twelfth- to thirteenth-century type. A third pit or cellar (F6) was not dated. The latest sherds were late medieval, probably fifteenth century, but there were no post-medieval finds.

Features and Layers

F1:   *A medieval pit in the eastern section*
    716.1.0/1.
    An eroded Saxo-Norman sherd and a rim of a colour-coated folded beaker.

F2:   *A medieval pit in the southwest part of the site*
    716.2.0/1. General infill of the pit.
    Cooking pot (Fig. 6:1). Saxo-Norman in very coarse version of the standard fabric.
    716.2.3/1. Filling above crushed chalk.
    Five sherds of grass-wiped pottery, thirteenth—fourteenth century.

F3:   *Modern drain trench*
    716.3.1/1, 716.3.2/1.
    Two late Roman flanged bowls and a late medieval handle.

F4:   *Burial 2*
    The skeleton of a male aged 17—18 years lay on its right side, head to the north, and with its legs slightly flexed. It is sealed by L4.
    716.4.0/1. Brown soil filling the grave.
    Flanged piedish (Fig. 6:2). Dull red, sand-tempered fabric with burnished surface.
    Cavetto rim jar (Fig. 6:3). Hard, light grey fabric with sparse, minute black flecks.

F5:   *Burial 3*
    The skeleton of a woman aged 25—30 years was lying on its back with its arms by its side. The legs ran into the side of the excavation and were not recovered. The grave was filled with gravelly soil and was sealed by L9.

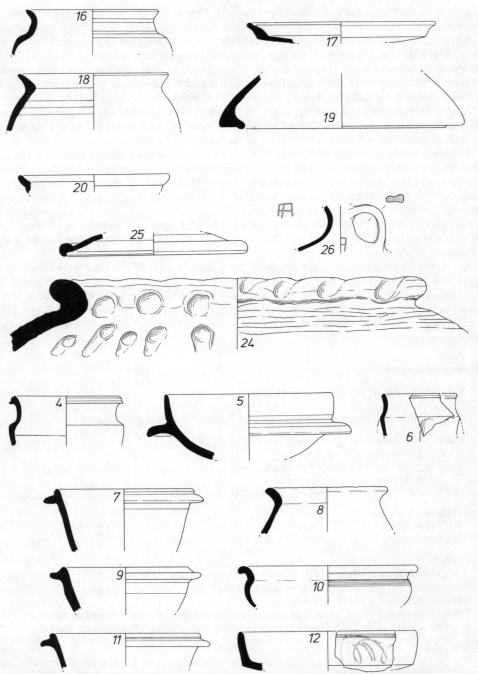

Fig. 5. Radley House: Roman pottery from L15 (16—19), L16 (20), L22 (25, 26), L19 (24) and L7 (4—12) (scale ¼).

F6: A pit in the northeast corner
No finds were recovered.

F7: Burial 1
This burial, a man aged 45—55 years, had been disturbed by the workmen, but apparently lay with its head to the southeast and feet to the northeast. The reports suggest that stone slabs (Fig. 3) lay over the head of the skeleton.

L1: Unstratified finds
716.00.1/1.
Of the surviving 50 sherds, 43 are late Roman including red colour-coat flanged bowls, purple colour-coat beakers, parchment ware with purple colour-coat, flanged bowl, jars, cooking pots, slipped grey wares, storage jar, and flanged dishes.
Two Roman coins of Tetricus II and House of Valentinian.
Of medieval date there are two rims and two body sherds in Saxo-Norman gritty ware, one sparse glazed 'Tripod Pitcher Ware' and one jug and one cooking pot of fourteenth-century date.
Three samian sherds.

L2: A dump of oysters
716.00.2/1.
A fragment from a grass-marked pot, thirteenth or fourteenth century.

L6: A mixed group from the southeast corner, including some from F1
716.00.6/1.
Of interest are an early Roman bead-rim vessel, a piedish, first-century samian, late Roman purple colour-coat.
Medieval in date is a sparse-glazed sherd decorated with a nine-pronged comb decoration under the glaze, and two fragments of cooking pots in Saxo-Norman gritty ware.

L7: Dark soil lying on natural gravel in the northern third of the site
716.00.7/1.
Bowl (Fig. 5:4). Hard, orange fabric with dull orange-red colour-coat.
Flanged bowl (Fig. 5:5). Hard, orange-buff ware with a grey core and white inclusions, orange-red colour-coat, burnished.
Folded beaker (Fig. 5:6). Steel-grey fabric with purple colour-coat.
Flanged dish (Fig. 5:7). Sandy, grey fabric with grey surface and a grey slip on the rim and interior.
Cooking pot (Fig. 5:8). Grey-black, gritty fabric, handmade, with burnished exterior.
Flanged dish (Fig. 5:9). Gritty, grey ware with black to reddish brown surface, burnished on the exterior.
Bowl (Fig. 5:10). Fine, grey-brown fabric with dull grey slip.
Flanged dish (Fig. 5:11). Fine, grey fabric with brown-grey surface and blue-grey to black slip on the rim and interior.
Piedish (Fig. 5:12). Harsh grey fabric, burnished exterior, with burnished pattern on the base and side and an internal black burnished slip.
Of the other ten sherds, two are bases of purple colour-coat beakers, a fragment of a grey slipped pitcher, and seven grey-ware sherds.
A coin of Valerian, and one sherd of Late Antonine samian.

L8: As L7 but on the west side
716.00.8/1.
The rim of a red colour-coat bowl.

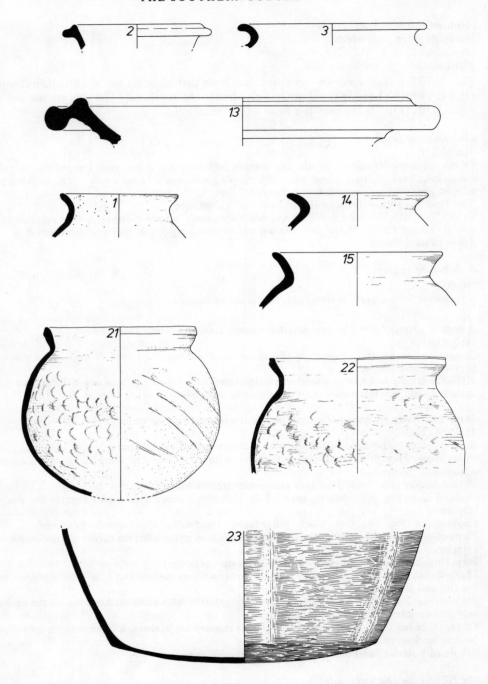

Fig. 6. Radley House: late Roman and early medieval pottery from F4 (2, 3), L9 (13), F2 (1), L12 (14, 15), L17 (21—23) (scale ¼).

L9: Above F5 in the northwest corner
716.00.9/1.
Mortarium (Fig. 6:13). Harsh white fabric.
There is also one fragment of an orange folded beaker.

L10: As L7, above L9
716.00.10/1.
A sherd of folded beaker in hard, purple colour-coat ware.

L12: Black soil in the northwest corner, above L7
716.00.12/1.
Cooking pot (Fig. 6:14). Saxo-Norman gritty ware.
Cooking pot (Fig. 6:15). As 14.

L14: A pocket of grey soil
716.00.14/1.
Fragments of two purple colour-coat beakers and a mortarium.

L15: Unstratified from the northern part of the site
716.00.15/1.
Jar (Fig. 5:16). Soft, grey to brown, sandy fabric, burnished grey surface.
Platter (Fig. 5:17). Fine, grey fabric with dark, burnished surface.
Cooking pot (Fig. 5:18). Harsh grey slightly gritty fabric, black surface, burnished.
Lid or bowl (Fig. 5:19). Harsh, grey fabric with dark grey, smoothed surface.
In addition there is late Roman material; a fine, burnished cavetto rim, a storage jar, and a
colour-coat base.

L16: Unstratified, low in the centre of the trench
716.00.16/1.
Girth beaker (Fig. 5:20). Hard, dull buff fabric with red inclusions, orange-brown slip.
The rest of this group is mainly late Roman, but with some early medieval sherds and a samian
sherd.

L17: Not closely stratified, on the east side
716.00.17/1—5.
Globular cooking pot (Fig. 6:21). In the grass-wiped tradition, but not so decorated. It has been
thrown on the wheel and then knuckled out. Fabric reduced, dark grey.
Globular cooking pot (Fig. 6:22). Similar vessel made by the same hand and method. Some
oxidation.
A large part of the base of a cooking pot or small storage jar (Fig. 6:23). In a reduced, semi-
oxidized, sandy fabric. It is decorated with an applied strip, put on very wet and thumbed into
place across the width. This decoration runs from the shoulder to the base of the pot. The surface
has been scraped with an edged tool which looks as if the pot had been fettled in sections as this
goes up quite high.
Other sherds include a finely made rim of a large vessel, outward flaring, with a square edge; two
glazed sherds in a white fabric with fine, oxidized, green (copper) glaze; and one with iron-green
glaze, reduced. Except for the latter, these vessels seem to form a fairly tightly dated group,
probably from the last quarter of the thirteenth century.
The rest includes much late Roman material, and an early Roman bead rim.

L18: Light-coloured soil, in middle of south side of the excavation
One fragment of samian, Drag. 37.

L19: Light-coloured soils in the southern section
716.00.19/1.
Rope-rimmed storage jar (Fig. 5:24). Harsh, sandy, light-grey fabric.

L22: Unstratified from the southeast corner
716.00.22/1.
Lid (Fig. 5:25). Fine, light-grey fabric, with dull grey surface, almost poor quality *terra nigra*.
Flagon (Fig. 5:26). Hard, orange-buff fabric with incised graffito.
There is also much late Roman material and some medieval.

The Finds

The Roman Coins by R. Reece

Provenance	Museum Coin Museum	Reference	Date A.D.
L1	C 1721	Tetricus II, RIC 254	270—73
L1	C 1719	House of Valentinian reverse illegible	364—78
L7	C 1720	Valerian I, RIC 126	253—59
L14	C 1859*	Constans, as CK 39(?)	346—50

*This coin is missing; identification by F. Cottrill.

The Samian by G. Dannell

Provenance	Museum Accession Number	Form	Date A.D.	Kiln
L1	716.00.1/2	27	Flavian	southern Gaul
L1	716.00.1/3	33	2nd century	central Gaul
L1	716.00.1/4	33	2nd century	central Gaul
L6	716.00.6/2	36 (?)	1st century	southern Gaul
L7	716.00.7/2	45	Late Antonine	central Gaul
L16	716.00.16/2	Chip	2nd century	central Gaul
L18	716.00.18/1	37	2nd century	Montans

The Glass by D. Charlesworth
Only one piece of glass has been recovered from the Radley House site. F3-2 has produced the centre of a base (716.1), probably from a bowl, made of green glass and showing signs of polishing on the outer surface. It can be dated to the first or second century.

The Burials by C. Wells
There are fragments of three human skeletons, all of which are in very poor condition.

Skeleton I (F7). Male, age 45—55 years. This skeleton is represented by a broken skull, including the calva, fragments of cranial base, and most of the jaws. There is also a damaged pelvis and several long bones.

The overall muscular development indicates that this was a strongly built man. The skull was ovoid in norma verticalis, but it is too defective to offer reliable measurements. The dental state was:

$$\text{R} \quad \frac{0 \quad 7 \quad 6 \quad 5 \quad 4 \quad 0 \quad 2 \quad 1}{\text{—} \quad 7 \quad 6 \quad 5 \quad 0 \quad 3 \quad 0 \quad 0} \quad \bigg| \quad \frac{0 \quad 0 \quad 0 \quad 4 \quad 5 \quad 0 \quad ? \quad ?}{0 \quad 0 \quad 3 \quad 4 \quad 5 \quad 6 \quad 7 \quad 0} \quad \text{L}$$

Caries was not present. Attrition of the teeth was light: the cusps were partly eroded to expose isolated areas of dentine but these exposed areas were limited to small discrete patches, with hardly any confluence between them.

Measurements of a few of the long bones were taken and are shown in Table 1. These measurements would correspond to a stature of about 1738 mm (5 ft 8½ in). The Meric Index

Table 1. Measurements of human long bones.

	Skeleton I		Skeleton II		Skeleton III	
	left (mm)	right (mm)	left (mm)	right (mm)	left (mm)	right (mm)
Clav L1	—	—	—	—	137·2	132·4
Hu L1	—	357·7	—	332·2	302·0	—
Ul L1	—	—	—	—	—	234·8
Ra L1	258·2	—	—	—	—	217·1
Fe L1	—	—	448·5	—	—	—
Fe D1	30·5	29·4	—	—	—	—
Fe D2	34·3	36·5	—	—	—	—
Ti L1	—	386·2	—	—	—	—
Ti D1	38·7	39·7	—	—	—	—
Ti D2	27·2	27·8	—	—	—	—
Fib L1	378·2	—	—	—	—	—

is 88.9 (L) and 80.5 (R), a high value on the left which indicates absence of antero-posterior flattening of the femoral shaft. There is slight flattening or platymeria of the right femur. The Cnemic Index is 70.2 (L) and 70.0 (R). This is eurycnemic and indicates no side to side flattening of the tibiae. The distal end of the left tibia is defective but the right is intact and shows no evidence of a squatting facet. There is no evidence of any pathological condition here.

A small fragment of ox skull is also present with this inhumation.

Skeleton II (F4). Male, age 17—18 years. This skeleton includes a much broken skull, but with most of the jaws intact; all vertebrae from the atlas down to L2, but many damaged; fragments of pelvis, scapulae and ribs; damaged left and right clavicles, humerus, ulna, radius and femur; a few tibial fragments and some small bones of hands and feet.

The dental state was:

$$\text{R} \quad \frac{\overset{8}{} \quad 7 \quad 6 \quad 5 \quad 4 \quad 3 \quad 2 \quad 0}{7 \quad 6 \quad 5 \quad 4 \quad 3 \quad 2 \quad 1 \underset{8}{}} \quad \bigg| \quad \frac{1 \quad 2 \quad 3 \quad 4 \quad 5 \quad 6 \quad 7 \quad \overset{8}{}}{1 \quad 2 \quad 3 \quad 4 \quad 5 \quad 6 \quad 7 \underset{8}{}} \quad \text{L}$$

Caries is not present. Attrition is very light, with only isolated patches of exposed dentine. There is well marked over-crowding of the anterior teeth of both jaws.

The epiphyses were unfused proximally on the humerus, distally on the femur. When these were placed in position the measurements shown in Table 1 were obtained. They correspond to a stature of about 1696 mm (5 ft 6¾ in), but some slight further growth might have occurred. Muscular development was light to moderate. The only pathology of any note is a rather large Schmorl's node on the superior surface of the T12 vertebra.

Also present are: a fragment of ox skull, ox rib and ox femoral head; and a piece of a sheep vertebra.

Skeleton III (F5). Female, age 25—30 years. This skeleton is represented by a fragmented skull, which includes broken but reconstructible jaws; vertebrae from C1 to T9, and L4—5; sacral, pelvic, and rib fragments; the clavicles and four arm bones.

The dental state was:

$$
\begin{array}{c}
\quad\text{C}\qquad\qquad\qquad\qquad\qquad\qquad\text{C} \\
R \quad \dfrac{?\ \ 7\ 6\ 5\ 4\ 3\ 2\ 1 \qquad 0\ 0\ 3\ 4\ 5\ 6\ 7\ -}{7\ 6\ 5\ 0\ 0\ 2\ 1 \qquad 1\ 2\ 3\ 4\ 5\ 6\ 7\ -} \quad L \\
8
\end{array}
$$

The caries is interstitial mesially on both the affected molars. Dental attrition is light, with only discrete exposure of the dentine. Small deposits of tartar are present. The 8̅| is impacted; and |8̲ and |8̅ have failed to erupt.

The measurements of the long bones are given in Table 1. They correspond to a stature of about 1578 mm (5 ft 2¼ in).

No pathology is recognizable but some trivial anatomical variants are present. Double foramina transversaria are present on the C5 vertebra, and there is a septal aperture in the olecranon fossa of the left, but not the right, humerus. These are presumably minor genetic variants.

Summary. The poor state of these burials reduces what can be said about them, but even if they were in better condition it does not seem likely that any very exceptional features would be identified.

The overall picture gives no grounds for supposing that they were suffering from poor nutrition or any disease until their final illness, if any.

The oldest of them was the man, Skeleton I. The fact that he, like the other two persons, had only very light dental attrition probably indicates a fairly refined, well-cooked diet, with no very tough or coarse food. This is perhaps further indicated by the dental decay of Skeleton III, in which two maxillary first molars are carious. This gives a frequency of 2 out of 22 erupted molars for the group, i.e. 9·1 per cent. The over-crowded, badly spaced teeth of Skeleton II are further evidence of indifferent functional use, as tends to occur with soft diets. Perhaps these people were of a relatively high social status, unaccustomed to the tough meats and crusty bannocks of the poor.

Some further support for this may be found in the absence of squatting facets in Skeleton I and the absence of arthritis in all three — though this disease would hardly be expected in the adolescent, nor probably in the young woman.

But the youth, at least, seems to have sustained some injury to his back, in view of the Schmorl's node which is present. Whether this was due to being made to work too hard or to some simple mishap such as a fall cannot now be determined but the condition points to rupture of an intervertebral disc as a result of some kind of strain or violence.

The absence of marked platymeria or platycnemia, especially in conjunction with moderate muscular development, may again indicate a relatively easy life as far as physical effort was concerned. But this is only a tentative inference.

78—79 KINGSGATE STREET
(78—79 KS, Site 717)

During 1964 new houses were constructed by Winchester College on the west side of Kingsgate Street, in a gap immediately adjoining the medieval Kingsgate. No archaeological excavation was possible beforehand, but the site was visited by Mr Cottrill, and he recovered finds from the digging of the house foundations. Permission to visit the site was given by the Warden and Fellows of the College, and they have donated the finds to the City Museum.

Summary

Both houses lie on the line of the City Ditch, and all finds can be assumed to be derived from its infill, though only a few items were found *in situ*. The finds are mainly of interest for dating the infill of the ditch which at this point seems to have been well underway in the thirteenth and fourteenth centuries.

Layers

L1: Unstratified material

717.00.1/1.

A mixed group of eleventh- to seventeenth-century finds.

717.00.1/2.

A white slip decorated bowl (Fig. 7:1) of late seventeenth or more likely of early eighteenth-century date. It is in a hard, salmon-pink fabric with an occasional lens of white clay in it. These lenses are quite thin and rare in the vessel, but noticeable, and should be a guide for grouping. The decoration is roughly trailed and irregular. The glaze is partially reduced as a result of horizontal stacking. The resulting colour scheme is dark yellow on dark brown/green.

717.00.1/3.

Fragments of German stonewares (Fig. 8:2—7) showing faces and medallions.

This box contains a number of fragments of German stoneware of sixteenth- to eighteenth-century date.

717.00.1/4.

Ten sherds of a very hard, thin pottery (Fig. 7:8) oxidized inside, the rest reduced and slate-grey in colour. The outside is covered with a fine, olive-green glaze over a decoration of horizontal or angular combing combined with applied strips, which are lightly slashed, and with tear-shaped pellets.

717.00.1/5.

This group of finds contains fragments of a large circular dish, a small plate, and a chafing dish in local red fabrics with a brown glaze. All could be late seventeenth or early eighteenth century. There is also the base of a Surrey greenware fabric with a light green glaze and a stamped combed decoration; a large handle in a fabric which has some local characteristics with a strong yellow glaze in patches with dark green overtones. There is a piece of Hispano-Moresque pottery from which the lustre has disappeared.

717.00.1/6.

A mixed group with black glazed ware fragments and tankards of mid eighteenth-century date, but also some seventeenth-century pieces including a cup base.

There are some tobacco pipes, a wig-curler, some glass fragments, an iron key, a bone spoon, three coins, and a leather belt.

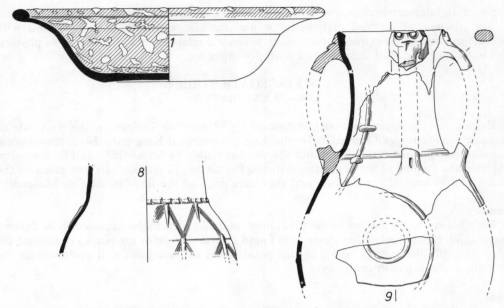

Fig. 7. 78—79 Kingsgate Street: medieval and post-medieval pottery (scale ¼).

L2: *Definitely from the infill of the City Ditch*
717.00.2/1.
Jug (Fig. 7:9) with hard, smooth, buff exterior, grey interior, dark iron-green glaze. It is decorated with a self-coloured, applied strip up the centre of the front of the vessel, probably supported by two scrolls at each side of the lower end of this strip. The strip has bars added at intervals along its length. The fragment of a large ear to one side of an auxilliary handle shows this vessel had a face mask in the front. There is evidence for four auxilliary and one proper handle. These handles are rod sectioned and slashed in the West Sussex Ware style. The upper fastening, which is at the top of the rim, is decorated with a face hand-moulded on the handle. The eyes are made with a ring-and-dot stamp.
717.00.2/2.
This is a collection of medieval jug fragments all in hard, lightly tempered fabrics with iron-green glazes. The quality of the jugs is in the main good, except for one poor base. One vessel has white slip under glaze. There is also a worn base of Winchester Ware. With this group there is a stone mortar, a ridge tile, and some iron objects.

L3: *From the infill of the City Ditch*
717.00.3/1.
Fragments of jugs of fourteenth-century date, probably earlier rather than later.
There is a single leather shoe.

L4: *Probably from the infill of the City Ditch*
717.00.4/1.
Fragments of a jug, similar to L3.
This group contains a wooden bowl and a penannular iron ring.

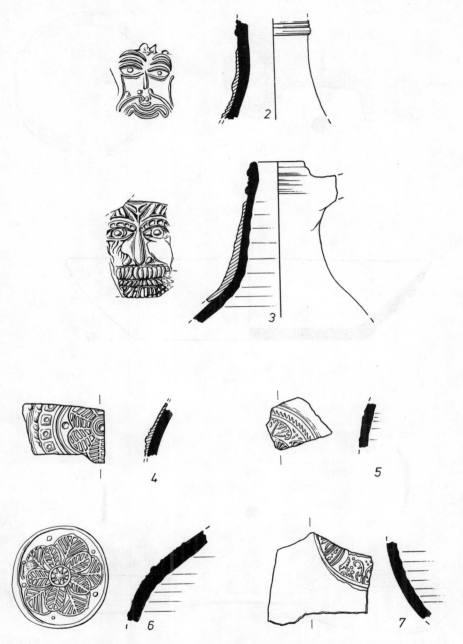

Fig. 8. 78—79 Kingsgate Street: medallions and masks on German stonewares (scale ½).

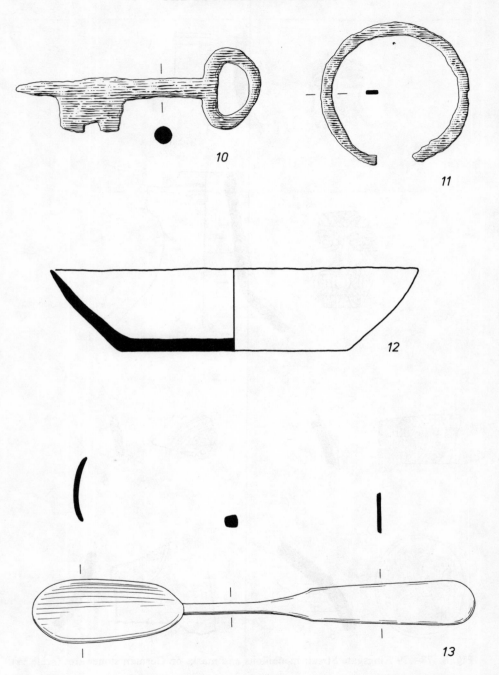

Fig. 9. 78—79 Kingsgate Street: objects of iron (10, 11), wood (12), and bone (13) (scale 10—12: ½, 13:1/1).

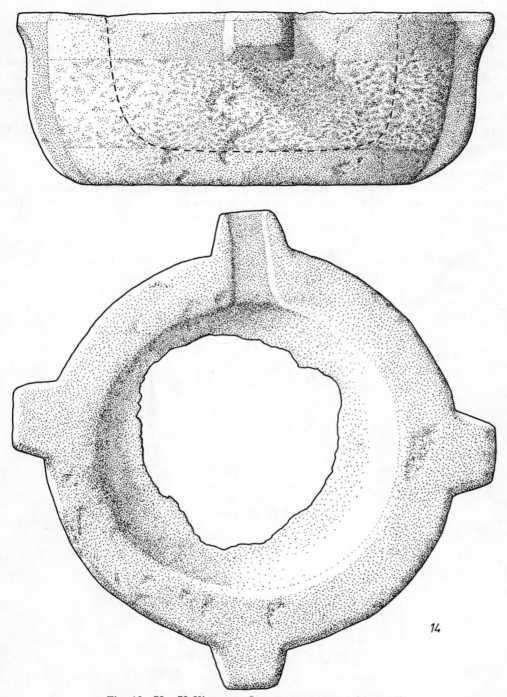

14

Fig. 10. 78—79 Kingsgate Street: stone mortar (scale ½).

The Finds

The Coins

Three coins come from L1 of the 78—79 Kingsgate Street site. There is a bronze coin, Spain, Philip II 1556—1598, obv. castle, rev. lion rampant (Heiss 1870, pl. 31:46), overstruck 1694 (identification by Miss M. Archibald, British Museum). The other two coins are a Charles I farthing (C 1857), and a silver groat (C 1856) of Henry VIII or Edward VI times.

The Iron Objects by I. Goodall

Only two iron objects come from this site. There is an iron key (717.7, Fig. 9:10) from L1 and a penannular ring (717.15, Fig. 9:11) from L4.

Miscellaneous Finds

There is a wooden bowl (717.16, Fig. 9:12) from L4. It is presumably late medieval. The wood has been treated and is unidentifiable. There is also a bone spoon (717.8, Fig. 9:13) from

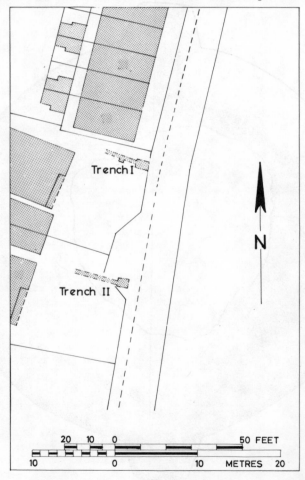

Fig. 11. Back Street, St Cross: location of Trenches I and II.

L1, presumably of late seventeenth- to eighteenth-century date; and a mortar (Fig. 10:14) of Purbeck limestone. The tobacco pipes, glass, and leather objects will be considered in a later volume.

BACK STREET, ST CROSS
(Site 650)

In 1958 several bungalows were constructed on the west side of Back Street, St Cross (Fig. 11). The bungalows stand some way back from the street frontage, and to connect the drainage to the main sewer system, four parallel trenches were dug east—west up to the street (Trenches I-IV), with large extensions at the eastern end. During the excavation of the northernmost of the trenches, the workmen unearthed a number of clay loom-weights which were reported to the Museum by the contractors, Messrs Bendall. The site was subsequently visited by F. Cottrill and A. R. T. Ball, who removed a number of loom-weights from a stack which had been disturbed by the workmen, and also dug a small trial trench (Trench V) to the south, with negative results. Subsequently I deepened the sewer trench, and found a number of weights which had obviously fallen from the loom. Excavation was restricted by the contractors' trenches, by adjacent walls, and by a lime tree, whose roots had greatly disturbed the deposits. The next trench to the south also produced evidence of occupation, but the others were sterile. The plan (Fig. 12) is based on measured drawings of the northern trench and a sketch plan of the southern trench.

Summary

The natural subsoil was a fine, clay-brown river silt, into which the floor of a hut had been cut. Only the northern limit was encountered, a sloping bank, 25 cm high, running east—west. The floor consisted of a chalky level up to 5 cm thick, which was found at 85 cm below pavement level in Trenches I and II. Above this in Trench I was a layer of ash 1 cm thick. With the exception of the dump of loom-weights, which lay on the ash deposit, the relation of these deposits to other features is unknown. In Trench II three post-holes (F1—3) were discovered, presumably contemporary, but neither their exact position nor details are recorded.

There were also three post-holes in Trench I. F6, of unknown function, narrowed markedly towards its base. F7 (53 cm deep) and the double post-hole F8 (25 cm deep) formed the posts for a vertical loom that had been in operation at the time of destruction. The majority of the bun-shaped loom-weights stood vertically in a line between these two post-holes (Plate Ia). There were about 22—23 with another two out of line at the eastern end and one near the centre lying on its side under the others. All were dull brown in colour and extremely friable, with roots from the adjacent lime tree actually running through the clay. Further loom-weights lay horizontally to the south and to the west against the bank at the edge of a hut, along with a stone 'foreign' to the area. At the east end of the trench was another batch of about 15 loom-weights lying in a heap (F9). Their condition contrasted strongly with those on the loom. They were hard, and bright red to orange in colour.

The loom-weights are of late Saxon type, though the sparse pottery might suggest a later date. The upper deposits, and a pit (F4) in Trench II cutting the floor, produced medieval pottery. The hut had apparently been destroyed by fire from the evidence of the layer of ash on the floor, and from the survival of the loom-weights in position. The heap of loom-weights, however, lay on top of the ash. Their bright red colour shows they had fired in an oxidizing atmosphere, and as there were no dark patches, they must have been hanging up in the hut. Those on the loom and on the floor must have been quickly covered by debris during the fire, producing a reducing atmosphere in which they were not so thoroughly burnt.

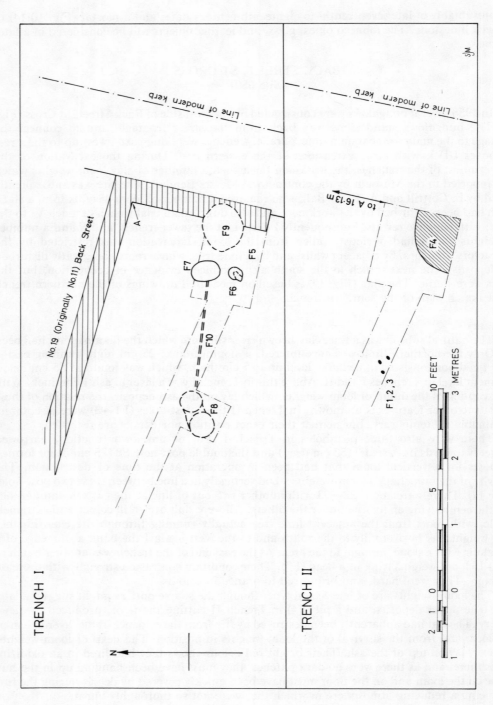

Fig. 12. Back Street, St Cross: detailed plans of Trenches I and II.

Features and Layers

F1, F2, F3: *Post holes in Trench II*
No finds or details.

F4: *Pit in Trench II*
650.4.0/1.
Late medieval to sixteenth- to seventeenth-century sherds.
One fragment of window leading (650.38).

F5: *Floor of the hut*
This is a chalky deposit up to 5 cm thick, lying on natural and 85 cm below the modern footpath.
650.5.1/1. Clearing down to the floor.
One late Roman burnished sherd.
There are fragments of bone, daub, and loom-weights.
650.5.2/1. Near the side of the hut, west of F8.
Loom-weight fragments.
650.5.3/1. Within 2—3 cm of natural near F8.
Two worn sherds, both probably medieval, perhaps thirteenth-century.

F6: *Post-hole*
Measures 20×25 cm at the top, and 7·5×18 cm lower down; depth unrecorded. No finds.

F7: *Post-hole*
Measures 40×30 cm at the top, and 50 cm deep below the floor. No finds.

F8: *Double post-hole*
Measures 33—35 cm across and 65 cm long, 25 cm deep. No finds.

F9: *Heap of loom-weights*
Loom-weights (650.1—650.37) found by the workmen, lying on floor F5.
650.9.0/1.
Contains a rim of a cooking pot and a glazed sherd, perhaps fourteenth century.

F10: *Row of loom-weights*
Loom-weights lying between F7 and F8 (650.10.0/1—16).

L1: *Unstratified*
650.00.1/1.
Mixed later medieval sherds and a fragment of a large Fareham greenware storage jar of late eighteenth-century date.

L2: *Dump from Trench I*
650.00.2/1.
Three sherds of early medieval gritted ware, but most from fifteenth century.

L3: *Dump*
650.00.3/1.
One early medieval cooking pot, one with internal glaze (fourteenth to fifteenth century), and an eighteenth-century Surrey Ware flanged bowl.

L4: *Dark, clay soil in Trench II, 30-75 cm deep*
    650.00.4/1.
    One or two early medieval sherds, but mainly fourteenth to fifteenth century. Also a bone handle
    (650.39).

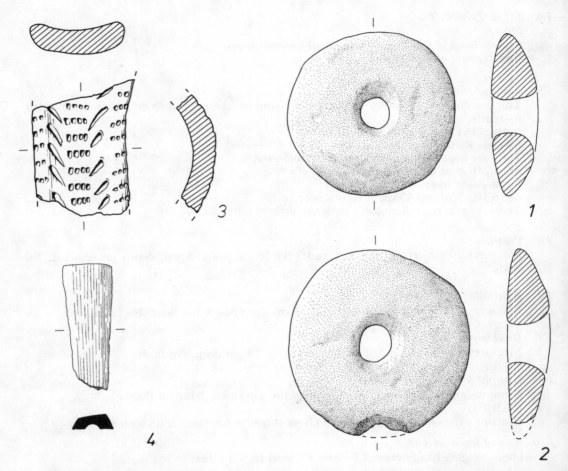

Fig. 13. Back Street, St Cross: loom-weights from F9 (650:1, 2), pottery handle from L6, and bone handle from L4 (scale ½).

L5: *Dump from Trench III*
    650.00.5/1.
    Four sherds of fourteenth-century date.

L6: *North—south trench just south of Trench I*
    Dark and light soils down to 60 cm.
    One handle (Fig. 13:3) from a Saxo-Norman storage jar in a very coarse, flinty-textured fabric, oxidized on the outside. The rest is thirteenth to fourteenth century.

L7:   Below L6, down to a level of cobbles
      650.00.7/1.
      These sherds including a tripod foot are late thirteenth to fourteenth century.

L8:   Below L7, just above natural
      650.00.8/1.
      One early medieval sherd.

The Finds

Miscellaneous Finds

Bone handle in L4 (650.39, Fig. 13:4). It is made from a length of long bone or cannon bone which has been trimmed to give it an angular cross-section. The medullar cavity has been drilled.

There is a fragment of window leading in F4.

The Loom-Weights by J. W. Hedges

The loom-weights, which presumably came from within the area of a single building, were found in four separate contexts. Some were in a single line (F10, Fig. 12) between post-holes (F7 and F8); a number of others were found in a heap (F9) to the west of this, while a few fragments were scattered over the hut floor (F5). Other fragments were recovered from the contractor's spoil (L2). Each of these groups is described separately below.

The line of loom-weights (F10). According to the original excavation records there appears to have been a line of either 22 or 23 weights in the 170 cm space between a single post-hole (F7) and a double one (F8) (Plate Ia). Unfortunately these were not numbered, lifted singly, or conserved, but were simply placed in fragmentary condition into sixteen bags seemingly with no intentional system although often the fragments from one weight were packed together. Full information could only be obtained for ten of the weights (Table 2) but these are so similar that they give a good idea of what all the members of the set must have been like originally. Their average weight is 308 g, and this was reasonably uniform (range 273 (est.)—339 g, while their diameters and thicknesses as well as the width of their central perforations varied little from the averages of 10·4, 2·8, and 2·7 cm.

These weights have already been referred to in passing as a set, and this is very much the impression they give. They are all rather crudely made out of poor clay which has not been properly fired; they all have finger-made perforations that give them a form like a doughnut; and their dimensions and weights vary little (Fig. 15).

At the time of discovery this find was recognised for what it was — the remains of a warp weighted loom that had been deserted for some reason when cloth was being woven on it. This is naturally a rare occurrence although similar finds have been made elsewhere (Table 3). While the presence of loom-weights on neolithic sites has been taken as sufficient evidence for the existence of the warp weighted loom, the form it is supposed to have taken has mainly been based on ones used in Scandinavia now and in the recent past (Hoffman 1964). Two particularly important assumptions are that the loom always sloped and that the warp was divided into two parts. This being the case, three shaft textiles could not be produced and their occurrence in Roman, Dark Age, and later contexts (Hedges 1973) could be cited as evidence for another type of loom. The archaeological evidence however is quite at variance with this idea, for while there are instances of collapsed looms where the warp was divided into two parts (represented by two parallel lines of weights), there is as good evidence that on occasions it was split into three systems or left as one. Although not as conclusive, the post-holes sometimes associated with such lines of weights and illustrations from the Classical period on (Hedges 1973) suggest that the loom may have been frequently, if not always, vertical.

Table 2. Loom-weights from the line (F10).

No.	Comments	Weight (g)	Diameter (cm)	Thickness (cm)	Diameter of Perforation (cm)
1	85% of one weight in fragments.	275 (324)*	10	2·4	2·2
2	One weight in fragments.	339	11	2·8	2·7
3	One weight in fragments. Mass reduced substantially by heavy washing.	279	10	2·9	3·0
4	One weight in fragments (Fig. 15).	313	10·4	3·0	2·4
5	90% of a weight in fragments.	252 (280)*	10	2·9	2·5
6	One weight in fragments (Fig. 15).	326	11·1	2·7	3·0
7	Fragments of more than one weight which could not be fitted together.	211 (total)	—	—	—
8	Fragments of more than one weight which could not be fitted together.	1136 (total)	—	—	—
9	95% of one weight in fragments.	276 (294)*	10	2·7	2·6
10	Fragments of more than one weight which could not be fitted together.	184 (total)	—	—	—
11	Fragments of more than one weight which could not be fitted together.	198 (total)	—	—	—
12	Fragments of more than one weight which could not be fitted together.	127 (total)	—	—	—
13	95% of one weight in fragments.	259 (273)*	10·3	2·7	2·7
14	One weight in fragments (Fig. 15).	330	10·2	3·0	2·7
15	One weight in fragments (Fig. 15).	323	10·8	2·8	2·0
16	Fragments of more than one weight which could not be fitted together.	2815 (total)	—	—	—

*Estimated weight of whole loom-weight.

The heap of loom-weights (F9). The loom-weights in the heap by the loom were, for the most part, distinctly different from those in use but again were so like each other as to suggest that they were a set. With the exception of two (16 and 18) they are very well made from hard, red clay with some grass tempering and are either lenticular in cross-section or have one

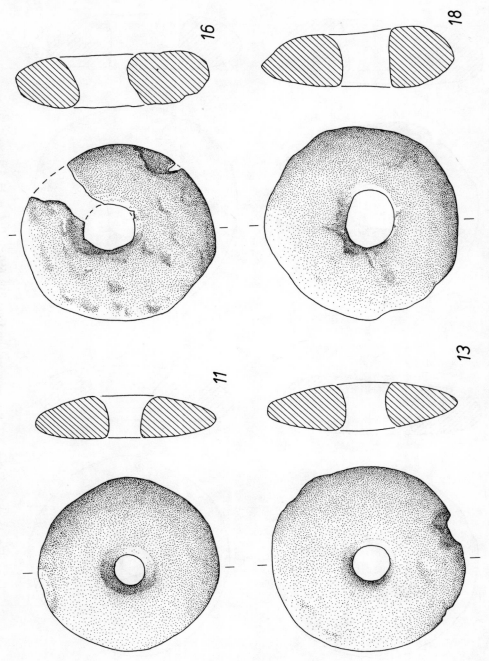

Fig. 14. Back Street, St Cross: loom-weights from F9 (650. 11, 13, 16, 18) (scale ½).

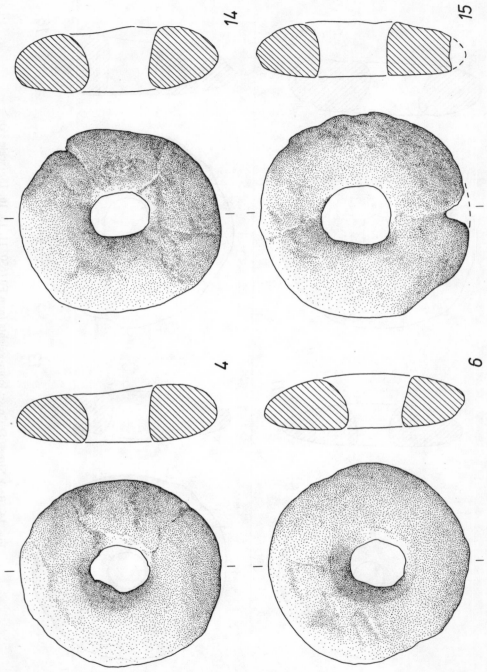

Fig. 15. Back Street, St Cross: loom-weights from F10 (650. 10.0/4, 6, 14, 15) (scale ½).

Table 3. Occurrence of lines of loom-weights on sites.

Site	Period	No. rows	Length* (cm)	Comments	Reference
Troy, Greece	Mid 3rd millennium B.C.	'several'	110	Post-holes	Blegen 1950: 350—353, Fig. 461
Niemitz, Guben, Germany	La Tène	2	60	—	Hoffman 1964: 312
Bornholm, Denmark	Migration	2	—	Post-holes	Ibid., Fig. 131
Grimstone End, Suffolk	Pagan Saxon?	2	244	—	Brown 1954: 198, Pl. XXIV
		2?	—	—	Ibid.
Upton, Northants.	Pagan Saxon	2	c. 100	—	Jackson 1969: 210, Fig. 4
		3	c. 40	—	Ibid.
West Stow, Suffolk	Pagan Saxon	1	c. 90	—	West 1969: Fig. 3
		1	c. 60	—	Ibid.
		1	c. 60	—	Ibid.
St Cross, Hampshire	Late Saxon Norman	1	170	Post-holes	—

*Distance between post-holes.

Table 4. Loom-weights in the heap (F9).

No.	Comments	Weight (g)	Diameter (cm)	Thickness (cm)	Diameter of Perforation (cm)
1	Complete (Fig. 13)	189	9·3	2·7	1·9
2	Chipped (Fig. 13)	223	10·0	2·2	1·3
3	Complete	199	9·5	2·3	1·8
4	Complete	248	10·3	2·9	2·4
5	Chipped	201	9·6	2·7	1·7
6	Complete	193	9·5	2·5	1·9
7	Complete	229	10·0	3·0	2·2
8	Complete	255	10·4	2·9	2·0
9	Complete	222	10·0	2·7	2·0

No.	Comments	Weight (g)	Diameter (cm)	Thickness (cm)	Diameter of Perforation (cm)
10	Complete	255	10·2	2·9	2·5
11	Complete (Fig. 14)	187	9·2	2·4	1·7
12	Complete	182	9·0	2·8	1·9
13	Complete (Fig. 14)	215	10·0	2·7	2·0
14	Complete	237	9·8	2·8	1·5
15	Complete	239	9·6	2·9	1·8
16	90% of one weight in fragments (Fig. 14)	266 (296)*	10·1	2·8	2·6
17	Chipped	204	9·8	2·5	2·2
18	Complete (Fig. 14)	318	10·1	2·8	3·2
19	One weight in fragments	229	9·7	2·6	2·2
20	One weight in fragments	216	10·1	2·5	1·8
21	One weight in fragments	219	10·0	2·3	2·3
22	One weight in fragments	236	9·9	2·4	1·8
23	90% of one chipped weight in fragments	216 (240)*	10·0	3·0	2·0
24	One weight in fragments	225	9·8	2·5	1·8
25	One weight in fragments	213	9·4	2·5	2·0
26	Chipped	208	9·7	2·5	2·0
27	One weight in fragments	221	10·0	2·4	1·9
28	One weight in fragments	219	9·9	2·2	2·0
29	One weight in fragments	215	9·9	2·4	2·2
30	One weight in fragments	204	9·5	2·5	2·0
31	One weight in fragments	234	10·0	2·3	2·5
32	80% of one weight in fragments	174 (218)*	9·4	2·7	2·2
33	75% of one weight in fragments	170 (227)*	9·8	2·5	1·7
34	50% of a weight; modern break	113 (226)*	9·7	2·3	2·0
35	One weight in fragments; modern breaks	218	10·0	2·4	1·7
36	One chipped weight in fragments	241	10·0	2·9	1·6
37	66% of one weight in fragments	177 (266)*	10·0	2·7	1·9
—	Fragments of more than one weight which could not be fitted together to any great extent	1843	—	—	—

*Estimated weight of whole loom-weight.

flattened side (Figs. 13 and 14). The central perforations are slightly wider at one end, but generally narrow, and give the impression of having been made with a finger. In weight the 35 most complete examples vary little from the average of 222 g (range 182—266 g), while their dimensions are constant around the averages of 9·8, 2·6, and 2·0 cm for diameter, thickness, and width of perforation respectively (Table 4). Numbers 16 and 18 are much more crudely made, and their overall similarity to those in the line suggests that they may have belonged to that set and for some reason were not being used (Fig. 14).

This feature is quite clearly a set of weights which had been put on one side against future use. How many there were is not known because of only partial recovery, but a minimum number of 43 (excluding 16 and 18) is given by dividing the weight of the fragments by the average for a complete specimen and adding this to the 35 that are whole or almost so. It is interesting that this is more or less double the number in the other set and that they are consistently of only about two-thirds the weight. It may be that they were intended for use when the warp was to be divided into two sheds, whatever the reason for that may have been, but this is pure supposition. This set, which were much cleaner than those from the loom when inspected, showed extensive wear marks running from the holes which had been caused by the loops of string to which the warp would have been attached.

Fragments of weights from the hut floor (F5). A total of 18 fragments came from the hut floor, all seemingly having come from weights similar to those in the line. For the most part the fragments are very small, but one-half of a weight is preserved and this must have had a diameter of 11 cm and a thickness and hole diameter of about 2.5 cm. In all, the fragments weighed 1238 g, which is equivalent to that of four whole weights.

Fragments of weights from the contractor's spoil heap (L2). Four very small scraps of no diagnostic value, weighing 37 g, were recovered.

Loom-weights are not useful for close dating, but the ones from St Cross have a form which suggests they were made late in the Saxon period, and this does not agree well with the limited pottery evidence. The earliest pottery is eleventh—twelfth century in date, and this implies the weights are among the latest known in this country, as the horizontal loom, which quickly ousted the warp weighted one, in less peripheral areas, arrived in Western Europe at about this time (Hoffman 1964).

CHAPTER 4

THE EASTERN SUBURB

The eastern suburb (Fig. 16), which might be expected to mirror the city on the opposing bank of the Itchen, is constrained by the steep bluff of St Giles's Hill which rises almost immediately from the river itself. A direct path to the east did exist at times, mounting straight up the hill, but houses could only be built on terraces on its lower slopes, and otherwise traffic and settlement were squeezed round the foot of the hill, whether along the gravel terrace of Chesil which carried the road to Portsmouth, or north and northeast towards the village of Winnall.

The Roman river crossing, whether by bridge or by ford lay close to and just south of the site of the modern City Bridge. Certainly a road ran from it southeast towards Portchester and Chichester, but whether the straight road running east over Magdalen Hill is of Roman origin or medieval origin is an unresolved problem, although the road *Portstret* certainly existed in the tenth century. No major road is known running north from the gate, though there are hints from the late Roman burials that some sort of track existed and there is a massive hollow way on Easton Lane. The farming settlement on the spur above Winnall (Winnall Housing Estate) dates back to the Middle Iron Age, and it seems to have survived as an independent settlement throughout most of the Roman period. A second settlement, again possibly independent, existed at Highcliffe on the southern slopes of St Giles's Hill, but the two widely separated burials from Highcliffe and Milland suggest it was something more than a mere farm.

Otherwise there are only hints from the unstratified pottery from Water Lane that extra-mural settlement was developing in the first century A.D. Second-century material is more common, with the suggestion of timber buildings, but by the end of the third century a substantial stone structure, a water tank or plunge bath, had been constructed on the Water Lane site. Nineteenth-century finds imply another stone building further south along Chesil Street, but Haverfield (1900) was more sceptical of the claim for a stone building at Highcliffe.

The pottery from Water Lane, Winnall, and Milland and the nineteenth-century finds from Highcliffe demonstrate domestic occupation at least until the middle of the fourth century. Burials within the suburb proper are unknown before the fourth century, although earlier ones occur both on the Winnall and Highcliffe settlements. But in the fourth century an extensive cemetery was established in the Water Lane—St John's Street area, on the slope running up from the river. The burials from the Blue Boar are unfortunately undated; they seem to be late, except for the evidence of an early Constantinian coin reported by Haverfield (1900). The evidence from Water Lane, however, suggests a date towards the end of the fourth century. Recently, burials have been excavated by the Research Unit on the hill north of Winnall, adjacent to the railway cutting (Biddle 1975a). Some, like the Lankhills burials, are enclosed within rectangular ditches. They, too, are late Roman, although this cemetery was presumably not linked directly with that in Water Lane (Biddle 1975a).

It is in this area that we have most evidence for early Saxon activity in the Winchester area (Meaney and Hawkes 1970). Two groups of sixth-century burials are known, one on St Giles's Hill, and the second on the hill north of Winnall (Winnall I), disturbed during the

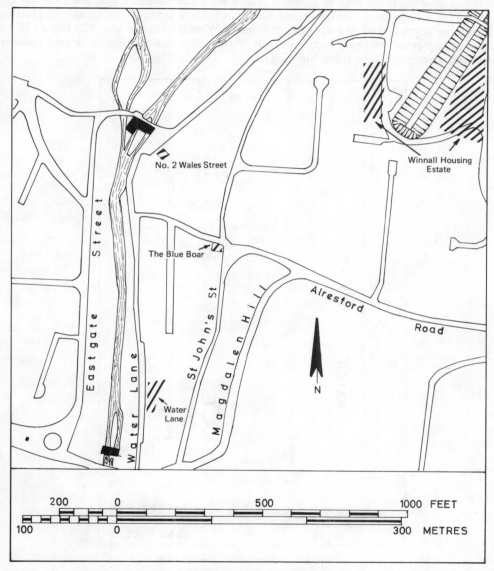

Fig. 16. Sites in the eastern suburb.

digging of the railway cutting. The latter may refer to an independent settlement, and since its seventh-century successor, Winnall II, is still further away from Winchester, one wonders if there was a ridge-top settlement under Winnall Industrial Estate, comparable to that from Chalton near Petersfield.

The medieval suburb was probably well established before the Norman Conquest. Its principle houses were aligned along the two main routes: Chesil Street, leading towards Portsmouth, and St John's Street, which skirted St Giles's Hill, led on towards Alresford, and was at this time the main road to London. There were also houses facing the river along the modern Water Lane, and cottages along the lanes leading from Water Lane and Durngate, and from the north end of St John's Street towards Winnall. On the top of St Giles's Hill was the site of the great medieval fair, occupied in the thirteenth century by a grid pattern of streets and numerous permanent buildings.

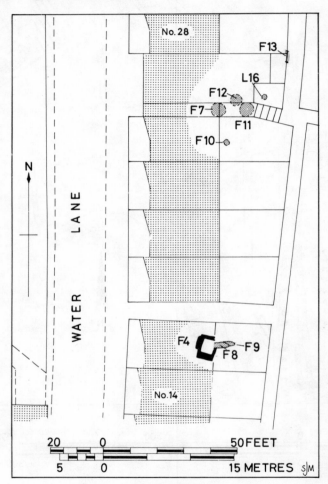

Fig. 17. Water Lane: general plan.

Although the suburb suffered some decline in the fourteenth century, it appears to have fared better than the other suburbs. On Speed's map of 1611 it is the largest of the four suburbs, and may well have exceeded its twelfth-century limits. Its resilience is also demonstrated by the survival of both its medieval parish churches, St John's and St Peter, Chesil, for few parish churches have survived elsewhere in the city. It also has more than its share of

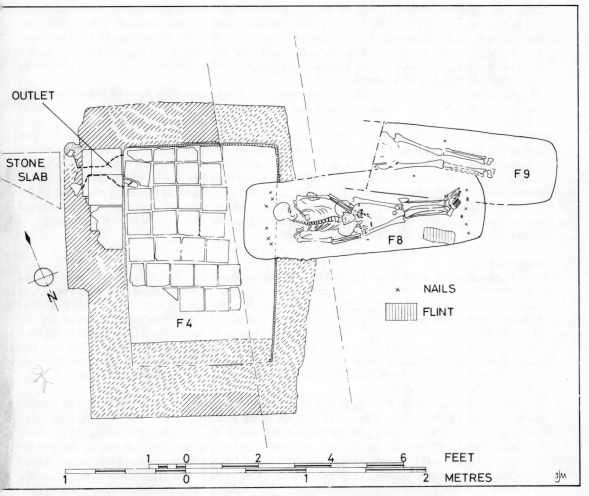

Fig. 18. Water Lane: stone-lined tank F4, and burials F8 and F9.

medieval buildings still standing — the Blue Boar, the Chesil Rectory, and the Tudor House in St John's Street, though this might really be a sign of recent poverty rather than ancient prosperity. At present, however, there is little archaeological evidence to place alongside the documentary and topographical evidence, which lies outside the scope of this study.

WATER LANE, 1958
(WLA 58, Site 718)

This site, on the east side of Water Lane (Fig. 17, Plate IIa), was observed during redevelopment, in the area of the new council houses now bearing the numbers 8—38. Three blocks of these houses were constructed, running north—south, and it was in the foundation trenches and the service trenches that observation was possible. A terrace had been cut by the builders back into the hillside removing up to a metre of top-soil on the eastern edge. The earth was removed by mechanical excavator, so observations were only made after trenching, but it was possible to follow up features with limited trenches and sondages. Our thanks are due to the former Chairman of the Housing Committee, the late Alderman E. C. Townend, and to the architect Mr A. H. Howard, L.R.I.B.A., for permission to investigate, and to the site contractors, Messrs Dunning, for their co-operation. The main observations were made by F. Cottrill, C. Burch, and myself.

At present the site lies on a terrace only about a metre above the level of the river Itchen which flows south, 20 m west of Water Lane. This high water-level is, however, the result of extensive schemes of management to provide water-power during the Middle Ages and later, and in Roman times the river perhaps ran in a channel 2 m lower than the present level. The line of the Roman and medieval defences ran along the western edge of the river, which here acted as the city ditch, and thus Water Lane lay outside, but facing the city. About 50 m to the southwest stands the City Bridge and East Gate of the medieval town, which formed a major point of access in the Roman period. The terrace itself has a subsoil of chalky clay, but to the east there has been some terracing into the hillside. Above it, to the west, lay a higher terrace along which runs St John's Street, after which the hillside rises steeply to the chalk ridge of Magdalen Hill and St Giles's Hill.

Summary

There are hints at first-century A.D. presence on the site — an unstratified bead rim and a possible sherd of girth beaker — but the earliest evidence for occupation is of second-century date. The only structural evidence consists of a single post-hole cut into the sub-soil (F1), but lying on the natural soil beneath and around the late Roman bath was an occupation deposit of brown clay with charcoal (L13) about 1.5 metres below the present surface. Finds from here are late second century. In the northern part of the site was a layer of burning (L12) and two pits, whose exact position is uncertain due to the loss of the original base plan made during excavations. Other later features (F3, F8, and F9) contained a certain amount of early Roman pottery as 'rubbish survival'.

The major structural feature found was a bath or tank constructed of flint and mortar masonry (Fig. 18, Plate IIb). There was no trace of the building to which it belonged; perhaps it was destroyed by the terracing of the hillside. Although there was some evidence, in the form of rendering of pink mortar on the external wall surfaces, to suggest that the contemporary ground surface was at the same level as the upper tiled floor, this seems unlikely, as one would expect a plunge bath to be sunk into the ground. The construction history was complex with a possible alteration of plan during construction. The original tiled surface was apparently laid on a bed of pink mortar lying on natural. This was subsequently raised on three occasions before the bath came into use, as the plaster rendering of each of the walls was found to correspond to a different level of pink mortar (Fig. 19). Perhaps the alterations were due to problems with the drainage of the tank. The only outlet for drainage was an irregular hole cut through the northern wall at the level of the upper tiled surface. Outside lay a sloping stone flag, but no trace of any drainage channel. In the final stage of use the outlet had been plugged by pink plaster applied from inside, suggesting a conversion to other uses.

The dating evidence suggests that the date of construction was late third century. The structure cuts L13 with second-century pottery, while from the first layer of mortar make-up (F4-8) came three radiate coins, the latest of Allectus c. A.D. 295. The black soil infill above the upper tiled floor produced late Roman pottery with two coins dated to c. A.D. 350, implying a half-century of usage.

All the finds up to the middle of the fourth century imply domestic occupation. At that point there was a radical change, and during the end of the Roman period the area became

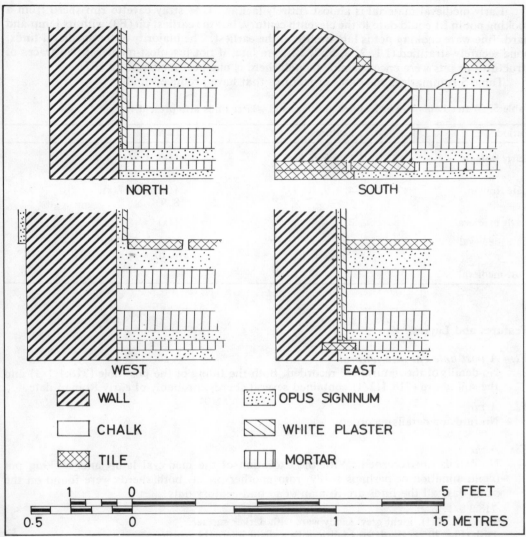

NORTH

SOUTH

WEST

EAST

	WALL		OPUS SIGNINUM
	CHALK		WHITE PLASTER
	TILE		MORTAR

Fig. 19. Water Lane: schematic sections of walls and floors of stone-lined tank F4, showing construction sequence.

part of an extra-mural cemetery. Remains of seven adults (three male, three female, one unsexed), one child, and an infant were found, and the graves are especially concentrated in a north—south line on the western part of the site continuing right up to its northern end. Only two burials were excavated archaeologically. Burials 1 and 2 (F8 and F9), the former cutting the latter. Both were extended inhumations, with heads to the east, and Burial 1 was certainly, Burial 2 possibly, in a coffin with iron nails. These two burials also provide the best dating evidence for the cemetery, as Burial 1 cut through the tiled structure and the deposit above it with its coins dated to c. A.D. 350. None of the burials could be definitely associated with grave goods, though there are stray finds of complete or relatively complete late Roman vessels which could have derived from the burials.

Early medieval material is almost entirely lacking. One stray cavetto rim sherd from a cooking pot in L1 could date to the eleventh century, but the earliest pit (F3) with its lamp and hard, fine-ware cooking pot is late twelfth at the earliest. The majority of the medieval finds, none securely stratified (L1, 2, 3, 5, 7, 10), are late, if not just post-medieval. No traces of structures or pits were encountered, though there is one post-medieval pit (F7).

Table 5 summarizes the dates of features that have produced finds.

Table 5. Water Lane: age of features and layers (x=later finds also present).

Period	Features	Layers
Early Roman	1, 3, 5, 6, 8(x)	1(x), 4, 6(x), 12, 13, 15
Late Roman	4, 8, 9, 10, 11	1(x), 2(x), 7(x), 8, 9
Early medieval	3	1(x)
Late medieval		1(x), 2, 3, 5, 6, 7, 10
Post-medieval	7	1

Features and Layers

F1: A post hole cut into natural

No details of the natural are recorded. Both the filling of the post hole (718.1.1/1) and the soil above (718.1.2/1) contained several sherds, probably of early Roman date.

F2: A pit

No finds or details recorded.

F3: A pit

No details are recorded. With the exception of the medieval lamp and cooking pot (contamination or perhaps really from another pit, as both sherds were found on the same day) all the finds are Roman of second-century date.

718.3.0/1.

Lid (Fig. 20:1). Light grey, sandy ware with darker surface.

Dish (Fig. 20:2). Hard, grey fabric with a slight internal burnish.

Bowl imitating Drag. 37 (Fig. 20:3). Grey to brown fabric with black surface.

Double-ended lamp (Fig. 22:4) in gritty Saxo-Norman ware.

Cooking pot (Fig. 22:5) in gritty Saxo-Norman ware.

F4: Stone-lined tank or plunge bath (Fig. 18, Plate IIb)

This was initially discovered during the excavation of the foundations for one of the back walls. No trace of the floor level associated with it was found, though where the wall survived above the tiled surface on the east and north sides the outer surface had a rendering of pink cement, as though it was meant to be exposed. There was however no other trace of the building. There was evidence of several changes during the construction. Originally all four walls were made about 0·3 m thick, of mortar and flint laid

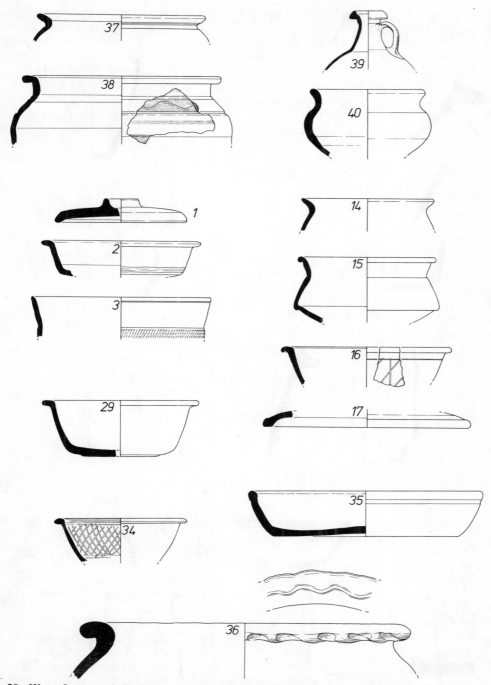

Fig. 20. Water Lane: early Roman pottery from L13 (37—40), F3 (1—3), F6 (14—17), L1 (29), L6 (34), L7 (35), and L9 (36) (scale ¼).

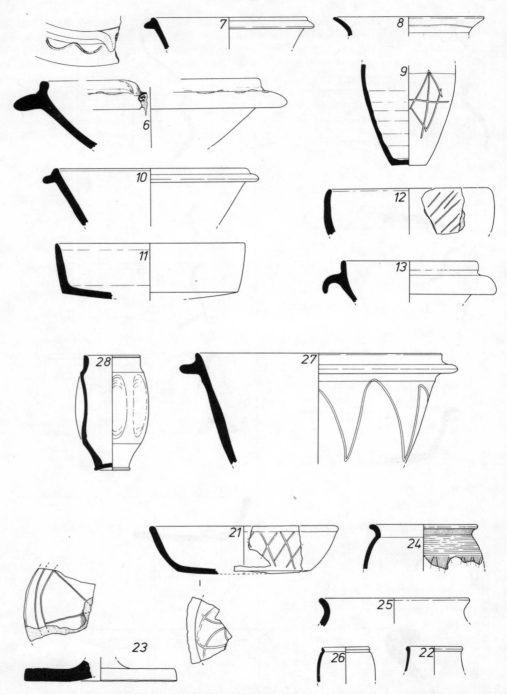

Fig. 21. Water Lane: late Roman pottery from F4 (6—13), F11 (27, 28), and F8 (21—26) (scale ¼).

directly on the bottom of the rectangular pit (Fig. 19). After the first course had been
laid, a floor of *opus signinum* (F4-9) was laid across the bottom of the trench. A bonding
course of tiles was then laid in the wall, and this projected over the floor in the east and
west walls, as though it were intended to make a tile floor at this level. The walls were
continued up, except that the south wall was considerably thickened internally. The east
wall was then given a rendering of *opus signinum* and white cement with brick chips
down to the level of the tile course. It was then decided to raise the floor level, and a
layer of mortar (F4-8), which contained three coins, was laid down with a second *opus
signinum* floor above it. The north wall was rendered with *opus signinum* and white

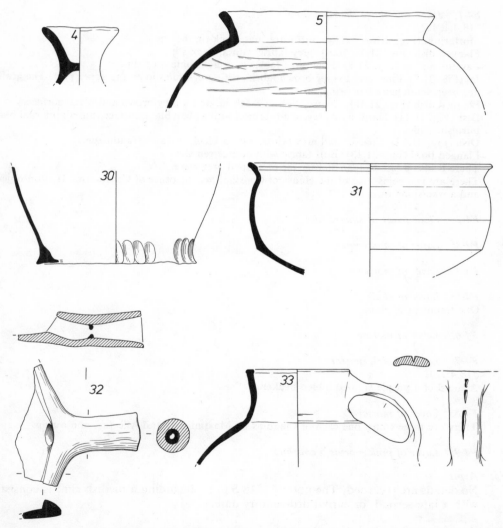

Fig. 22. Water Lane: medieval pottery from F3 (4, 5), L2 (30, 31), and L3 (32, 33) (scale ¼).

mortar with brick lumps. Finally the floor was again raised with layers of chalk and
mortar, and a third and final *opus signinum* floor with a roughly laid floor of square
tiles completed the sequence. The south wall was narrowed down to its original width at
this level, though there is an illogicality in the records here, as the rendering of the east
wall (carried out in the first stage) runs right up to this corner. The west wall was also
rendered in pink and white concrete, and a hole was punched through to form an outlet,
but it was later plugged with some *opus signinum*. Outside the water drained on to a
stone slab, but no traces of a drain were noted. Finally the tank went out of use, and
black soil, containing mid fourth-century coins, accumulated in it. It was later cut by
burials F8 and F9.

F4-1:   *Dark soil above the tiled floor*
718.4.1/1,2.
Mortarium (Fig. 21:6). Sandy, buff ware, but black on the rim.
Flanged dish (Fig. 21:7). Hard, grey fabric with a black slip.
Cavetto-rim jar (Fig. 21:8). Fine, grey fabric with light blue-grey slip.
Jar (Fig. 21:9). Fine, grey to grey-brown fabric, with grey-blue slip on the upper part. The graffito
has been scratched after firing.
Flanged dish (Fig. 21:10). Coarse, dull grey fabric, and a grey-brown and black surface.
Dish (Fig. 21:11). Hard, light grey, sandy fabric, with a plain black surface, but an internal black-
burnished slip.
Dish (Fig. 21:12). Coarse, dull grey fabric, with a black surface. Handmade.
Flanged bowl (Fig. 21:13). Buff fabric with orange-red slip.
There is also a late Roman storage jar of slipped grey ware.
There are two coins, one of the House of Constantine, the other of Constantius II, iron objects,
and a whetstone fragment.

F4-2:   *Floor made of square tiles*

F4-3:   *Layer of pink cement*

F4-4:   *Layer of mortar*

F4-5:   *Layer of chalk*
One fragment of glass.

F4-6:   *Layer of mortar*

F4-7:   *Layer of pink mortar*
718.4.7/1.
A sherd of a purple slipped folded beaker.

F4-8:   *Layer of mortar*
There are three coins, one each of Claudius II, Maximian I, and Allectus, and a ring.

F4-9:   *Layer of pink mortar 5 cm thick*

F5:   *A pit*
No details are recorded. The pottery (718.5.0/1), including a piedish rim, is consistent
with a late second- or early third-century date.

F6:   *A pit or ditch*
No details are recorded.

718.6.0/1.
Jar (Fig. 20:14). Slightly gritty, grey-brown fabric, grey surface, burnished outside.
Bowl (Fig. 20:15). Hard, light grey fabric with a brown-black surface.
Piedish (Fig. 20:16). Hard, harsh, grey fabric, black to light grey exterior with burnished decoration, and brown burnished interior.
Lid (Fig. 20:17). Harsh, brown fabric with a brown surface.
There is a second lid as well as beaker and jar rims, all of second- to early third-century date.

F7: *Pit, under the footpath*

718.7.0/1. A group of pottery apparently from this pit.

A German stoneware jug (Fig. 23:18) of sixteenth-century date.
Dripping dish (Fig. 23:19) thrown as a tube and cut into two, with a flattened base. It had at least one strap handle on the edge of the rim. Untempered, brick-red fabric with a fine, lustrous brown glaze. There are two other post-medieval sherds, a base in similar fabric and glaze, the other similar but unglazed, and a jug handle, probably from a chamber pot.
Dripping dish (Fig. 23:20), as above (Fig. 23:19).

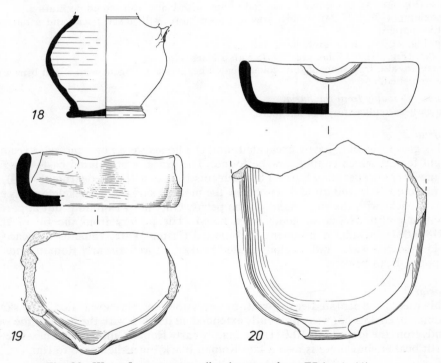

Fig. 23. Water Lane: post-medieval pottery from F7 (scale ¼).

F8: *Burial 1 (Fig. 18)*

The burial, orientated east—west, was in a subrectangular grave with rounded corners, and lay over 1·20 m below the present road surface. It cut through another burial (F9) and a tiled structure (F4). The skeleton, a woman aged 35—60, was extended on its back with the head at the west end facing left. The left hand lay on the pelvis, the right on the femur. There were no grave goods, but there were traces of a coffin or bier with 14 iron nails or fragments around the skeleton. Another burial, a newborn baby, lay above the adult. Little is recorded of the infill of the grave, except the presence of eight chalk blocks on the right of the skeleton some 15 cm above the bottom of the grave.

F8-1:   General filling of the grave
718.8.1/1—2.
Dish (Fig. 21:21). Hard, harsh, slightly coarse, dark grey fabric with a burnished surface. There is also a fragment of a late Roman, grey flagon of New Forest type, including the handle, and two Antonine samian fragments.

F8-2:   Grave fill less than 1·20 m deep
718.8.2/1.
Beaker (Fig. 21:22). Fine, orange-buff fabric with a brown, slightly metallic slip.
There is also a fragment of a metallic, purple slipped beaker, and a second-century samian chip.

F8-3:   Fill of the grave around the skeleton
718.8.3/1.
Base (Fig. 21:23). Brick-like fabric, red to brownish black with scored decoration.
Cooking pot (Fig. 21:24). Sandy, grey to brown fabric with black flecks and a burnished lattice pattern.
Jar (Fig. 21:25). Hard, grey, harsh fabric.
Beaker (Fig. 21:26). Fine, grey fabric with a black slip.
There are also fragments of soft, colour-coated beakers and flagons with a dull brown slip, one rouletted.

F8-4:   Probably from the burial
An early second-century samian sherd.

F9:   **Burial 2**
This grave was only partly excavated, and the bones were not removed, except for the right femur, which cannot now be found. The grave is orientated east—west and lies some 20 cm deeper than burial F8 which cuts it. It cuts the tiled structure (F4), and the infill could be traced up to 40 cm below the modern surface. The skeleton was extended on its back, with the right hand on the pelvis. One nail was found, but apparently not from a coffin. No grave goods were noted. The pottery from the fill of the grave (718.9.0/1) includes a fragment of rouletted Castor Ware, rouletted, micaceous, red colour-coated ware, and a colour-coated beaker, as well as early Roman finds such as a poppy-head beaker.

F10:   **Burial 3**
This was also orientated east—west, but only the feet were excavated. The skeleton, a woman aged 35—55, was apparently extended on its back with the head to the west. The finds from the grave (718.10.0/1) are mainly early Roman, including a possible sherd of girth beaker, but there is also a late Roman black burnished cavetto rim.

F11:   **Burial 4**
The burial or burials were totally disturbed by workmen digging an east—west trench, so presumably that was the orientation. One skeleton was female aged 40—60, the other probably a male adult.

F11-1:   Found near the skeleton
718.11.1/1.
Flanged bowl (Fig. 21:27), about half complete. Fine, hard, sandy, grey ware.

F11-2: From the dump nearby
718.11.2/1.
Folded beaker (Fig. 21:28), half complete. Hard, grey to buff fabric with dull brown slip.
There is a rim of a second beaker and part of a painted New Forest flagon.

F12: Burial 5
No details or finds recorded. It is a male, aged 35—45.

F13: Burial 6
No details or finds are recorded. The burial is of an adult male, but there is a fragment
of another adult and of a child.

L1:   *Unstratified material from the whole site*
718.00.1/1—6.
Piedish (Fig. 20:29). Slightly coarse, hard, grey-black fabric with black to buff exterior, and
light grey interior.
The rest of the finds are a considerable mixture including a couple of first-century sherds, such
as a bead rim. Early Roman sherds are well represented. Of the medieval, there are some sherds of
Saxo-Norman gritted ware including a cavetto-rim form and a decorated rim of a Tripod-Pitcher-
Ware vessel. One of the latest finds is an early Crosse-and-Blackwell lid.
Other finds include an unidentifiable Roman coin, samian, a key and a buckle of iron, a shale
fragment, and a clay-pipe bowl.

L2:   *Medieval infill above the tiled structure (F4)*
718.00.2/1.
Mixed medieval jugs, probably late thirteenth and into the fourteenth century.
718.00.2/2.
Fragment of a wide-bodied jug (Fig. 22:30) of fine quality, smooth, pink fabric. Splash green
glaze outside only.
Wide-mouthed cooking pot (Fig. 22:31) in a grey, hard, coarse, sandy fabric with green glaze
inside.

L3:   *From a drainage trench behind the middle block of houses*
718.00.3/1.
Handle of a skillet (Fig. 22:32) in red, sandy fabric with brown glaze inside, heavily trimmed on
the outside of the handle.
Jug (Fig. 22:33) in oxidized painted ware with a bib or collar, glazed area on neck.
There is also a reduced painted-ware handle, and all three vessels are fifteenth century.
There are two samian sherds.

L5:   *Drainage trench north of 8—16 Water Lane*
A bronze buckle and three fragments of medieval glazed jug.

L6:   *From a sewer trench 16—17 m from the north end of the site*
718.00.6/2.
Dish (Fig. 20:34). Very fine, light grey fabric with a black slip and burnished decoration.
718.00.6/1.
A lid and a pie dish, both of the second century, a Hadrianic samian sherd, and a jug with pale
green glaze and a cream-coloured fabric with evidence of black slip decoration on the top of the
handle (thirteenth century).

L7: As L6, but stratified, near the street frontage

718.00.7/1.
A complete dish (Fig. 20:35), presumably from a burial. Hard, dark brown to black fabric, with internal burnish. The concave base is usually a late Roman feature.
718.00.7/2.
Fragment of a red-ware, medieval jug, thirteenth century, and a second-century samian sherd.

L8: Stratified below L7

718.00.8/1.
Rim of a large, early Roman jar.

L9: Stratified on natural below L8

718.00.9/1.
Rope-rimmed storage jar (Fig. 20:36). Harsh, grey fabric with inscribed decoration.
The other finds include rims of a bowl, a dish, and a storage jar, and a fragment of a slipped grey-ware jar, all probably of the third century; and a late Antonine samian mortarium sherd.

L10: From a trench behind 26 Water Lane
Fragments from a jug, very damaged, completely oxidized, and covered with an orange glaze, and speckled black.

L12: A thin charcoal spread in the northern half of the site
There are fragments of a second-century piedish.

L13: Light-brown clay soil, lying on natural
About 1·20 m below street surface, cut by F4, F8, and F9.

718.00.13/1.
Jar (Fig. 20:37). Similar fabric to above, grey surface.
Necked jar (Fig. 20:38). Slightly gritty, red-brown fabric with a grey core, black surface, and burnished on the neck and part of the shoulder.
Flagon (Fig. 20:39). Fine, hard, off-white fabric.
Bowl (Fig. 20:40). Dull grey, hard, slightly coarse fabric, with a dull grey to black surface.
There is a decorated base of a piedish and a folded beaker in soft, red-buff fabric with a black burnished slip outside.
All the finds are probably of the second century.

L15: Putty coloured soil beneath and to the south of Burial 3 (F8, F10)
Iron nails and strip, and one samian sherd.

L16: North of footpath leading to St John's Street
Substantial fragment of a louvre which will be discussed by Mr G. C. Dunning in a forthcoming volume.

The Finds
The Roman Coins by R. Reece

Provenance	Museum Coin Number	Reference	Date A.D.
F4-1	C 1723	Constantius II, CK 32	348—50
F4-1	C 1722	House of Constantine, as CK 25	350—60
F4-8	C 1724	Claudius II, reverse illegible	268—70
F4-8	C 1726	Maximian I, RIC V 559	286—94
F4-8	C 1725	Allectus, RIC 97	293—96
L1	C 1727	3rd—4th C, illegible	
L1	C 1804	Constantine II, HK 198	330—35

The Samian by G. Dannell

Provenance	Museum Accession Number	Form	Date A.D.	Kiln
F6	718.6.0/3	35/6	2nd century	central Gaul
	718.6.0/4	18/31	Hadrianic	central Gaul
F8-1	718.8.1/3	38	Antonine	central Gaul
	718.8.1/4	chip	Antonine	—
F8-2	718.8.2/2	chip	2nd century	central Gaul
F8-3	718.8.3/2	33	Hadrianic/ Antonine	central Gaul
F8-4	718.8.4/1	42	late 1st—early 2nd century	southern Gaul
L1	718.00.1/6	38	Antonine	central Gaul
	718.00.1/7	18/31	Hadrianic/ Antonine	eastern Gaul
L3	718.00.3/2	38	Antonine	central Gaul
	718.00.3/3	27	Antonine	central Gaul
L6	718.00.6/3	38	Hadrianic	central Gaul
L8	718.00.8/2	18/31	Hadrianic/ Antonine	central Gaul
L9	718.00.9/2	chip	2nd century	central Gaul
L15	718.00.15/1	45	Late Antonine	central Gaul

The Glass by D. Charlesworth

Provenance	Museum Accession Number	Date A.D.	Description
F4-5	718.5	3rd—4th century	Window glass. Edge fragment, blown glass, smooth on both sides.
F8-1	718.10.11	—	3 fragments, 2 certainly from the same vessel; thin, nearly colourless, unidentifiable.
F8-3	718.12—14	—	Fragments from the same vessel as F8-1.
		3rd century (?)	1 very fine colourless fragment.
		1st century (?)	1 fine amber fragment.
L11	718.23	modern	

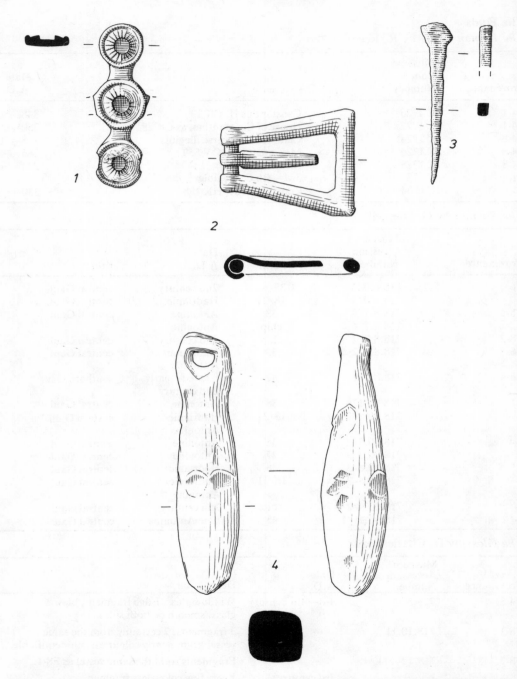

Fig. 24. Water Lane: bronze objects and iron nail; Wales Street: lead plumb-bob (scale: 1, 2, 4:1/1; 3:½).

Miscellaneous Finds

Bronze object from F3-0 (718.9, Fig. 24:1). Dr Graham Webster writes: 'A bronze mount consisting of a strip of three attached circles, the central one being larger than the other two. There are circular cavities in each of the three roundels which could have been settings for coloured stones or enamel, and the fact that no trace of the latter survives may indicate the stronger possibility of the former. The only parts of attachment to the rest of the mount are on each side of the centre roundel. The decoration round the sunken areas is typical of medieval work (cf. London Museum 1940: pl. LXX). It is suggested that this could have been part of a cross for a rosary.'

Bronze buckle from L5 (718.22, Fig. 24:2). A medieval type.

Other objects of note (not illustrated). A plain bronze ring from F4-8 (718.6); a whetstone fragment from F4-1 (718.7); a ring of Kimmeridge shale from L1 (718.19); and a quern fragment from F8-3 (718.28).

Iron objects. Dr Manning notes that the iron objects include the head and part of the stem of a small Class I nail from F1-2. There is a Class II nail (718.29, Fig. 24:3), length 8·8 cm, from F8-1. Nail types are discussed in Frere (1972) and illustrated in Fig. 69. A fragment of iron strip (718.16) with two rectangular nail holes through it, length 4·5 cm, comes from F10-1.

The Burials by C. Wells

This material consists of five inhumations, mostly in very defective and poor condition. The following is a brief account of each.

Burial 1 (F8). Two individuals are identifiable here: (*a*) female, age 35—60, and (*b*) a newborn baby.

(*a*) The female is represented by a damaged skull which is lightly built, ovoid in norma verticalis, with a frontal bone rising steeply from negligible brow ridges. There is a shallow sagittal sulcus between the posterior halves of the parietal bones but no tuber occipitale. The mastoid processes are small. The mandible is damaged but the dental state is:

```
R   0  .  .  .  .  0  0  |  .  .  .  .  .  .  0  .     L
    _____
    8  .  .  5  .  .  .  .  |  0  0  0  0  .  .  .  .
    C     P                 |        P
```

Attrition is heavy on the surviving teeth. The caries is occlusal. There has been extensive infection of the alveolus, with a large periodontal abscess around 5̅ and a small one around |4̅. Two loose premolars and one maxillary molar have hypercementosis of their roots, indicating reaction to alveolar infection.

The following cranial measurements were obtainable:

Maximum sagittal length	181·9 mm
Maximum parietal breadth	134·8 mm
Least frontal breadth	95·1 mm
Maximum frontal breadth	119·2 mm
Cranial index (dolichocranial)	74·1 mm

Post-cranial remains include: fragments of most vertebrae, sacrum, most long bones (extensively damaged), most of the carpal and tarsal elements, all metacarpals and metatarsals, and a few other scraps in poor condition. The following measurements were taken:

	left (mm)	right (mm)
Clav L1	133·8	134·5
Hu L1	298·2	305·4
Ul L1	239·6	244·2
Ra L1	217·2	224·1

This would correspond to a stature of about 1595·0 mm (5 ft 2¾ in).

There are anomalies and pathology observable in this skeleton. The sacrum has six segments instead of five; the distal ends of both tibiae have large squatting facets; and neither humerus has a septal aperture. Osteophytosis is widespread in the vertebral column: it is slight on the cervicals and on T6, 7, 8, 11 and 12, and on L3, 4 and 5; it is severe on T9 and 10. A defect of the body of the L1 vertebra is difficult to assess owing to post-inhumation changes. It consists of an erosion of the inferior part of the left side and is about the size of a cherry, i.e. 18 mm in diameter. This lesion might have been due to invasion of the bone by a localized aneurysm of the abdominal sorta. However, other possibilities exist and there seems no way of deciding between them in view of the uncertainty about the extent of the post-inhumation changes. Both maxillary antra have their floors roughened by sinusitis. This was presumably associated with the alveolar infection, because a fistula extends from the left antrum to the socket of the M3 tooth. Slight osteoarthritic lipping is present at the right shoulder joint around the margin of the glenoid fossa and on the head of the humerus.

(b) This consists of 12 fragments of cranial vault of a newborn baby. There is no way to decide whether these two burials are to be interpreted as due to some such hazard as a puerperal death of a mother and child after a difficult delivery. It may be noted, however, that a six-piece sacrum, deepens the cavity of the pelvis and thus may tend to produce a long and hard labour. The osteophytosis of the woman's spine and her arthritic shoulder suggest that she led a hard-working life, and she may have been prematurely exhausted and unfit to resist the demands of a difficult birth. But as she could have been from 35 to 60 years old, she may have been beyond the childbearing age.

Three fragments of animal bones were also present: a scapula and rib of a small lamb and a fragment from a small ox.

Burial 3 (F10). Female, age 35—55 years. There are a few very damaged fragments of cranial vault and a broken and defective mandible. The dental state is:

0 7 6 0 0 0 0 0	0 0 0 0 5 6 7 0

Attrition is heavy; caries absent; and there are moderate deposits of tartar. A fragment of the occiput shows the anatomical variant of her sagittal sinus turning left instead of right.

Post-cranial remains include: vertebrae C1—3, T1—2, L4—5, and S1—2 segments; also a few small fragments of pelvis, scraps of ribs, the damaged shafts of arm bones and three metacarpals. This was a lightly built woman, and she was probably about 1534 mm (5 ft 0½ in) tall. She had some osteoarthritis, and slight osteophytosis of her cervical vertebrae. A small fragment of a middle left rib shows a well-healed fracture.

Burial 4 (F11). Remains of two persons are present.

(a) Female, age 40—60 (?) years. There is the posterior two-thirds of a cranial vault. This has a shallow sagittal sulcus in the posterior half of the parietal region, and there is a low tuber occipitale. A fragment of maxilla shows the dental state:

Attrition on the surviving tooth is moderate. There is well-marked sinusitis in the left maxillary antrum associated with a fistula, about 6 mm in diameter, at the site of the missing 6.

Post-cranial remains include: fragments of sacrum, innominate, right clavicle, left and right humeri, left ulna, left and right femora and tibiae. All are extensively damaged and eroded.

(b) Male (?), adult. This consists only of a damaged pair of tibiae. Their measurements were:

	left (mm)	right (mm)
Ti L1	356·8	—
Ti D1	33·4	33·3
Tl D2	26·3	26·6
Cnemic Index	78·7	79·8

This is eurycnemic indicating no flattening of the bones from side to side. Stature can be estimated to have been about 1683·0 mm (6 ft 6¼ in). A medium sized squatting facet is present on the left tibia.

Burial 5. Male, age 35—45 years. This consists of the damaged innominates and major leg bones of a fairly well-built man. The left cnemic index was obtainable: Ti Dl 36.8 mm. Ti D2 28.3 mm. Index 76.8. This is eurycnemic. A medium sized squatting facet is present on the left tibia, a small one on the right tibia.

Pathology is present in the form of slight osteoarthritis present at both sacroiliac joints. There is also a small exostosis, rather like a 'rider's bone', on the medial side of the linea aspera of the right femur. This was probably due to a tear of the insertion of the adductor longus muscle. There is also a very small bony 'tag' or exostosis anteriorly on the distal end of the left fibula, which was probably the result of tearing a ligament.

Burial 6. Male, adult. This consists of a damaged calvarium. It is ovoid in norma verticalis. The following cranial measurements could be obtained: L 180·2 mm, B 145·6 mm, GB 94·0 mm, NH 49·1 mm, NB 23·2 mm. This gives a cranial index of 80.8 (brachycranial) and a nasal index of 47.2 (mesorrhine). From the maxilla the dental state is seen to be:

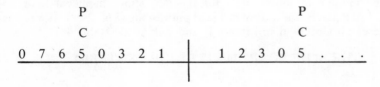

Attrition is moderately severe. The caries on the premolar teeth was occlusal and small periodontal abscess cavities surround their roots. Tartar is present but light. The interior of the left maxillary antrum shows evidence of sinusitis. This may be related to the dental caries and alveolar abscess.

A right clavicle, 143·9 mm long, and 6 rib fragments are also present.

A fragment of a second calva is present with this inhumation. It appears to be from a child of about six or seven years. There is also another fragment of maxilla.

Summary. The extremely defective state of these remains does not allow much to be inferred from them. In the five burials at least eight persons are represented: three male, three female, a child, and a newborn baby. As far as it is possible to judge there was moderate diversity of physical type amongst them, e.g. the skull of Burial 1 was dolichocranial, the skull of Burial 6 was brachycranial.

In all there were 21 surviving teeth, of which 3 (14·3%) were carious, and 4 had associated periodontal abscesses. This points to a rather low level of oral and dental hygiene. Further substance is given to this by the presence of maxillary sinusitis in three of these persons. This is a condition which is often associated with general ill health and chronic infection of the respiratory tract, etc. There is insufficient surviving material to establish this in detail but it is notable that most of these persons seem to have been of rather light build, with no great development of their musculature. They were of average height. Further comment on their dental condition shows that of 79 tooth places that can be identified in their jaw fragments, 31 (39·2%) had lost their teeth before death. Much of this loss seems to have been related to alveolar infection and serves, to some extent, to indicate a poor level of general health. The presence of osteoarthritis and osteophytosis in many vertebrae, a shoulder joint, etc. (when so many post-cranial bones are absent or defective) indicates that these persons led a fairly heavy and strenuous life, which exposed them to abundant physical strains. This is reinforced by the exostoses, presumably traumatic, present in Burial 5.

Where it is possible to examine for the feature, large squatting facets are found and these indicate, in general, a low social status associated with a lack of chairs or benches in their houses or else point to the practice of occupations, probably humble, which involved grovelling or squatting. The presence of sinusitis in three of these individuals may have been aggravated by living in poor, ill-ventilated huts, full of smoke from a central hearth, where over-crowding led to para-nasal disease from droplet infection. Their diet was probably tough and coarse, in view of the fairly heavy dental attrition that was present on most teeth. But it was probably adequate in amount, because the group as a whole does not show any well-marked evidence of chronic malnutrition.

The sum of the evidence suggests that these people were a fairly poor, hard working community of humble status who, if not exposed to severe food shortage, nevertheless were of only medium physique and suffered from a considerable amount of chronic, low-grade illness.

No. 2 WALES STREET

Wales Street is a continuation of Water Lane, the junction being near the Durngate Mill. In 1962 during the digging of foundations for the new shop, medieval floor levels were exposed. The only find made by the author is a lead plumb-bob (Fig. 24:4). It was passed on to the Winchester Research Unit who still retain it under the code BSSC 497.

THE BLUE BOAR, 24—25 ST JOHN'S STREET

Summary
This familiar timber-framed building was threatened with demolition in 1963—4, a threat which fortunately never materialized. A survey by Mr W. J. Carpenter Turner suggests its origin as a medieval hall-house, with a number of later additions. In 1964 Miss Brenda Toogood, on behalf of the City Museum, carried out an excavation inside the building, to elucidate some of its internal lay-out. This excavation is not considered here as it is only meaningful taken in conjunction with a survey of the standing building, which lies beyond our present scope.

During the final phases of restoration, in April 1971, workmen were digging a soakaway in the back garden when human bones were discovered at a depth of 1·20 m below the ground surface. The police were informed and made some preliminary investigations. Subsequently Mr J. Dockerill of the City Museum visited the site and excavated the remnants of the burials. The hole in which they were found is orientated north—south, parallel with the west and north walls of the garden. The northwest corner of the hole is 4 m from the west wall, and 5 m from the north wall. Four intersecting burials were discovered, all in the southeast corner, and all with the head approximately to the east northeast. The chronological sequence seems to be Burial 4, 3, 2, 1, with Burial 1 being the latest. They are presumably late Roman, as Burial 2 is a 'boot burial' typical of that period. It has not proved possible to locate the human bones among the Museum's collections.

The Features

F1: *Burial 1*
The grave fill is slightly chalky. There are no details of the lay-out of the skeleton, and the head end could not be excavated.

F2: *Burial 2*
Only the feet and the left tibia and fibula were left *in situ*. The right leg had been removed either in the digging of Burial 1, or by the police. The grave fill was more earthy than that of Burial 1 and was apparently cut by it, and it seems to cut Burial 3. The head was to the east, but the burial had been extensively disturbed by the mechanical excavator. There were hobnails at the feet, and supposedly one coffin nail with a rounded head, but as 'boot burials' usually lack coffins, this observation must be treated with reserve.

F3: *Burial 3*
This was completely excavated. It is an extended inhumation, the head to the east, and the hands apparently on the thighs. The skull was badly fragmented, and the right femur was missing (removed by Burial 2?), as were the tibia and fibula which had been disturbed by the mechanical excavator. The burial had a coffin with oval-headed nails. These were undisturbed on the south side, implying that it is later than Burial 4.

F4: *Burial 4*
The top of a femur and some finger bones were exposed in the section in the southeast corner of the hole, but no excavation of this burial was possible.

WINNALL HOUSING ESTATE
(WHE 55, 59, Site 719)

Discoveries were first reported to the City Museum in the autumn of 1955, when the digging of drainage sumps for a new Winchester City Council housing estate revealed a group of early Roman pottery vessels. Mr F. Cottrill and Miss M. A. Bennet-Clark (Mrs Carey), and later Mr B. Cunliffe carried out some initial excavation on the ditched enclosures which lie east of the railway cutting. Further vessels and some inhumation burials were unearthed in the same area in 1959, and further records were made during the excavation of house foundations. At the same time finds were made west of the railway. The recording of these later discoveries

was done by Miss Brenda Capstick and Miss Mavis Wood, assisted by Mr A. R. T. Ball and
the writer, supervised by Mr Cottrill.

Owing to the pressure of other work in Winchester at the time, opportunities for
excavation and keeping a watching brief were restricted. This report is based mainly on the
field notes made by Mr Cottrill. Throughout there was excellent co-operation from the City
Engineer, Mr L. M. Perkis, and his staff.

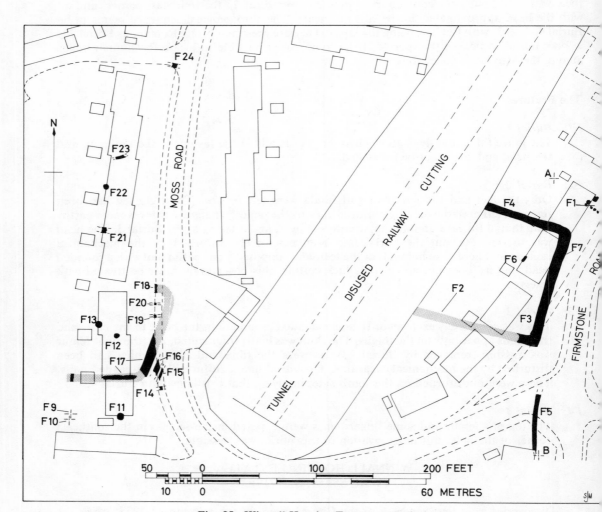

Fig. 25. Winnall Housing Estate: general plan.

Summary

Despite its proximity to the city walls, the site seems to represent a totally separate
settlement throughout its history, except perhaps in the late Roman period when the town's
cemeteries began to encroach on this general area. The siting is fairly typical for a rural

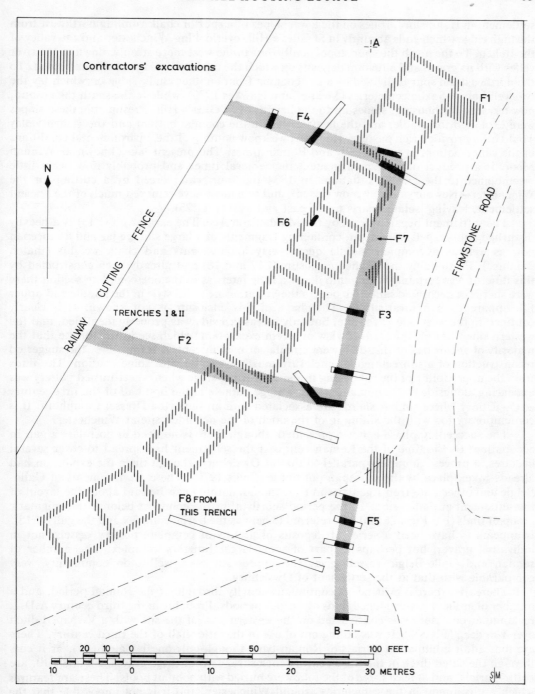

Fig. 26. Winnall Housing Estate: plan of the area east of the railway.

settlement in Hampshire. It lies on the lower slopes of a spur of chalk running northwest from the high ridge which ends abruptly in St Giles's Hill, overlooking Winchester and the valley of the Itchen. To the north the spur slopes gently, but to the west more steeply, down to the river valley with its gravel and alluvium deposits on which the medieval village of Winnall stood. To the northeast the spur is divided by a dry coombe from another chalk ridge on which lay the two well-known Saxon cemeteries (Meaney and Hawkes 1970), while to the south the ground, now terraced for housing, slopes up to the heights of St Giles's Hill. Presumably these slopes were exploited for arable, and the heavier soils in the coombe bottom and the Itchen valley would have provided rich pasture. However, we know nothing of the environmental conditions in the valley bottom in pre-Roman and Roman times. The present lake, known as Winnall Moor, is a product of river management in medieval times and probably now bears little resemblance to the former situation. In 1884 the spur was pierced by a cutting for the Winchester—Newbury railway (now closed), and this must have removed much of the ancient settlement, leaving isolated parts to the east and west (Fig. 25).

The settlement began at least by the Middle Iron Age. The earliest pit (F13) is a heavily disturbed bell-shaped storage pit, containing fragments of a large storage jar and a saucepan pot, as well as a complete saddle quern, clay loom-weights and chalk weights (thatch weights?). Presumably the ditched enclosure (F17 and 18) had already been constructed by this time. It was certainly falling into decay a little later, as in the one complete section there were sherds of decorated saucepan pots in the St Catherine's Hill style in the middle and upper fill, apparently a natural silting. The shape .of this enclosure is not known. It is clearly confined to the west side of the site, but only its eastern side was properly identified, and the western side was only inferred. In view of recent excavation, which seems to indicate that the majority of enclosures of this date were circular or oval in central Hampshire, the suggested reconstruction of a subrectangular enclosure must be treated with some caution. The finds from the upper filling of the silt belong to the interesting stage when wheel-turned pottery was appearing alongside the handmade wares, a stage datable to the first half of the first century at Owslebury where similar sherds are associated with an imported Dressel I amphora. It is contemporary too with the silting in of the ditch of the defended site at Winchester.

The succeeding phase is not represented, though there is no need to postulate a gap in occupation. By the time of the Roman conquest the settlement had spread to cover several hectares, a process doubtless parallel to that at Owslebury, though there the expansion had already taken place by the saucepan-pot phase (Collis 1970). There are fragments of Gallo-Belgic and other Late Iron Age types in F11, though nothing can be said about the layout of the settlement at that period. To the period shortly after the conquest belongs the enigmatic group of finds (F1, Figs. 26 and 27), referred to here as the burial complex and the gully (F15). It appears to have been a series of deposits of groups of complete pottery vessels, not in individual graves, but perhaps as part of some larger funerary complex. The number of samian and Gallo-Belgic vessels gives the impression of a well-to-do community, very comparable with that at the settlement of Owslebury.

Thereafter there is evidence of continuous activity throughout the Roman period, and a number of gullies have produced finds of various periods. Probably in the third century A.D. a rectangular enclosure was constructed on the western part of the site with a V-shaped ditch over 1 m deep (Fig. 26). It was falling out of use in the latter half of the third century. There are four adult inhumation burials of Roman type, though only one is dated (F7), as it cuts through the silted ditch of the third century enclosure. Two of these graves, F9 and F10, are coffin burials, and at least three of the four were buried with hobnail boots. These are features which are common in the cemeteries around Winchester, and it is not impossible that the settlement was now on the fringe of the urban cemeteries which seem to have extended out beyond the church at Winnall in the fourth century. However, it seems most likely that they belong to the settlement which was certainly still occupied. All four are male burials, and it has been noted at Owslebury (Collis 1977b) that in the later Roman period there is a great

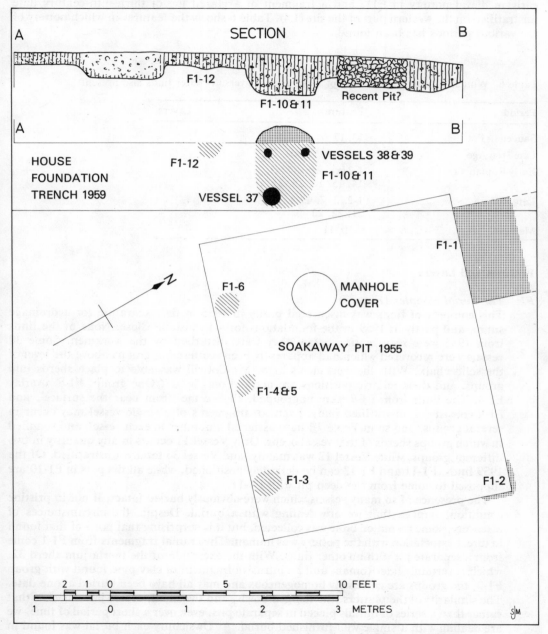

Fig. 27. Winnall Housing Estate: plan and section of burial complex F1.

preponderance of male burials which, on the evidence of burial site and the physical condition of the individuals, were of low social status.

After the Roman period there is little evidence for occupation. There are a few sherds of early medieval pottery in F11, and a fragment of a glazed jug of thirteenth-century date unstratified on the western part of the site (L4). Table 6 shows the features in which pottery of the various periods has been found.

Table 6. Winnall Housing Estate: age of features and layers (x = later finds also present)

Period	Features	Layers
Saucepan Pot	13, 17	
Late Iron Age	1-1, 2-5, 11 (x)	
Early Roman	1-2 (x), 2 (x), 7 (x), 14, 15, 16, 18, 21 (x)	
Late Roman	1-2, 2, 7, 17-4, 19 21, 22, 23	
Medieval	2-10, 11	4

Features and Layers

F1: The burial complex (Fig. 27)

This complex of finds was discovered partly in 1955 in the excavation for a drainage sump, and partly in 1959 in the foundations for 4 Firmstone Close. None of the finds from 1955 were seen *in situ* before they were disturbed by the workmen. Some 30 vessels were recovered which had apparently been scattered in groups above the level of the solid chalk. With the workmen's help, Mr Cottrill was able to place sherds into groups, and their relative positions are marked on Fig. 27. One group, F1-5, overlay F1-4. The finds from F1-7 were ungrouped, F1-8 came 'from near the surface', and F1-9 consists of unstratified finds. Even so, fragments of a single vessel may occur in several groups, and so in Table 7 I have assigned a number to each vessel, and signified in which groups sherds of that vessel occur. Only Vessel 11 occurs in any quantity in two different groups, while Vessel 12 was mainly, and Vessel 36 totally, unstratified. Of the 1959 finds, F1-11 and F1-12 can be definitely positioned, while all the pots in F1-10 are supposed to come from the deep pit with F1-11.

The presence of so many vessels which were obviously buried intact, if not in pristine condition, implies that we are dealing with a burial. Despite the circumstances of discovery, some cremated bone was collected, but it is surprising that none of that found in direct association with the pottery was human. The cranial fragments from F1-1 come from a separate pit with no other finds. With the exception of the mortarium sherd 32, which is certainly late Roman, and an intrusive fragment of clay pipe found with group F1-3, the groups are extremely homogeneous and may all have been buried at one date. The similarity of the platters, the flanged bowls, and the small, coarse jars suggests that rather than a series of burials placed in separate pits, even over a short period of time, we are dealing with a single well-furnished burial. At Owslebury each burial was found in its own isolated pit, but assuming the population on the two settlements to have been

Table 7. Occurrence of sherds and vessels in F1 (+ = single or few sherds, ★ = many fragments).

Vessel No.	1	2	3	4	5	6	7	8	9	10	11	12	13	14	15	16	17	18	19	20	21	22	23	24	25	26	27	28	29	30	31	32	33	34	35	36	37	38	39	40	41	42	43
F1-3	★	★	★	+	+	★	★	★	★	★	★	+	+	+																													
F1-4															★	★	+	+																					+				
F1-5											★	+		★	★	+	+																										
F1-6										+								★	★																								
F1-7											★	★																									+						
F1-8										+																											+						
F1-9									+							+																				+							
F1-10																				★	★	★	★	★	★	★	★	★	★	★	★	★	+	★	+								
F1-11																																					★	★	★				
F1-12																																								★	★	★	★

similar, the calculations of population size and the chronological spread of the burials in the Owslebury cemetery make it extremely unlikely that four or five people, as implied by the Winnall grouping, would be likely to die and be accorded such rich burial in so short a space of time.

As for absolute dating, Mr Hartley's report on the samian would suggest 55—65 A.D. He further notes that the footrings of vessels 1, 2, 3, and 21 are unworn, implying they were relatively new when buried. The Gallo-Belgic wares would agree with this dating, for instance the high percentage of illiterate and geometric stamps is considered a late feature, and of all the vessels hopefully termed *terra nigra* in the descriptions below, only one or two would be acceptable to all scholars as true *terra nigra* (e.g. vessel 9) and those are of poor quality. However, the remaining vessels are all in a very hard fabric with well-purified clay, which contrasts strongly with the local, generally rather gritty versions of the Belgic platters. Most of the vessels were apparently new when buried, and the wear which has been noted on the upper surface of several of them is almost certainly due to this being exposed to natural weathering, especially by roots, while the unweathered appearance of others implies that some of the vessels were piled one on top of the other. The vessels are described in numerical order and illustrated on Figs. 29—31 with these numbers, and as far as possible mounted in their supposed groups.

F1-1
The only finds from this pit were some cremated bone which Calvin Wells identifies as seven small pieces of cranial vault and three small fragments of long bone of an adult.

F1-2
719.1.2/1.
This pit produced two small sherds of gritted prehistoric pot.

F1-3 to F1-12
719.1.3/1.
Vessel 1 (Fig. 29:1). Samian cup, form Ritterling 8, of mid late-Neronian date (see p. 83).
719.1.3/2.
Vessel 2 (Fig. 29:2). Samian cup, form Ritterling 8, dating to *c*. A.D. 50—65 (see p. 83).
719.1.3/3.
Vessel 3 (Fig. 29:3). Samian cup, form Drag. 27, dating to *c*. A.D. 50—65 (see p. 83).
719.1.3/4.
Vessel 4 (Fig. 29:4). Samian fragment, Drag. 18, probably pre-Flavian.
719.1.3/5.
Vessel 5. Samian fragment, Ritterling 8 or possibly Drag. 27, pre-Flavian.
719.1.3/6.
Vessel 6 (Fig. 29:6). *Terra nigra* platter or imitation of *Camulodunum* form 16Ac. Hard, fine, light brown fabric with black smoothed surface. Internal concentric burnished lines at 25 and 18 mm radius. Internal surface worn. Stamped IIVLI.
719.1.3/7.
Vessel 7 (Fig. 29:7). *Terra nigra* platter, *Camulodunum* form 16Ac. Soft, fine, grey ware, dark grey-black surface, internal surface worn. Illiterate stamp.
719.1.3/8.
Vessel 8 (Fig. 29:8). *Terra nigra* platter, ware and stamp as 6, but surface lighter grey, internal surface worn.
719.1.3/9.
Vessel 9 (Fig. 29:9). *Terra nigra* flanged bowl. Light grey-brown, hard fabric, with dark-grey coating. *Camulodunum* form 58A. Stamped.

719.1.3/10.
Vessel 10 (Fig. 29:10). Flagon neck and handle, hard, sandy, buff ware.
719.1.3/11.
Vessel 11 (Fig. 29:11). Ovoid beaker, of *Camulodunum* form 92. Sandy, orange ware with buff surface, occasional grey flecks. Decoration is with an 8- or 9-toothed comb, in zones defined by shallow grooving. Very abraded.
719.1.3/12.
Vessel 12. Shallow bowl. Soft, brown ware with grog, black surface.
719.1.9/1.
Vessel 13 (Fig. 29:13). Lid, black, cinder-like texture, probably handmade.
719.1.9/2.
Vessel 14 (Fig. 29:14). Colour-coated bowl. *Camulodunum* form 62Ae. Fine, soft, cream ware, with purple-black, rough-cast surface, badly worn.
719.1.4/1.
Vessel 15 (Fig. 29:15). Butt-beaker. Hard sandy ware with fine rounded grit, grey core and grey-brown surface. Dribble of white slip inside. Badly warped. Cf. Vessel 43.
719.1.4/2.
Vessel 16 (Fig. 29:16). Pear-shaped, cordoned jar with burnished chevron. Hard, sandy ware with fine rounded grit. Grey core, brown under-skin, and grey-brown surface.
719.1.6/1.
Vessel 17. Flagon, neck only. Fine, sandy, light-buff ware with grey core.
719.1.6/2.
Vessel 18 (Fig. 31:18). Small jar. Hard, sandy ware with fine rounded grit, grey-brown with black burnished surface.
719.1.6/3.
Vessel 19 (Fig. 31:19). Small jar. Hard, sandy ware with fine rounded grit, light grey.
719.9.
Vessel 20 (Fig. 30:20). Glass flask. See p. 85.
719.1.10/1.
Vessel 21 (Fig. 30:21). A samian dish similar to form 36. Probably pre-Flavian. See p. 85.
719.1.10/2.
Vessel 22 (Fig. 30:22). *Terra nigra* platter, *Camulodunum* form 8. Hard, light grey-brown fabric with black smoothed surface, inner surface not weathered. The stamp was broken during excavation and only half was recovered.
719.1.10/3.
Vessel 23 (Fig. 30:23). *Terra nigra* platter, as Vessel 22.
719.1.10/4.
Vessel 24 (Fig. 30:24). *Terra nigra* platter, *Camulodunum* form 16Ac. Hard, reddish-brown fabric with black surface. Stamped.
719.1.10/5.
Vessel 25 (Fig. 30:25). *Terra nigra* platter, *Camulodunum* form 16Ac. Fine, soft, light grey fabric with black surface, upper surface worn.
719.1.10/6.
Vessel 26 (Fig. 30:26). *Terra nigra* platter, *Camulodunum* form 16Ac. Hard, light brown fabric with black surface, inside unworn. The stamp is purely geometric and apparently a woodcut.
719.1.10/7.
Vessel 27 (Fig. 30:27). *Terra nigra* flanged bowl, *Camulodunum* form 58A. Hard, light brown fabric with black surface. The inside is worn but the footring is not. The stamp is apparently geometric.
719.1.10/8.
Vessel 28 (Fig. 30:28). *Terra nigra* bowl as Vessel 27, again worn internally.
719.1.10/9.
Vessel 29 (Fig. 30:29). *Terra nigra* flanged bowl, fine, soft, grey ware, grey inside and black outside.

719.1.10/10.

Vessel 30 (Fig. 30:30). Small jar. Hard fabric with fine rounded grit. The core is grey, the under-skin red-brown and the surface dark grey and burnished.

719.1.10/11.

Vessel 31 (Fig. 30:31). Ovoid jar with burnished decoration. The fabric is hard and sandy with fine rounded grit and grog. In places the core is light grey with reddish under-skin and grey-black surface, in other places chocolate-brown throughout.

719.1.10/12.

Vessel 32 (Fig. 30:32). Mortarium of Ashley Rails (New Forest) type. Soft, brick-red with white coating. This is obviously an accidental intrusion.

719.1.4/3.

Vessel 33 (Fig. 30:33). Large, heavy bowl. Hard, sandy fabric with some coarse, black grit. Grey to grey-brown ware with a black external surface.

719.1.10/13.

Vessel 34. Ovoid jar fragments, similar in ware to Vessel 31.

719.1.10/14.

Vessel 35 (Fig. 30:35). Rim sherd of a small jar, hard, sandy, grey-brown ware with fine grit.

719.1.10/15.

Vessel 36 (Fig. 31:36). Small open dish, hard, sandy ware with a fine, white grit. The fabric is chocolate brown, with a black or reddish-black surface. All the fractures are recent, suggesting that the remainder of the pot was missed.

719.1.11/1.

Vessel 37 (Fig. 31:37). Almost complete flagon. Fine, orange-buff ware with red specks, with light buff surface.

719.1.11/2.

Vessel 38 (Fig. 31:38). Small rough-cast jar. Orange-buff ware with red specks.

719.1.11/3.

Vessel 39 (Fig. 31:39). So-called feeding bottle. The ware is very hard, orange-buff with red specks. The surface is smoothed and has traces of mica-dusting. This coating suggests that the traditional interpretation of these vessels is wrong, and some form of pourer, perhaps a lamp filler, is more likely.

719.1.5/1.

Vessel 40. Samian rim, Ritterling form 8, pre-Flavian, see p. 85.

719.1.12/1.

Vessel 41 (Fig. 31:41). Samian cup, form 35. See p. 85. Probably Claudio-Neronian. The footring of the cup seems to be moderately worn, as if it had been in use for a time before incorporation in the burial. It may have been used as the lid for Vessel 42.

719.1.12/2.

Vessel 42 (Fig. 31:42). Ovoid jar. Hard, buff ware with black, fumed external surface. On the shoulder and rim is a black varnish. It is broken but substantially complete. The footring is unworn.

719.1.12/3.

Vessel 43 (Fig. 31:43). Jar. Hard, sandy, grey fabric with reddish core. At one point there is a streak of white slip, and this and general fabric are closely similar to the butt-beaker, Vessel 15. The reconstruction is tentative.

719.1.3/12.

Vessel 44 (Fig. 31:44). Small open bowl in reddish-brown fabric tempered with fine sand and red specks. Dark grey surfaces.

There are cow and pig bones in F1-10 (see p. 92), and chicken bones in F1-3, and F1-5 (see p. 93).

F2, 3, 4: *The enclosure ditch*

In the autumn of 1955 a number of trenches were dug to establish the line of the enclosure ditch, and these have been plotted on the plan (Fig. 26). Further trenches on

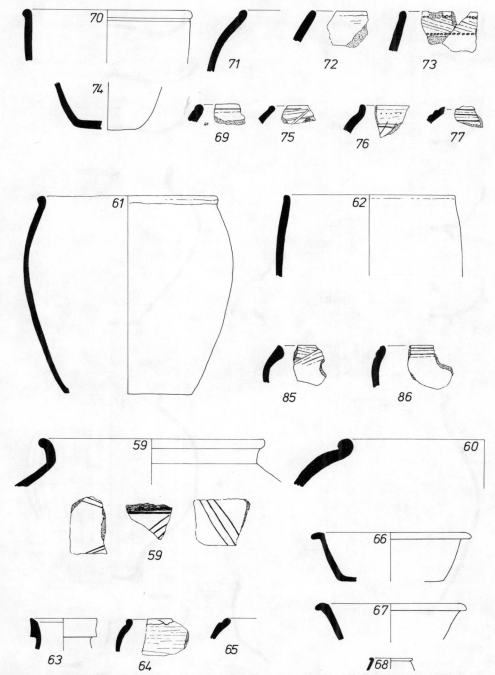

Fig. 28. Winnall Housing Estate: Iron Age and early Roman pottery F17-1 (69), F17-2 (70—77), F13 (61, 62), F21 (85), L2 (86), F11 (59, 60), F15 (63—65), F16 (66—68) (scale ¼).

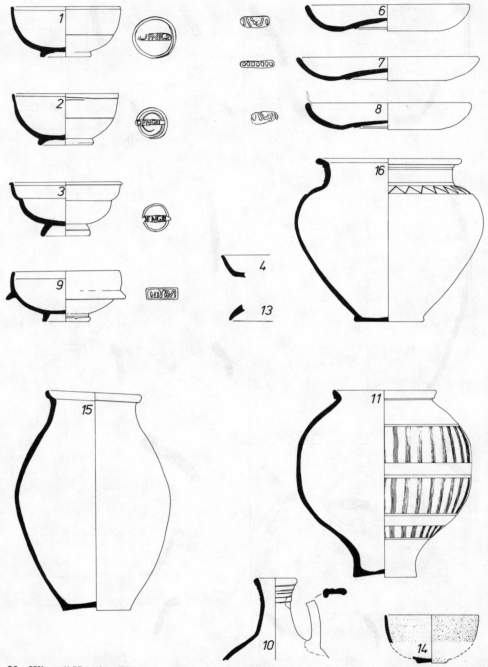

Fig. 29. Winnall Housing Estate: early Roman pottery from the burial complex F1, F1-3 (1—9, 13, 16),
    F1-4 (15), F1-5 (10, 11, 14) (scale ¼).

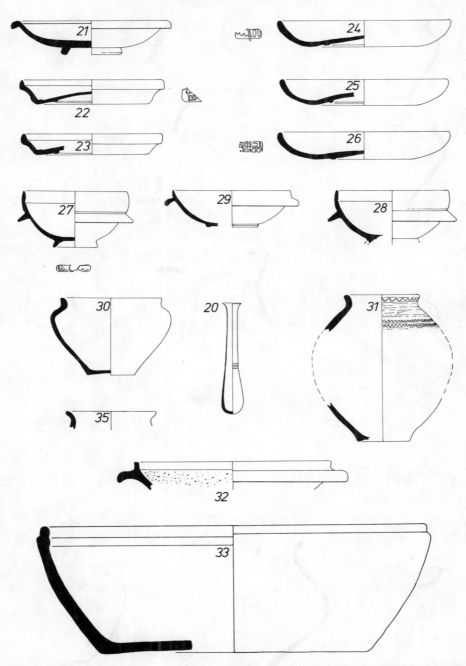

Fig. 30. Winnall Housing Estate: early Roman pottery and glass from the burial complex F1-10 (scale ¼).

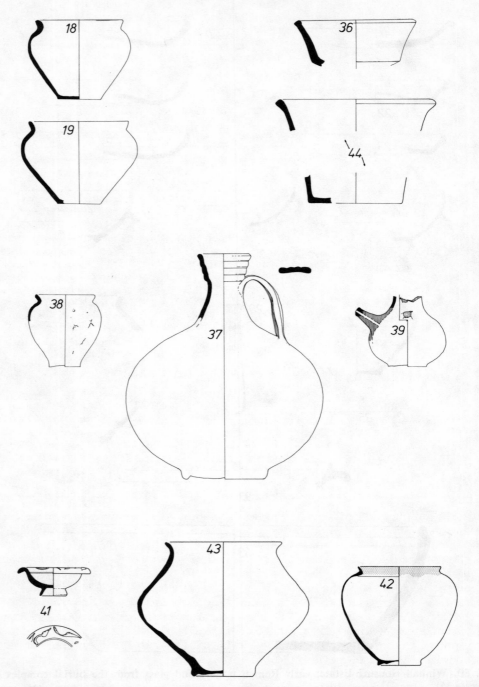

Fig. 31. Winnall Housing Estate: early Roman pottery from the burial complex F1, F1-6 (18, 19), F1-9 (36), F1-10 (21), F1-11 (37—39), F1-12 (41—43) (scale ¼).

Table 8. Winnall Housing Estate: correlation of finds from the ditch of the rectangular enclosure (F2, F3, F4).

	Plus Material	Top Fill	Upper Fill	Upper Main Fill	Lower Main Fill	Rapid Silt	Primary Silt	Quarry	Trench No.	Description of Trench
F2-1	+								I	A few feet from railway
F2-2		+	+						—	Near railway cutting
F2-3		+	+						—	—
F2-4			+						I	A few feet from railway
F2-5			+						I	A few feet from railway
F2-6				+					I	A few feet from railway
F2-7								+	II	10 paces from railway cutting
F2-8			+						II	10 paces from railway cutting
F2-9				+					II	10 paces from railway cutting
F2-10					+				II	10 paces from railway cutting
F2-11						+			II	10 paces from railway cutting
F2-12							+		—	Near fence
F2-13			+						—	Near railway
F2-14	+								—	Trench
F3-1	+								—	Eastern lip of ditch
F3-2	+								III	Just south of corner
F3-3		+							—	—
F3-4					+				III	Just south of corner
F4-1			+						IV	Trench nearest railway cutting
F4-2				+	+				IV	Trench nearest railway cutting
F4-3			+	+					IV	Trench nearest railway cutting
F4-4					+				IV	Trench nearest railway cutting
F4-5						+			IV	Trench nearest railway cutting
F4-6						+			—	20 feet from railway cutting
L1	+								—	—

the line of the southern ditch dug in the following winter, however, were not accurately recorded. The pottery from all these trenches was placed in paper bags on which were written details of which trench and at what depth the finds were made. In Table 8 an attempt is made to summarize the information in tabular form, and also to assign trench numbers, I to IV, where the location can be defined, and these are also marked on the plan. No drawn sections of the ditch exist except for a sketch showing the relationship of Burial 2 (F7) to the filling, and there are no descriptions of layers.

For the dating of the ditches, F2-12 from the primary silt is clearly most important, as it contains two sherds which cannot at present be dated earlier than the late third century. The finds have been published fairly fully, because in our present state of knowledge it is hardly possible to be more precise with groups than to describe them as late Roman. The absence of both the coarse jar with a simple everted rim and of the piedish with a short stubby flange would suggest a late third- or early fourth-century date rather than later, and the coin of Tetricus II from F2-6 would confirm this.

F2: The south ditch of the rectangular enclosure

F2-1: Unstratified
719.2.1/1.
A small rim fragment of samian from Curle form 23 in east Gaulish Ware. Late second or early third century.

F2-3: Top and upper main fill
719.2.3/1.
Flanged bowl (Fig. 32:44). Hard, fine, creamy ware with light grey core.
Also a fragment of a hard, straight-sided dish.
Perforated bronze disc (see p. 86).

F2-4: Upper fill
716.2.4/1.
Jar (Fig. 32:45). Light grey ware with yellow tinge and black specks, smoothed, grey surface. There are also another hard, grey-ware vessel with similar profile, two with less curled rims (short cavetto), and two with thickened rims.
Jar (Fig. 32:46). Coarse, lumpy, grey ware with red-brown patches and smoothed surface.
Open bowl (Fig. 32:47). Hard, grey ware with black, smoothed surface and lightly tooled decoration.
There is a thick, white sherd with black colour-coat and rouletting, probably Castor ware; a mortarium of fine, buff ware with slight traces of a red colour-coat; a storage jar; a flagon like Clausentum FNFGI (Cotton and Gathercole 1958); a coarse, grey, straight-sided dish with burnished surface; a small sherd of samian, Form 45, after A.D. 150; and a pre-Flavian samian sherd. There is also a shale bracelet fragment, a stone slab, oyster shells, and animal bones.

F2-5: Upper fill
719.2.5/1—2.
Small jar (Fig. 32:48). Red to brown-red ware with fine grog and maroon surface.
Also two short cavetto rims, and a late second-century samian sherd, form 36.
There is a rotary quern, a stone slab, and a mussel shell.

F2-6: Upper main fill
719.2.6/1.
Thumb-pot (Fig. 32:49). Soft ware with grey core, light yellow surface and light to dark brown colour-coat.
Piedish (Fig. 32:50). Light grey core with drab, smoothed surface.
Lid (Fig. 32:51). Fine, smooth, orange-buff ware with some rounded grit inclusions.
Straight-sided dish (Fig. 32:52). Hard, grey ware with smoothed, dark grey surface.
Jar (Fig. 32:53). Fine, soft, grey ware with large, black grit. Also fragments of a large storage jar of hard, grey fabric with tooled surface, pierced with small holes; jar with a short cavetto rim and two jars with rolled-out rims, sherd of hard, sandy ware with a black external slip, like vessels from Sloden (New Forest). There is a coin of Tetricus II (A.D. 270—273).

F2-7: Quarry or pit in Trench II
719.2.7/2.
Sherds of a Belgic or early Roman jar.
719.2.7/1.
A samian sherd form 27, probably Trajanic-Hadrianic.

F2-8: Upper fill
719.2.8/1.
Storage jar with thick, square-sectioned rim formed by turning the clay over; fine, sandy ware.

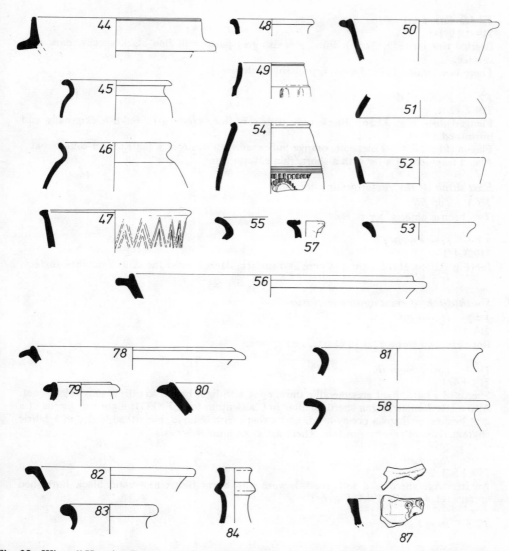

Fig. 32. Winnall Housing Estate: late Roman and medieval pottery F2-3 (44), F2-4 (45—47), F2-5 (48), F2-6 (49—53), F2-9 (54), F2-11 (55), F2-12 (56, 57), F3-4 (58), F17-4 (78—80), F18 (81), F19 (82—84), L2 (87) (scale ¼).

F2-9:   Upper main fill
719.2.9/1.
Beaker (Fig. 32:54). Hard, grey ware with metallic-purple colour-coat.

F2-10:   Lower main fill
719.2.10/1.
The sherds are mainly Roman, but there is a fragment of the handle of late medieval pitcher.

F2-11: Rapid silt
719.2.11/1—2.
Everted rim jar (Fig. 32:55). Fine, greenish-grey paste with fine black specks, dark grey surface.
There is a samian flake, form 33, probably Antonine.

F2-12: Primary silt
719.2.12/1.
Flanged dish (Fig. 32:56). Black ware with very fine, sandy grit, reddish externally and burnished.
Flagon (Fig. 32:57). Fine, soft, orange-buff ware with traces of a matt brown colour-coat.
Also a fragment of a jar with a short, thin cavetto rim.

F3:   *East ditch of the rectangular enclosure*
      F3-3: Top fill
      Two bronze objects, see p. 86.

      F3-4: Lower main fill
      719.3.4/1.
      Jar (Fig. 32:58). Hard, light grey core and surface, darker under the skin. Smoothed surface.

F4:   *South ditch of rectangular enclosure*
      F4-2: Upper fill
      719.4.2/1.
      Rope-rimmed storage jar in coarse, gritty ware.

      F4-4: Lower main fill
      719.4.4/1.
      Sherds of a hard, light grey metallic thumb-pot with light brown to purple-grey colour-coat. Also a late Roman flagon sherd, similar to Clausentum form FNFG1; eight rim sherds of a grey beaker, perhaps a poppy-head; and a sherd with oblique, burnished lattice in a fabric characteristic of cavetto-rim jars. There are some animal bones.

      F4-5: Rapid silt
      719.2.5/1.
      An Iron Age sherd of a soft, reddish ware with burnt flint temper and black burnished surface (cf. Cunliffe 1964, Fig. 6:3).

      F4-6: Rapid silt

F5:   *Ditch*
      This north-south ditch is recorded on the 1955 plan, but there are no details of its dimensions or records of finds.

F6:   *Burial 1*
      This burial lay within the rectangular enclosure. It was exposed during the digging of the foundations for houses in Firmstone Road, and had been partly disturbed by workmen. The skeleton, male, aged 40—55, lay on its back, head to the south, facing east, and feet to the north, with the legs slightly flexed to the left, right leg over left. The upper right arm was parallel to the body, with the hand on the pelvis; the arm was flexed with the head on the abdomen. The only finds were boot nails, *in situ* under the feet, and this

heavy footwear supports Calvin Wells's remark about the 'punishment' the feet had received. The grave itself, 45 cm below the chalk surface, was filled with chalk rubble. The boots imply a late Roman date, but there is no direct dating evidence.

F7: Burial 2

The grave for this burial was cut from a high level into the filling of the east ditch of the rectangular enclosure (F3). The grave was just under 1 m deep, and was sealed by a humus layer caused by undisturbed worm action. The skeleton was a man aged 35—45, and only the upper half, to just above the pelvis, was excavated. The head was at the north and facing east. The left arm lay parallel to the body, while the right forearm lay across the body to grasp the left arm above the elbow.

From the fill comes a samian fragment from the wall of a cup of form 33 in Lezoux fabric, typical of the Antonine period. There is also a handle in dark grey ware with soft, grey grits, perhaps grog (cf. Cotton and Gathercole 1958, Fig. 28: 8—9); and a thick sherd with reddish-brown paste and backing of red and grey grog. The other finds are all grey or black, featureless, sandy sherds. The stratigraphy and finds all suggest a date in the second half of the fourth century.

F8: Burial 5

This child, aged about 18 months, was found during the mechanical excavation of a trench across Firmstone Road, but no details of its position are recorded, and there was no dating evidence.

F9: Burial 3

The more northerly of these two burials (F9, F10) lay extended with head to the west and hobnails at the feet. The grave was cut about a foot into the solid chalk, which lay 15 cm below the modern surface. It was disturbed during the excavation of a contractor's trench. It is a child aged about 12—13 years.

F10: Burial 4

This burial lay nearly parallel to F9, a little to the south, and was also found in the contractor's excavations. The head was to the east, and again there were hobnails. The grave depth was 30 cm below the chalk surface. The skeleton is male, aged 30—40.

F11: Pit

Pit 1·40 m wide in section and 45 cm deep, cut by a house foundation. It only extended 30 cm back from the section.

719.11.0/1.
Rim and other sherds of a large jar (Fig. 28:59). Hard ware with much fine sand, dull light brown. The surface varies from light orange-brown to black. The decoration is burnished, and in black areas it comes out orange. An identical vessel from Mill Plain, Christchurch, is in the Red House Museum at Christchurch.
Bead-rim jar (Fig. 28:60). Grey-brown, gritty ware with light brown to black burnished surface. Many fragments.
Imported wares consist of fragments of a girth beaker in pink-orange fabric with a fumed surface and several fragments of a pitcher in pink-buff ware with drab surface and external white colour-coat. Some of the sherds in this group were picked up on the dump and there is some later material, notably an orange-glazed sherd in an early medieval fabric, probably from a tripod pitcher, and the rim of a cooking pot in sandy ware, of Dunning's 'Saxon aspect' type (Dunning 1960).

F12: Pit

No finds or details.

F13: Pit

Circular pit 1·70 m in diameter and 1·20 m deep below the modern surface, 70 cm below
the chalk surface. It was disturbed by workmen.

719.13.0/1—2.

Large storage jar with bead rim (Fig. 28:61). Hard, brown to grey-brown ware with black core
and surface, fine white angular flint. The internal and external surfaces are matt and have been
wiped, perhaps with coarse cloth or a piece of wood with fine grain.

Saucepan pot (Fig. 28:62). Black to brownish-black ware with fine, white, angular grit. The
surface is a variegated dark brown and light brown to buff in streaky lines, perhaps caused by
burnishing over a patchy, light slip. A similar technique has been noticed on a pot from
Owslebury, associated with wheel-turned pottery. There are fragments of two other vessels, both
8 mm thick, in similar ware to 62 and with matt surface, but one has a burnished outer surface
and a little rounded grit.

Also a complete saddle quern, two chalk weights, clay loom-weights, and cob.

F14: A gully southeast of the Iron Age enclosure

719.14.0/1.

A few nondescript Roman sherds.

F15: Gully

A small gully at the east end of the 1959 trench. It is probably Neronian in date.

719.15.0/1—3.

Flagon rim sherd (Fig. 28:63). Hard, light grey to white ware.

Bead-rim jar (Fig. 28:64). Hard, grey-brown ware with chocolate-coloured surface that has been
heavily tooled.

Bead-rim jar (Fig. 28:65). Hard, grey fabric.

Imported sherds include a broad, fluted handle with four mouldings, perhaps from a flask of
Hofheim type, in pinkish ware with a grey core; a fragment of *terra rubra* platter, inner surface
patchy orange and red, the outer buff orange; one fragment of a soapy, pink ware with grey core;
and one fragment of amphora.

One fragment of a thick bead-rim jar, in hard, grey ware with coarse, flint grit and black surface,
has a shoulder formed apparently by irregular cutting with a knife, a very distinctive ware and
technique noticed several times in Winchester.

There are two samian sherds, one form 29 of Neronian date, and an Antonine form 31, which does
not conform to the early date of the rest of the group.

F16: Gully

A small gully which cuts F17. It is probably second or third century in date.

719.16.0/1.

Piedish (Fig. 28:66). Hard, light, sandy ware with black burnished surface.

Piedish (Fig. 28:67). Dark grey ware with red to black burnished surface.

Flask (Fig. 28:68). Fine, hard, grey ware with black burnishing.

F17: East ditch of the Iron Age enclosure

The ditch has a V-shaped profile and is over 1·20 m deep. The lowest filling produced
saucepan-pot material, and the ditch had largely silted up while such pottery was still in
use. The upper fill contains Roman material.

The rim sherd from F17-1, which was found about 30 cm above the bottom of the ditch, is typical of the late phases of the so-called saucepan-pot tradition, such as is commonly associated with the decorated vessels best known in central Hampshire from St Catherine's Hill. The group from the higher filling of the ditch is especially interesting, as it seems to mark the very last phases of the tradition. The saucepan pots have fairly deeply grooved decoration which seems to be a late characteristic, and this is here confirmed by the presence of a sherd of definitely wheel-turned pottery. The potter's wheel seems to appear first in this country in the ports of the south coast, such as Hengistbury Head, before the middle of the first century B.C., and such a date would not be amiss for the group here. The presence of vessels not in the black burnished ware shows that even though the saucepan-pot tradition was dominant in this area, other workshops were producing other types with distinctive decoration.

F17-1: Primary fill
719.17.1/1—2.
Jar (Fig. 28:69). Dark purple-brown fabric with white grit and black burnished surface.
There are some animal bones.

F17-2: Main fill
719.17.2/1.
Most of the finds were removed from the side of a contractor's excavation and only two sherds, 71 and 72, are from the trench, but all are well stratified.
719.17.2/1.
Saucepan pot (Fig. 28:70). Fine, hard, grey-brown ware with a little white grit, surface dark, burnished; could be wheel turned.
Bead-rim bowl (Fig. 28:71). Dark grey-brown ware with much fine grit, external surface black and burnished.
Jar (Fig. 28:72). Dull purple-brown fabric with much fine, white grit; burnished black surface.
Saucepan pot (Fig. 28:73). Reddish ware with much grit, burnished black surface.
Saucepan pot base (Fig. 28:74). Dull brown core, grey-brown to black burnished surface. Finely gritted.
Jar (Fig. 28:75). Black ware with a little grit, surface dark, well burnished.
Jar (Fig. 28:76). Red to grey-brown ware with much white- and grey-flint grit; black to reddish-brown surface with burnishing. The decoration consists of scratching and pin-pricks below the rim.
Shoulder sherd with grooves (Fig. 28:77). Soft, reddish-brown ware with white grit.
There are several body sherds of a chocolate-brown ware with some red grog. The surface is orange red and has been given a fine rustication; the fabric is soapy to the touch. Also one hard sandy sherd which is certainly wheel turned.
There are some animal bones.

F17-3
Group 1 contains sherds of soapy, rusticated ware.

F17-4: Top fill
719.17.4/1—2.
Flanged bowl (Fig. 32:78). Pinkish ware with fine grog, black to grey burnished surface.
Flask neck (Fig. 32:79). Hard, grey ware with black, colour-coated surface.
Flanged bowl (Fig. 32:80). Grey ware with large, white grit.
There is also the rim of a coarse, gritty, rope-rimmed storage jar and fragments of folded beakers and a flagon. A samian sherd is of form 18 or 18R of pre-Flavian or Flavian date, and a coin of Constantine II, A.D. 337—340.

F18: Ditch

This ditch was sectioned in a sewer trench, and from its dimensions is probably the north ditch of the Iron Age enclosure. The finds are all from the upper fill.

719.18.0/1.

Jar (Fig. 32:81). Hard, grey ware with very fine grit; surface dark and carefully polished.

Also a coarse, gritted, bead-rim jar, a fragment of amphora, and a fragment of a rotary quern.

F19: Gully exposed in the section of a sewer trench

719.19.0/1.

Piedish (Fig. 32:82). Hard, grey, sandy ware with smoothed, light grey to black surface.

Flask (Fig. 32:83). Hard, grey ware with smoothed surface.

Flagon (Fig. 32:84). Creamy-buff ware with orange to dull orange colour-coat.

Also a fragment of a thumb-pot in hard, reddish-orange fabric with steel-grey core in places and drab brown colour-coat.

This pottery suggests that the field observation that this might be the same gully as F16 was wrong.

F20: Gully

Exposed in sewer trench. No finds.

F21: Ditch

Exposed in a foundation trench; 1·40 m across north—south.

719.21.0/1.

Bowl (Fig. 28:85) of hard, grey-brown ware with much white, angular grit, burnished black surface.

Finds from here also include a neck of a Roman two-handled flask in white ware, a sherd of a late Roman flanged bowl and a sherd of a flagon of orange ware with a white slip.

There is one animal bone.

F22: Pit

Exposed in a foundation trench, about 1 m across.

719.22.0/1.

There are some Roman sherds.

F23: Gully

About 0·70 m wide.

719.23.0/1.

The finds include a cavetto rim.

F24: Gully

Exposed in a sewer trench. No details or finds.

L1:   From the upper fill of F2, 3, 4

Fragment of bronze ligula and a bronze buckle plate.

L2:   Unstratified, from the western part of the site

719.00.2/1.

Bowl (Fig. 28:86). Soft, purple-brown fabric with chert temper. Black burnished surface.

There is a coin of Valentinian I.

L3: *Unstratified, from the northeastern corner of the western part of the site*
A coin of Maximian.

L4: *Unstratified*
719.00.4/1.
A bridge-spout (Fig. 32:87) with a face on the rim, of Bristol-Redcliffe type, A.D. 1275—1300.
Pale buff fabric with pale apple-green glaze.

The Finds

The Roman Coins by R. Reece

Provenance	Museum Coin Number	Reference	Date A.D.
F2-6	C 1735	Tetricus II, RIC 259	270—73
F17-4	C 1736	Constantine II, HK 93	337—40
L2	C 1784	Valentinian I, as CK 506	367—75
L3	C 1734*	Maximian I, RIC VI London 15	296—305

*Donated by Mr Steptoe.

The Samian by B. R. Hartley

From F1-3 come fragments of three complete, or nearly complete, vessels (719.1.3/1—3). All have unworn footrings suggesting that they were new when buried.

Vessel 1 (Fig. 29:1). A cup of Ritterling 8 by Niger, stamped OFNIGR. The die in question was generally used on dishes, but occasionally appears on cups, as at Vechten (Ritt. 8 and 27) and Nijmegen (27). It was also found on form 29 at La Graufesenque. Records with some degree of independent dating include Valkenburg Period 2 (A.D. 43—47 according to van Giffen), the filling of the fort ditch at Cirencester with a group of unused samian (Wacher 1962) of *c.* A.D. 55—65, and a slightly doubtful example at Caerleon.

The Valkenburg stamp is a crux, but it may be noted that stamps attested there in Period 2 frequently are in Neronian groups in Britain, such as the Boudiccan burnings at Colchester and Verulamium. It is, therefore, not easy to accept van Giffen's estimate, and it may be permissible to ask whether Period 1 at Valkenburg belongs after all to the Claudian retrenchment of A.D. 47 (Tacitus, *Ann.* XI. 19) with Period 2 falling in the fifties.

The Cirencester record certainly suggests that the Winnall cup belongs to the same period as the others of Niger, and, if weight is allowed for the Caerleon piece, a mid or late Neronian date, *c.* A.D. 55—65, becomes likely.

Vessels 2 and 3 (Fig. 29:2, 3). Cups of Ritterling form 8 and Dragendorff 27 respectively, both stamped OFNGRI by Niger of La Graufesenque. This particular stamp is always on cups and the forms involved, including Ritterling 8 (also at London and Richborough), Ritterling 9 (London and Poitiers), and form 24/25 (frequently) show that it is firmly pre-Flavian. Nevertheless, stamps from the same die are known from barracks in the fortress at Chester and also from Nijmegen fortress (not however necessarily Flavian), so that a Claudian date is improbable and the period A.D. 50—65 the most likely for its use.

Vessel 4 (F1-3, 719.1.3/4). A fragment of form 18, south Gaulish and probably pre-Flavian.

Vessel 5 (F1-3, 719.1.3/5, Fig. 29:5). A fragment from a south Gaulish cup, more probably Ritterling 8 than form 27. The fabric is a pre-Flavian one.

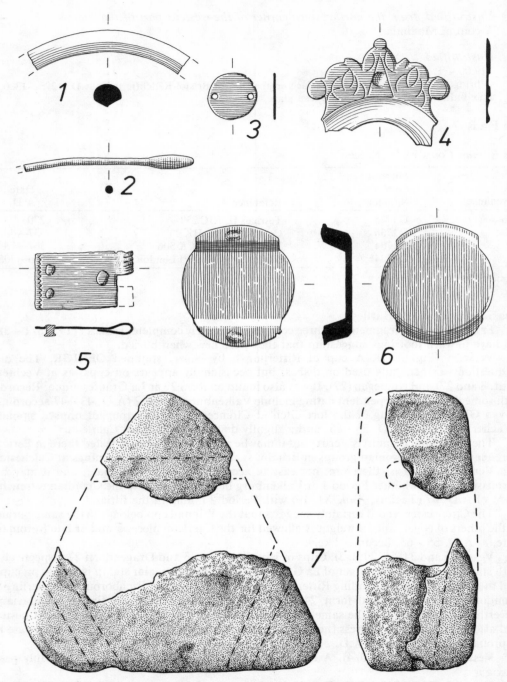

Fig. 33. Winnall Housing Estate: small finds and clay loom-weight F2-4 (1), L1 (2), F2-3 (3), F3-3 (4,.6), L1 (5) (scale 1/1); F13 (7) (scale ½).

Vessel 40 (F1-5, 719.1.5/1). Ritterling form 8 rim, south Gaulish and pre-Flavian.

Vessel 21 (F1-10, 719.1.10/1, Fig. 30:21). A dish approximating to form 36, but with a stubby rim without barbotine leaves. This should perhaps be regarded as the dish of the same set as Hermet form 7 (Hermet 1934, Pl. 2). The fabric is undoubtedly south Gaulish and, since the standard form 36 was dominant by the Flavian period, this dish is likely to be pre-Flavian.

Vessel 41 (F1-12, 719.1.12/1, Fig. 31:41). Samian cup, form 35 in south Gaulish fabric, almost certainly of La Graufesenque. This small cup, virtually complete, is unusual in two ways. First, although the fabric is undoubtedly south Gaulish, the glaze has some plates of mica included, which suggests a lower temperature of firing than was usual in southern Gaul. Secondly, the footring is grooved in the manner of form 27. Although the form itself is rarely closely datable, the two departures from the norm probably indicate a Claudio-Neronian date. The footring of the cup seems to be moderately worn, as if it had been in use for a time before incorporation in the burial.

A small rim fragment (F2-1, 719.2.1/1) from Curle form 23 in east Gaulish ware. Late second or early third century.

Two fragments of samian come from F2-4 (719.2.4/1).

(i) A small sherd from a gritted samian mortarium, probably central Gaulish. Form 45, the commonest samian mortarium, was not in use before about A.D. 170, but other forms were probably introduced slightly earlier (Curle 21, form 43). A date after A.D. 150 is, however, certain.

(ii) A fragment of a dish of south Gaulish origin, probably pre-Flavian.

A fragment (F2-5, 719.2.5/1) from a variant of form 36 with a groove above the internal carination on a rim with rather straight profile. The fabric is east Gaulish and a date near the end of the second century is likely.

A wall fragment of form 27 (F2-7, 719.2.7/1) with flat upper profile typical of central Gaulish examples. The fabric is best matched by cups of the Trajanic and Hadrianic periods from Les-Martres-de-Veyre.

A flake (F2-11, 719.2.11/1) of a central Gaulish cup of form 33. Probably Antonine.

Fragment (F7, 719.7.0/1) from the wall of a cup in Lezoux fabric, typical of the Antonine period.

A small fragment (F15, 719.15.0/2) from the lower zone of form 29 showing a continuous wreath above a series of vertical wavy lines. The decoration is too fragmentary and too banal to suggest a maker, though a Neronian date is most likely for this style.

A rim fragment (F15, 719.15.0/1) from a standard example of a central Gaulish form 31 of Antonine date, not, however, closely datable within the period.

A sherd from a dish (F17, 719.17.1/1) of form 18 or 18R, more probably the latter, in south Gaulish ware. This could equally well be pre-Flavian or Flavian.

Roman Glass by D. Charlesworth

A glass flask (719.9, Fig. 30:20) was recovered from F1-10. These things are difficult to date, and I would not like to suggest a date closer than the first or second century A.D. It is blown, a natural green glass with a knocked off rim, smoothed in the flame.

Miscellaneous Finds

Fig. 33 no.	Provenance	Museum Accession Number	Description
1	F2-4	719.2	Fragment of a shale bracelet (Fig. 33:1)

Fig. 33 no.	Provenance	Museum Accession Number	Description
2	L1	719.4	Fragment of a bronze ligula
3	F2-3	719.5	Perforated bronze disc
4	F3-3	719.7	Decorated bronze object Dr Graham Webster writes: 'Part of a thin decorated bronze mount; from a piece of furniture such as a handle or lock escutcheon, and probably 18th century'
5	L1	719.6	Bronze buckle plate
6	F3-3	719.8	Bronze attachment with traces of iron on the back

The Loom-Weights from F13 by J. W. Hedges

The fragments of loom-weights recovered during excavation came from pyramidal chalk weights and triangular, baked-clay ones, both of which are common on sites of Early Iron Age date (Hedges 1973: 119—120, Fig. 34; 116—117, Fig. 30).

Eighteen of the chalk fragments fit to form an almost complete loom- or thatch-weight (719.2, Fig. 34) 24 cm in height, 19 cm in width, and 9 cm thick, with a perforation 1·5 cm across. Although the weight of this, 3260 g, is about a third or half of the total weight of each set of the late Saxon ones from St Cross (p. 33), this is not unusual for this type. The other 14 fragments, weighing a total of 818 g are equivalent to only part of a weight; one piece shows a perforation 2·5 cm wide and is 6·5 cm thick. The clay fragments vary greatly in the degree to which they were fired, but five, weighing a total of 300 g, fit to form two-thirds of a triangular weight with sides 16 cm long. It is 6 cm thick and perforated at each corner by a hole 1·5 cm in diameter (719.3, Fig. 33:7). The estimated weight, 450 g, is very light for this type and means that the remaining 2375 g of fragments, which show similar features, come from at least four or five other loom-weights.

Stone objects by F. R. Hodson and I. M. West

Small slab, perhaps building stone (F2-4, 719.14). Dark, shelly limestone, externally oxidized, with reddish tint. Probably Purbeck marble.

Fragment of a rotary quern (F2-5, 719.15). Calcite-cemented, well-sorted, medium-grained sandstone with much evenly distributed glauconite. A limonitic concretion is present, perhaps formed by the oxidation of a pyrite nodule. The glauconite in this sample is not greatly oxidized and thus the material has not been very extensively weathered. Upper Greensand of southern England. Many possible localities.

Slab, perhaps building stone (F2-5, 719.16). Middle Purbeck ostracodal limestone with *Ostrea distorta*. Ostracods are mostly *Cypridea*, possibly *C. fasciculata*. The specimen appears to have been burnt. The sample comes from the Upper Building Stones of the Purbeck Beds. These are exposed on the coast at Durlston Bay, Swanage, where they are 15 m thick. They also occur in the cliffs at Worbarrow Bay and thin in the direction of Lulworth Cove where they are 3 m thick. They also occur in the region of Poxwell and Upwey, north of Weymouth, but are poorly exposed except in modern cuttings and quarries. Similar Purbeck limestone might also be found in the area of Battle in Sussex, but exposures are very poor and an origin in the Swanage area is much more probable.

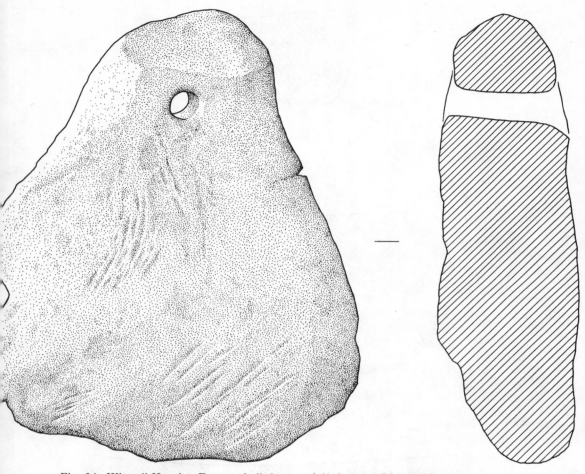

Fig. 34. Winnall Housing Estate: chalk loom-weight (see pp. 86 and 87) (scale ½).

Saddle quern (F13, 719.11, Fig. 35:2 and 3). The quern is complete, though broken, and is formed of a block 30·5×38×15 cm. Calcite-cemented, well-sorted, medium-grained sandstone with much evenly distributed glauconite. This is probably Upper Greensand, like the quern fragment listed above, but in rather oxidized condition. Presumably this is the result of burning if the black coating is carbon. Oxidation by weathering usually gives a more brown and less reddish colour.

Loom-weight (F13, 719.10, Fig. 34, see also p. 86). This hard, grey chalk, is probably Lower Chalk of southern England. Fragments of the bivalve *Inoceramus* occur. Calcispheres are unusually abundant and foraminifera are present. The label states that the specimen is burnt, but definite evidence of burning was not seen. Lower Chalk may have been a suitable material that is sufficiently soft to shape into loom-weights but harder and stronger than Upper Chalk.

Fragment of a rotary quern (F18, 719.18). Red-brown, coarse to pebbly grit. Probably Old Red Sandstone from Herefordshire.

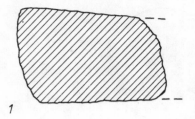

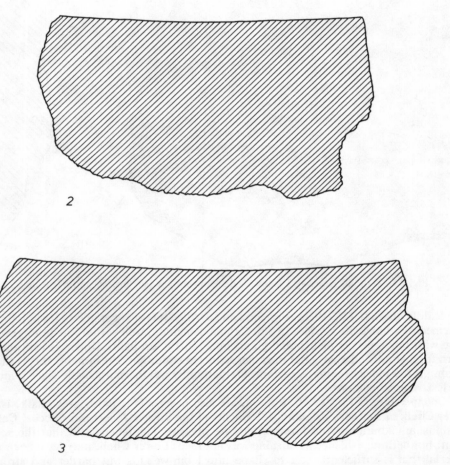

Fig. 35. Winnall Housing Estate: sections through querns from L3 (1) and F13 (2 & 3) (scale ½).

Fragment of rotary quern (L3, 719.17). Glauconite sandstone with sponge spicules. It is decalcified Upper Greensand.

Fragment of rotary quern (L3, 719.12, Fig. 35:1). Coarse felspathic sandstone. Many of the quartz grains show crystal faces developed. These are either original faces preserved or due to secondary overgrowths of silica. No such felspathic sandstone occurs in the Hampshire Basin area. It is unlikely to have come from southern England but resembles the Millstone Grit of the Pennines or possibly South Wales.

Burials by C. Wells

Seven small pieces of cranial vault and three small fragments of long bone of an adult were recovered from F1-1. All were well cremated, and there is little to say about them.

Burial 1 (F6). This consisted of a much damaged, though substantially complete, skeleton of a male, aged 40—55. About 50 fragments of skull were present. These were too broken to make reconstruction worthwhile, but it could be seen that the brow ridges were of slight to moderate development, the mastoid processes were small but craggy, the areas for attachment of nuchal muscles were strongly developed, so too were those for the temporal muscles. The orbits may have been rather low (chamaeconch). The skull was probably mesocranial. The palate survived and had lost all teeth ante-mortem except the left canine which had been lost post-mortem. The broken mandible had lost all teeth ante-mortem except the right central incisor lost post-mortem. The gonial angles were strongly developed and everted. Much old periodontal infection was present in both jaws with some periostitis covering most of the anterior two-thirds of the palate.

Much of the post-cranial skeleton was intact. All the vertebrae were present. They showed extensive osteophytosis on the bodies of the T7 to T12 and on all lumbar vertebrae. There was also slight osteoarthritis on the posterior joints of L3 and L4 and on the costal head facets of a few thoracic vertebrae. There were about 40 rib fragments. Some of these showed osteo-arthritis of the head and transverse process articulations — occasionally severe. One rib fragment from the middle of the series showed a well-healed fracture. The sacrum had almost completely disintegrated, but the remainder of the broken pelvis showed it to be a strongly android type. There was a trace of osteoarthritis of the left acetabulum.

Both scapulae and clavicles were damaged. Mild osteoarthritis was present at the right acromioclavicular joint. The humeri and damaged forearm bones survived: also 12 carpals, 10 metacarpals and about 24 phalanges of fingers.

The femora could be reconstructed. The left femoral head had slight osteoarthritis. Both patellae and tibiae were undamaged: the fibulae broken. An area of periostitis and osteitis with thickening of the bone was present in the middle of the shaft of the right tibia. It was most pronounced on the subcutaneous surface but it also encircled the bone. It covered about 10 cm of the shaft. There was a similar but less severe area of periostitis on the right fibula at about the same level. No squatting facets were present on the tibiae.

The tarsal and metatarsal bones were almost complete. Extensive generalized osteo-arthritis was present in many intertarsal joints and also on the heads of both first metatarsals. A few phalanges of toes survived: those for the hallux were craggy and deformed at the base. The fifth and also fourth metatarsals of both feet were strongly bowed medially.

Measurements of long bones are shown in Table 9. Stature would have been about 1651 mm (5 ft 5 in).

The muscle markings for the lower limbs were strongly developed; those for the upper limbs were of moderate development only. This may imply that this man had, throughout his life, been accustomed to perform long walks or climb rough and hilly country. This impression

Table 9. Measurements of human long bones.

| | Burial 1 | | Burial 4 | |
	left (mm)	right (mm)	left (mm)	right (mm)
HuL1	—	302·8	—	—
FeL1	432·7	—	—	—
FeD1	25·2	26·1	—	—
FeD2	33·6	36·0	—	—
TiL1	343·0	344·2	376·5	—
TiD1	37·8	38·2	39·8	38·4
TiD2	23·3	22·9	27·1	25·7
Meric Index	75·0	72·5	—	—
Cnemic Index	61·6	59·9	68·1	66·9

is reinforced by the extensive osteoarthritic changes in his feet, which seem to have taken heavy 'punishment' (but his ankle and knee joints had developed no arthritic changes). The osteitis of his right tibia and fibula are of uncertain origin. They may indicate some old injury or could perhaps have arisen from a deep varicose ulcer which produced secondary inflammation of the bone. The strongly bowed lateral metatarsals may possibly have resulted from the frequent use of a tight sandal thong or similar constriction to his feet.

His strong temporal muscles, everted gonia and virtually edentulous jaws probably indicate that he was used to a tough diet which had eroded his teeth until pulp exposure initiated the alveolar infection which led to the shedding of his teeth. It is clear that all the molars, at least, had been lost long before death.

The osteoarthritis and osteophytosis of his spine may have been the result of habitually carrying heavy burdens or packs on his back. If so, this may have been a further factor in producing the strong muscular development of his legs.

Too little survives to justify any estimate of his racial type but the suggestion of a low orbital height would fit well with many Iron Age groups.

Burial 2 (F7). This consisted of a much damaged and defective skeleton of a male, aged 35—45. There were numerous small fragments of cranial vault and a few of base and face. Sutural fusion was well established endocranially. There was evidence of a distinct tuber occipitale. The mastoid processes were craggy; brow ridges moderately well developed. The areas for attachment of the nuchal muscles were strongly developed. Part of the maxillae and part of the mandible were present from which the dental state could be in part determined:

```
          .   .   .   .   0  2  1  |  0  2  3  .   .   .   .   ?
  R       ──────────────────────────────────────────────────────     L
          ?  ?  ?  ?  ?  ?  0  0  |  0  2  .  4  5  6  .  8
                                 p              c
```

A large paradontal abscess cavity had surrounded the root of the shed mandibular left canine. The caries cavity on the M3 was on the buccal surface of the tooth. Dental attrition was heavy on the occlusal surfaces of surviving teeth.

Post-cranial remains included a few much damaged vertebral fragments; rib fragments; fragments of both humeri, ulnae. and radii; and some carpals, metacarpals, and phalanges. The arm bones were of only moderate build and their muscle markings not particularly well developed. There was some very early osteoarthritic change on the heads of two metacarpals and the bases of two phalanges.

Burial 5 (F8). This consists of 10 small fragments of a child, aged about 18 months. Present are 5 small pieces of skull, 1 of ilium, 2 of femur and 1 of tibia. There are no special anthropological or pathological features about these fragments and there is little that can be profitably said of them.

Burial 3 (F9). This was a damaged and defective skeleton of a child (probably male) aged about 12—13 years. Most of the cranial vault was present, but this was broken into many fragments. Most of the face and mandible were preserved. The dental state was:

—	7	6	5	4	0	2	1		1	2	3	4	5	6	7	—
—	7	6	5	4	3	2	1		0	2	3	4	5	6	7	—

No caries was present. Early attrition was present on the M1 teeth.

Post-cranial bones present were the atlas, the axis, and parts of three other cervical vertebrae; the distal halves of both femora; the left and right tibia, fibula, talus, and calcaneus; and a few of the metacarpals and metatarsals. All epiphyses were still unfused. No pathology was noted and no cause of death could be identified.

Burial 4 (F10). This consisted of the much damaged skeleton of a male, aged 30—40. There were a few fragments of cranial vault showing progressing sutural fusion; a few fragments of cranial base and substantial parts of the facial skeleton including most of the maxillae and mandible. The cranial muscle markings were prominent. The mastoid processes were large and craggy. The dental state was:

R	8	7	.	5	4	0	0	0		1	2	3	4	.	.	.	?	L
	.	7	6	5	4	3	2	1		0	2	3	4	5	6	7	8	

The dental arcade was a divergent U-shape. Attrition on the occlusal surfaces of the teeth was slight to moderate. The mandibular left M3 had a cervical caries cavity and the alveolus around the shed right M3 revealed a small paradontal abscess cavity. Small deposits of tartar occurred on several teeth and had probably produced gingivitis (inflammation of the gums) during life. There was some over-crowding of teeth in the anterior part of the dentition. Enamel hypoplasia was recognizable on the canines, first premolars, and central incisors.

Post-cranial remains included parts of probably 18 vertebrae, with slight osteoarthritis of the posterior intervertebral articulations in the lumbar region. A small Schmorl's node is present on the superior surface of L4. Pelvic and rib fragments survive, in addition to the damaged scapulae, clavicles, the right humerus, the proximal part of the left humerus, and the left and right ulnae; and femoral fragments. The tibiae were sufficiently well preserved for the measurements shown in Table 9 to be obtained. Both proved to be mesocnemic. Stature can be estimated to be about 1730 mm (5 ft 8 in). Muscle markings were rather light on the humeri and ulnae, but strongly developed on the pelvis, femora, and tibiae. This suggests that habitually greater strain was imposed on legs than on arms, probably as a result of much walking and climbing over rough or hilly ground. The osteoarthritic changes in the spine, together with the Schmorl's node, suggest the possibility that heavy burdens may often have been carried by this man or that he may have followed some occupation involving torsional strains.

Faunal Remains

Provenance	Museum Accession Number	Species	Anatomical Element
Mammals			
F1-2	719.1.2	roe deer	1 right mandible with P2, 3, 4, M2 (all worn)
F1-10	719.1.10	cow	1 lower M2 (worn)
			1 lower M3 (worn)
		pig	4 skull fragments
F2-4	719.2.4	sheep/goat	2 radius shaft fragments
			1 upper M3 (front cusp only in wear)
F4-4	719.4.4	sheep/goat	1 metapodial (proximal end)
		horse	1 metapodial (distal end)
		cow	1 radius (proximal end)
F4-6	719.4.6	horse	1 lower P1 (worn)
		cow	1 lower M1 (very worn)
		pig	1 upper canine (worn)
F17-1	719.17.1	sheep/goat	1 tibia shaft
			1 radius shaft
		cow	1 metatarsal (proximal end)
		horse	1 mandible with dp4; M1, 2, 3 erupting
F17-2	719.17.2	cow	1 metatarsal shaft
			1 mandible fragment
			1 scapula (proximal end)
			1 horn core/skull fragment
		dog	1 left mandible with P1—4, M1, 2
		pig	1 skull fragment
F21	719.21.0	sheep/goat	1 first phalange

Provenance	Museum Accession Number	Species	Anatomical Element
Birds by G. Cowles			
F1-5	719.1.5	domestic chicken	1 left femur 1 right femur (proximal end) 1 left ulna (proximal end) 1 right tarsometatursus (proximal end)
F1-6	719.1.6	domestic chicken	1 left humerus (distal end)
Molluscs			
F2-4	719.2.4	mussels and oysters	A small group of shells has been preserved, but mention is made in the notes of similar finds elsewhere in same ditch
		garden snail	Some shells of *Helix aspera* which appear at Owslebury first in the early Roman period, but only become common in the later levels
F2-5	719.2.5	mussel	1 shell

MILLAND
(Site 328)
by V. Jones

In October 1930, while digging a manhole, workmen unearthed a Roman cremation burial. The discovery of some forty vessels was made between St Catherine's Road and Milland Road, about 90 m south of All Saints School (Fig. 36).

Summary

The pit lay at a depth of 0·80 m, and was 0·80 m in diameter. A cinerary urn was found, but this and its contents disappeared soon afterwards and was presumed to have been taken by a workman. Some bird bones were found lying on a platter. An iron stud, a piece of stone (whetstone?), *opus signinum*, and fragments of wood were also uncovered.

The finds as preserved fall clearly into two groups. Firstly there are the vessels which are substantially complete comprising coarse vessels (Fig. 37), samian (Figs. 39, 40, 41), and a glass vessel (Fig. 40). These, with the possible exception of vessel number 20, form a homogeneous group and must belong to the burial, which on the samian evidence is datable to the late Flavian period (*c*. A.D. 75—100). The second group are stray sherds (Fig. 38:26—36) which are later, including some fourth-century sherds. These and the fragment of *opus signinum* clearly relate to later domestic activity.

In 1930 a coin of Domitian A.D. 81—96 (C1212) was found in the mouth of a skeleton in the Corporation Housing Estate, Milland.

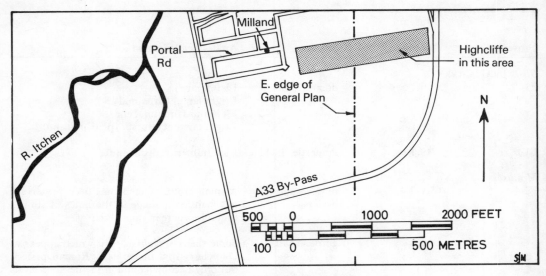

Fig. 36. Milland and Highcliffe: location map.

The Features

Presumably from the burial

This includes the samian vessels (pp. 98—101), the glass vessel (p. 102), and the bird bones (p. 103).

328.00.1/1.
Carinated grey-ware bowl (Fig. 37:1). Fabric quite heavily sanded with colourless grains 0·2—0·3 mm in size, occasional iron compounds, and particles of chalk up to 0·2 mm in size. The bowl is roughly burnished on the exterior below the carination.

328.00.1/2, 3, 26, 36, 37.
Carinated grey-ware bowls (Fig. 37: 2—6). Fabric finely sanded with colourless water-worn sands up to 0·2 mm. Particles of organic chalk up to 0·2 mm.

328.00.1/5.
Carinated grey-ware bowl (Fig. 37:7). Fabric sanded with white and colourless water-worn sands up to 0·3 mm, iron compounds up to 0·5 mm, and particles of organic chalk up to 0·2 mm.

328.00.1/38, 24.
Carinated grey ware bowls (Fig. 37:8—9). As vessel 2.

328.00.1/6.
Carinated grey-ware bowl (Fig. 37:10). Fabric quite heavily sanded with white and colourless water-worn grains up to 0·5 mm in size, iron compounds up to 0·5 mm, and particles of organic chalk up to 0·2 mm. The bowl is very lop-sided. The lower half of the bowl has been burnished on the exterior, and above the carination there is a burnished zig-zag line.

328.00.1/31.
Small platter (Fig. 37:11). Grey ware, quite heavily sanded with colourless grains 0·2 to 0·3 mm in size, iron compounds and organic chalk particles up to 0·2 mm. Rough burnishing on the interior, and on the exterior around the base.

328.00.1/10.
Grey-ware lid/bowl (Fig. 37:12). Fabric sanded with white and colourless sands up to 0·4 mm, iron compounds up to 0·7 mm, and organic chalk compounds up to 0·2 mm. This forms a lid for vessel 15, but it has also been used as a bowl, as the four prongs which form the handle/foot show signs of wear.

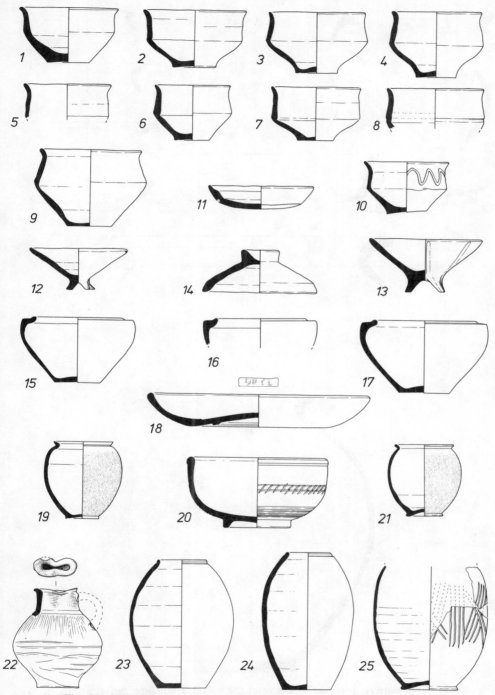

Fig. 37. Milland: coarse pottery, presumably from the burial (scale ¼).

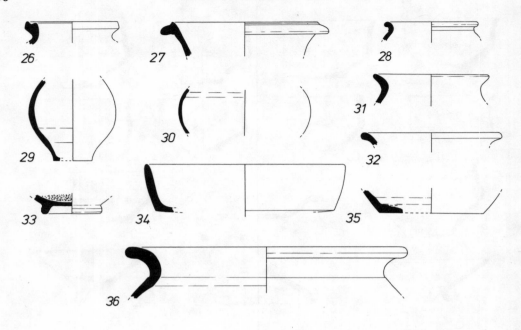

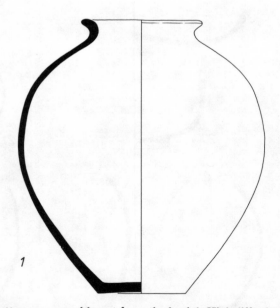

Fig. 38. Milland: pottery, presumably not from the burial; Highcliffe: burial urn (scale ¼).

328.00.1/13.
Grey-ware lid/bowl (Fig. 37:13). Fabric heavily sanded with white and colourless water-worn sands up to 0·3 mm and iron compounds up to 1·1 mm. This forms a lid for vessel 17, but also shows wear on the four prongs, as 12. Irregularly placed burnished lines radiate from the centre top of the outer surface of the lid.
328.00.1/39.
Grey-ware lid (Fig. 37:14). Fabric sanded with unevenly sized, colourless grains up to 0·2 mm, iron compounds up to 0·5 mm, and particles of organic chalk up to 0·2 mm.
328.00.1/12.
Grey-ware bowl/jar with lid-seating (Fig. 37:15). Fabric as 13.
328.00.1/40.
Grey-ware jar as 15 (Fig. 37:16). Fabric finely sanded with colourless water-worn sands up to 0·2 mm in size, particles of organic chalk up to 0·2 mm.
328.00.1/11.
Grey-ware jar as 15 (Fig. 37:17). Fabric as 13.
328.00.1/9.
Terra nigra platter (Fig. 37:18), severely excoriated. Fine, pale fabric with occasional sands up to 0·5 mm, very occasional iron compounds up to 0·3 mm. The stamp was examined by Valery Rigby, who states that it is

either CATIRIOS or CATIXOS, neither of which is recorded elsewhere. The *Camulodunum* form 16 platter was standardized by A.D. 30, but very few, if any, examples from British sites were pre-conquest imports. The majority fall in the period *c.* 45—75 A.D. The size and shape of the stamp suggest it should be a Claudian product, but until more evidence concerning this stamp is produced it is safer to say Claudio-Neronian.

328.00.1/35.
Jar (Fig. 37:19). Very fine, off-white fabric containing minute colourless sands (less than 0·1 mm) and iron compounds. Rough casting of clay particles on the exterior. Mid-brown colour-coat.
328.00.1/34.
Bowl (Fig. 37:20). Orange fabric with occasional white and colourless sands up to 0·3 mm, iron compounds up to 0·6 mm. Worn, light orange-brown colour-coat. Roughly incised decoration on the exterior.
328.00.1/4.
Jar (Fig. 37:21). Very fine, buff fabric with colourless sands up to 0·1 mm, though occasionally larger. Outer surface rough-cast with clay particles. Dark brown colour-coat.
328.00.1/7.
Grey-ware jug, handle missing (Fig. 37:22). Fabric sanded with white and colourless grains up to 0·3 mm, iron compounds up to 0·9 mm, and organic chalk up to 0·2 mm. The neck of the vessel is pinched. Horizontal burnished line around the upper shoulder. Vertical burnished lines decorate the upper portion of the jug, and there are roughly impressed, haphazard lines around the lower portion.
328.00.1/8.
Grey-ware jar (Fig. 37:23). Fabric finely sanded with colourless water-worn sands up to 0·2 mm, iron compounds up to 0·5 mm, and particles of organic chalk up to 0·2 mm.
328.00.1/25.
Grey-ware jar (Fig. 37:24). Fabric finely sanded with colourless water-worn sands up to 0·2 mm in size, iron compounds up to 0·5 mm, and particles of organic chalk up to 0·2 mm.
328.00.1/27.
Jar (Fig. 37:25). Fine, orange-buff fabric with minute colourless sands (less than 0·1 mm) and minute iron compounds. Dark brown colour-coat. Barbotine 'hair-pin' decoration on the exterior. There are fragments of at least four to five more carinated bowls similar to vessels 1—9.

Finds probably not from the grave group

328.00.1/41.
Grey-ware jar (Fig. 38:26). Fabric sanded with minute colourless grains less than 0·1 mm, many iron compounds up to 0·7 mm.

328.00.1/41.
Grey-ware flanged dish (Fig. 38:27). Fabric sanded with white and colourless sands up to 0·6 mm, iron compounds up to 0·5 mm, and organic chalk up to 0·2 mm.

328.00.1/47.
Grey-ware jar (Fig. 38:28). Fabric finely sanded with white and colourless water-worn grains to 0·5 mm and iron compounds to 0·4 mm.

328.00.1/43.
Grey-ware base (Fig. 38:29). Fabric sanded with colourless water-worn sands up to 0·2 mm.

328.00.1/30.
Sherd of fine white/pink fabric (Fig. 38:30) with occasional colourless sands up to 0·1 mm, iron compounds up to 0·8 mm.

328.00.1/45.
Grey-ware jar (Fig. 38:31), fabric grogged.

328.00.1/46.
Grey-ware jar (Fig. 38:32). Fabric finely sanded with white and colourless water-worn sands up to 0·3 mm, and iron compounds up to 0·4 mm.

328.00.1/32.
Mortarium (Fig. 38:33). Fine, orange fabric with occasional white and colourless sands up to 0·2 mm, and some iron compounds up to 0·3 mm. Worn pink/red colour-coat on the exterior.

328.00.1/44.
Grey-ware dish (Fig. 38:34). Sparsely sanded with colourless grains up to 0·3 mm, occasional iron compounds. The outer surface is smoothed.

328.00.1/48.
Grey-ware base (Fig. 38:35). Fabric finely sanded with colourless grains up to 0·1 mm and iron compounds up to 0·2 mm.

328.00.1/45.
Grey-ware storage jar (Fig. 38:36). Fabric heavily sanded with white and colourless grains up to 1·8 mm.

Grey-ware storage jar rim, very badly worn. Fabric sanded with white and colourless sands unevenly sized up to 0·9 mm, Iron compounds to 1 mm. Black slip on the exterior.

The Finds

The Samian by G. Dannell and B. R. Hartley

Form	Museum Accession Number	Figure Number	Date A.D.	Kiln	Comments
15/17	328.00.1/23 328.00.1/21	39:37 39:38	c. 75—100		Two vessels stamped from same die, OFVIRILI. Virilis. Stamps from other dies of the same potter are at La Graufesenque. There are many records from Flavian foundations, the latest being Corbridge, Holt and Saalburg.

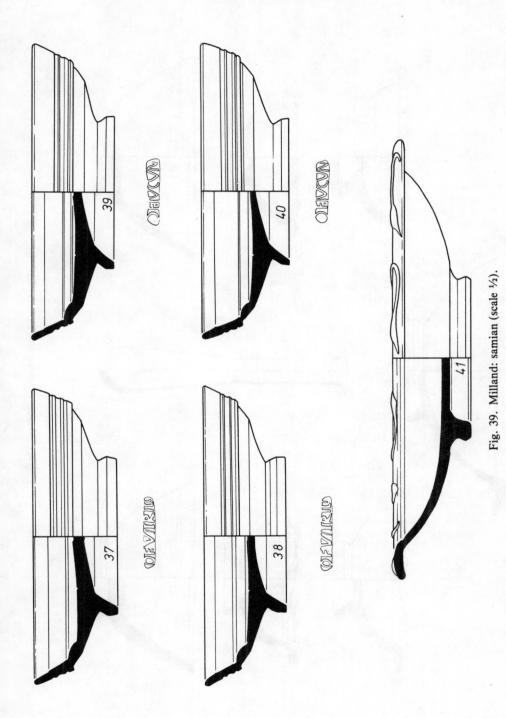

Fig. 39. Milland: samian (scale ½).

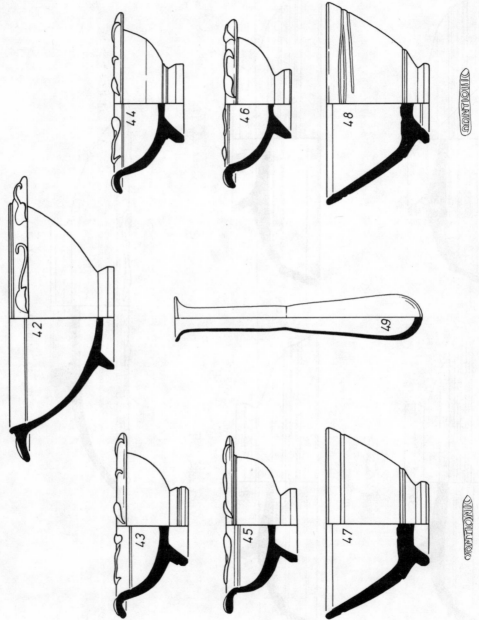

Fig. 40. Milland: samian and glass (scale ½).

Form	Museum Accession Number	Figure Number	Date A.D.	Kiln	Comments
	328.00.1/22	39:39	c. 75—90		Two vessels stamped
	328.00.1/28	39:40			OF. IVCVN. Iucundus. Stamps from the same die have been discovered at La Graufesenque. Dated sites include Nijmegen (*Ulpia Noviomagus* site) and Valkenburg period IV.
	328.00.1/49	41:50	c. 75—90		Stamped [O]FPONTI[, Pont(h)eius. Found at La Graufesenque, Brecon, Ilkley, Inchtuthil, and the Nijmegen fortress. This stamp is from the die after it had become worn.
27	328.00.1/52		1st century	southern Gaul	
33	328.00.1/14	40:47	c. 65—85	southern Gaul	Two vessels stamped
	328.00.1/15	40:48			DONTIOIIIC. Dontio of La Graufesenque. The stamp is almost invariably on cups, rarely on dishes, or on Form 29, the latter showing use before c. A.D. 85. Many records from Flavian foundations, including Brough-*Petuaria*, Caerleon, Chester, and Rottweil, but there is a possibility that Dontio moved to Les-Martres-de-Veyre.
	328.00.1/50	41:51	c. 65—85	southern Gaul	Two vessels stamped
	328.00.1/51	41:52			DONTIOIIICI. As vessels 47 and 48.
35	328.00.1/17	40:43	—	—	
	328.00.1/18	40:44	—	—	
	328.00.1/19	40:45	—	—	
	328.00.1/20	40:46	—	—	
36	328.00.1/29	39:41	Flavian	southern Gaul	
	328.00.1/52	—	1st century	southern Gaul	4 fragments from same vessel, including rim sherds.
Curle 11	328.00.1/16	40:42	Flavian	—	

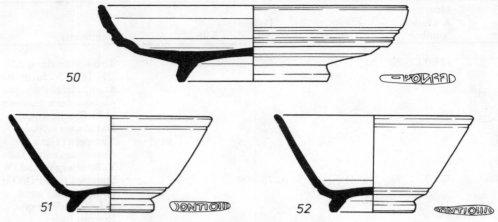

Fig. 41. Milland: samian (scale ½).

The Glass Flask by J. Price

This vessel (Fig. 40:49) was found unlabelled, but appears to be that recorded from the Milland grave. It is a complete tubular unguent bottle, of bluish-green glass, with a few elongated bubbles (height 13·0 cm, diameter of rim 2·5 cm). It has an everted rim, the edge cut off and fire-rounded, narrow neck and body expanding outwards slightly to a maximum width above a very small flattened base. About halfway between rim and base the tube is constricted to mark the junction between the neck and the body. The vessel is blown.

This was a very common form of unguent bottle in the first century A.D., and is found in great quantities in most provinces of the Roman Empire; it is nearly always made from ordinary bluish-green glass. The form has been discussed by Isings (1957: Form 8,24; 1971; Maastricht no. 3, 6—7), who has recorded many examples in contexts dating from the reign of Tiberius to the end of the first century A.D., and a few which survive into the second century A.D. The main period of production seems to have been during the second half of the first century, and the form disappeared almost completely thereafter.

Unguent bottles were not specifically funerary objects, but it is rare to find complete specimens except as grave goods, and the small fragments found on many habitation sites often cannot be identified with certainty. However, large numbers of these vessels have been found in the cities of Pompeii (e.g. Charlesworth 1965: 233—4, Fig. 2, and Pl. XIII:8—9) and Herculaneum, and it is clear that they were also used in everyday life. The unguent bottles were probably manufactured in several places, and traded for their contents, which are likely to have been small quantities of perfumes and other cosmetic preparations.

Comparatively few examples from sites in Roman Britain have been published. These include several from Colchester (May 1930:254—73, Graves 7, 29, 32, 44, 56 and 72; Harden 1947:304—5, Pl. 88:85, Brailsford 1958:44, and Pl. XII:16), mostly from Claudio-Neronian to late first-century A.D. contexts, though one comes from a burial early in the second century. Other published finds from London, mid first century (Wheeler 1928:159, Fig. 65:28); York, early second century (Harden 1962:85, 137, Fig. 89 H.G.32); Caerleon, unstratified (Murray Threipland 1966:48, Fig. 5:13); and Winnall, Winchester (see pp. 85). However, others have been found and specimens exist in many of the archaeological museums in Britain (e.g. Charlesworth 1959:54, Fig. 10:3 and Pl. V:2).

The Faunal Remains

Provenance	Species	Anatomical Element
Mammals		
Apparently on platter 18	pig	left ulna, proximal and distal ends, unfused left radius, proximal and distal ends, unfused, less than 1 year (Silver 1969)
Birds by G. Cowles		
Apparently on platter 18	woodcock	one individual including: left humerus right humerus sternum, incomplete left tibiotarsus left carpometacarpus right carpometacarpus fused thoracic vertebrae
	domestic chicken	one individual including: left humerus left femur left coracoid left scapula right proximal end of carpometacarpus
	domestic chicken(?)	right scapula, immature

HIGHCLIFFE
(Site 1232)
by V. Jones

A group of pottery was uncovered in June 1911 by Mr A. Green while he was working in his allotments in the Highcliffe area of Winchester. The vessels lay some 0·50 m below the surface. The discovery was recorded as lying on Mr Green's land 'near Charlie Salter's shed' (Fig. 36). The precise location was not noted, and searches through Winchester City Record Office, Hampshire Record Office, and the Winchester and District Allotment Society records failed to supply any information useful in locating this site.

The Finds

The Coarse Pottery
Grey-ware urn (1232.00.1/1, Fig. 38:1). Fabric sanded with white and colourless water-worn grains up to 0·2 mm, and iron compounds to 0·9 mm.

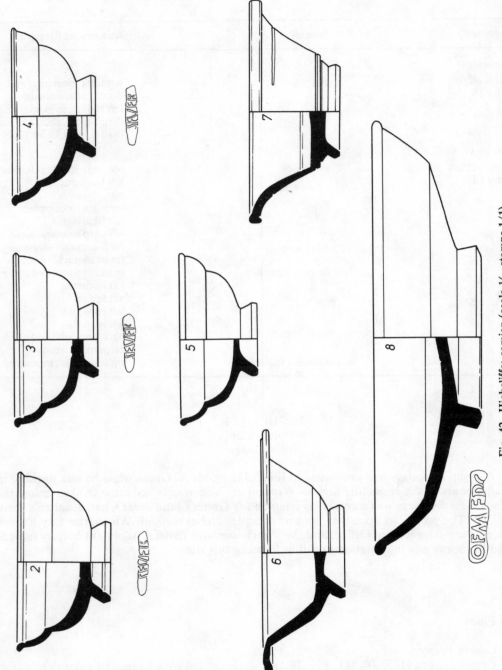

Fig. 42. Highcliffe: samian (scale ½, stamps 1/1).

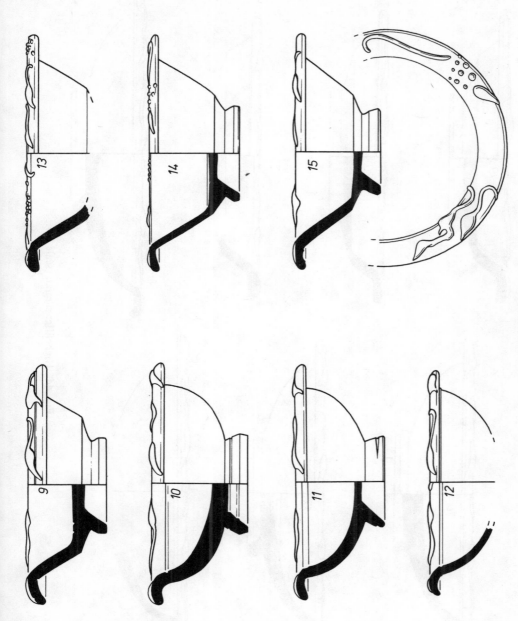

Fig. 43. Highcliffe: samian (scale ½).

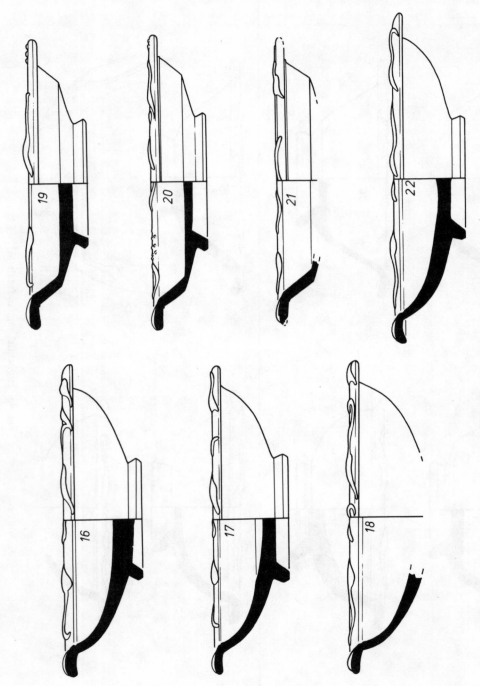

Fig. 44. Highcliffe: samian (scale ½).

The Samian by G. Dannell and B. R. Hartley

Form	Museum Accession Number	Figure Number	Date A.D.	Kiln	Comments
18R	1232.00.1/4	42:8	*c.* 90—110		Stamped **OFMERC**. Mercator. Stamps from other dies of this potter are recorded at La Graufesenque. Other records from Chester, Corbridge, and Saalburg.
27	1232.00.1/9 1232.00.1/10 1232.00.1/11	42:2 42:3 42:4	*c.* 75—90		Three vessels stamped **SEVERI**. Severus. Stamps of other dies of this potter recorded from La Graufesenque. Newstead gives latest dated site, with records from Caerleon, Carmarthen, the Nijmegen fortress, Ribchester, and Valkenburg IV, confirming Flavian date. Same stamp is in Winchester-Crab Wood burial (Collis 1977c).
	1232.00.1/17	42:5	pre-Flavian(?)	southern Gaul	
35/36	1232.00.1/8	42:6	1st century	southern Gaul	Flat rimmed, with no barbotine.
	1232.00.1/6	43:9	Trajanic	Martres-de-Veyre	With rounded rim.
35/36	1232.00.1/13 1232.00.1/12 1232.00.1/18	43:10 43:11 43:12	1st century	southern Gaul	
	1232.00.1/19 1232.00.1/20	43:13 43:14	1st century	—	With flat rim.
	1232.00.1/3	43:15	1st century	southern Gaul	With rounded rim.
	1232.00.1/15 1232.00.1/16 1232.00.1/22	44:19 44:20 44:21	1st century	—	With flat rims.
36	1232.00.1/14 1232.00.1/15 1232.00.1/21	44:16 44:17 44:18	1st century	southern Gaul	With flat rims.
	1232.00.1/23	44:22	1st century	southern Gaul	With rounded rim.
46	1232.00.1/7	42:7	late Flavian	southern Gaul	
	1232.00.1/24	—	1st century	—	Fragment with barbotine vine leaf (?).

The Cremation by C. Wells

This cremation consists of about 50 fragments of bone, with some tiny splinters and dust. The following are a few of the identifiable fragments: 3 scraps of cranial vault, one with a few millimetres of unfused suture; pieces of long bone shafts including humerus, radius and ulna, femur with linear aspera, tibia with part of the medial condyle, distal tibia, fragments of tibial and fibular shafts. Fragments from the body of both clavicles are recognizable; also the trochlear and lateral surfaces of a talus.

The unfused cranial suture may suggest that this was a young person but the proximal and distal tibial fragments show that the epiphyses were already fused: an age between *c.* 19 and 30 years is a likely range.

The bones are gracile and lightly built without strong muscle markings, but the cortex is fairly thick relative to the medulla. Stature cannot be estimated but was certainly not great. This was probably a woman or a very lightly built man of small size and weak development.

Firing had been carried out with great efficiency. Collection, or at least preservation, of the remains was inadequate. Only one individual is detectable, and no animal bones were identified.

CHAPTER 5

THE NORTHERN SUBURB

It is the northern suburb which has seen the largest amount of archaeological activity in the last few years. Other than the sites described here (Fig. 45), and the casual observations made by Ward-Evans during the construction of the cattle market in the 1930s, there has been extensive excavation of the late Roman cemetery at Lankhills (*Winchester Studies* 4). Also three sites have been excavated by K. Qualmann, a Roman settlement site at Hyde Abbey, and Roman and medieval road frontages at Victoria Road and Hyde Street/Swan Lane.

The northern limit of the Iron Age enclosure and the Roman and medieval town was defined by a shallow east—west valley in which flowed a small stream, the Fulflood. The flanks of this valley outside the North Gate were especially suited to occupation, and our earliest evidence, from 82 Hyde Street, is of Middle Bronze Age date, although it was not until the Roman period that intensive occupation took place.

The importance of the area where later the North Gate was to be built began in the Claudian period with the intersection of two major roads, those from Cirencester and Silchester. Which of these roads is the earlier and why they follow their alignments is still far from clear. Both seem to be Claudian, and certainly predate the construction of the Roman defences by at least a generation, so that the siting of the gate has nothing to do with their alignment, though it is possible they are heading for a gate in the Iron Age defences. Equally, wherever one wishes to postulate a fort (see p. 6 above), one of these roads must bypass it. It is possible they are aligned on an entrance in the Iron Age earthwork which seems to be on approximately the same line as the later defences at the North Gate, but the other Roman roads into the city take little cognizance of it. All this demonstrates how little we know of the formative years of Roman Winchester.

Even before the construction of the Roman defences in the late Flavian period a cemetery had begun to develop in the angle between the Cirencester and Silchester roads, and this cemetery continued in use into the second century. The present excavations have also revealed the stone foundations of a mausoleum, unfortunately heavily disturbed by medieval pits. However, in the second century there was also domestic activity, and along the sides of the Cirencester road, in the area between the cobbled surface and the side gullies there are rectangular areas of chalk, apparently small buildings of some kind. The more scrappy evidence from 82 Hyde Street suggests similar structures along the Silchester Road, and again they primarily belong to the second century, continuing a little into the third.

However, there were settlement areas further north along the Silchester road. Recent excavations near Hyde Abbey gateway have produced some first-century occupation (Wilson 1973:318), and about half a kilometre to the north there is an isolated burial from Nuns' Walk which could relate to this settlement. Occupation was continuous in this area into the fourth

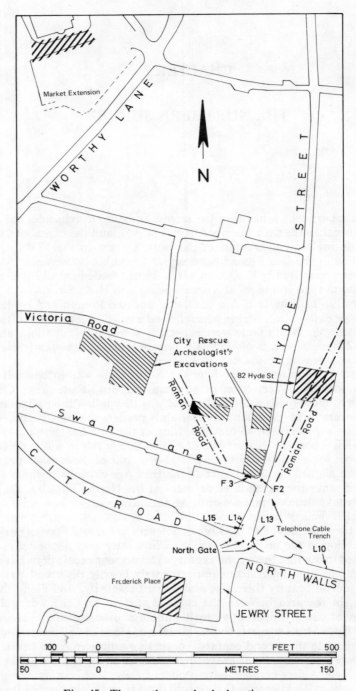

Fig. 45. The northern suburb: location map.

century, with the settlement expanding to the south. In its final phase in the fourth century there was a subsidiary east—west road with at least two timber buildings alongside it, and one suspects this was something more than a farming settlement. Along the Cirencester road there is no evidence for a separate settlement until Berwick House, about a couple of kilometres from the town.

Near the North Gate there is some evidence for the realignment of the Roman roads, but the details are still far from clear. Though there is evidence for the continued use of the early Roman cemetery in Hyde Street, the main cemetery excavated in Victoria Road belongs to the fourth century. It lies well back from the road frontage. The main cemetery areas lie further north along the Cirencester road. Numbers of graves turned up in the 1930s under the cattle market, and they may be essentially third century as may those published here from the Market Extension site. Recent rescue work on this site has produced more burials, and there seems to be a very extensive cemetery, though of low social status. Further north again is the large cemetery of Lankhills (Clarke, G. N., in Biddle 1969, 1970, 1975a) which was started in the 320s, and which continued in use until after the end of the century.

In the post-Roman period the system of roads approaching the town from the north was greatly altered. The medieval and modern road starts to deviate from the line of the Silchester road as far out as Kings Worthy; nearer the city, and before the late ninth century, this road appears not to have headed for the North Gate but to have followed the line of the modern Worthy Road and Worthy Lane. The modern Andover Road diverges westwards from the Roman Cirencester road about a half kilometre short of the gate. The two routes from the north merged to form the south end of Andover Road, and ran up the hill towards the Westgate along the line of modern Sussex Street. The implications are that the North Gate had ceased to function.

When the city was reorganized in the late ninth century new elements appeared in the street pattern of the suburb. With the presumed reopening of the North Gate a road appeared connecting it with Worthy Road, and Hyde Street became the main artery of the suburb. The 'twitchen' running along the outer edge of the defensive ditch connecting Hyde Street with Sussex Street survives in the modern Swan Lane, and it presumably continued westwards along the valley of the Fulflood towards Weeke. Church Lane which linked Worthy Lane and Hyde Street opposite the abbey was probably the latest element of the medieval street pattern to be established. Of these roads, Hyde Street was the most densely built up, and in the twelfth and thirteenth centuries houses extended along it at least as far north as the junction with Worthy Lane. In the same period there were also houses along Swan Lane and Worthy Lane. Near the important junction of Swan Lane and Sussex Street stood the parish church of St Mary in the Vale. Further west, near the railway line, was Bar Ditch which marked the north-western boundary of the suburb. It continued in a northeasterly and then in a northerly direction parallel to Worthy Lane as far as a plot of land known as *Palliesputte,* where the limit of the city liberty was defined by a boundary stone. This stone was almost certainly the large sarsen found in no more than a slightly displaced position in Edington Road (p. 156).

Not much early medieval material has so far been found in this suburb. The earliest feature on 82 Hyde Street was a ditch running parallel with the modern road, and this could mark the eastern limit of the suburb in the tenth—eleventh centuries. The site has also produced a small number of eleventh- or twelfth-century pits. The recent excavations on the corner of Swan Lane and Hyde Street have produced little material of this date, whereas thirteenth-century and later material is plentiful, mainly from pits, but few other structures have survived.

In 1110 the New Minster, which had previously occupied a constricted site in the centre of the city, was moved to a new site at Hyde. The new church stood on the western margin of the water meadows and some of its monastic buildings extended towards Hyde Street. After its dissolution the abbey buildings largely fell into ruins, but the extra-mural settlement survived both this and the earlier economic crisis in the fourteenth century. There was some contraction in the area occupied, but Hyde Street continued to thrive as the archaeological finds adequately testify.

TELEPHONE CABLE TRENCH
(TCT55 Site 723)

Between May and October 1955 an extensive series of trenches was dug in the northern and eastern part of the town for the laying of a new telephone cable (Fig. 44). A number of observations were made by Mr Cottrill, the most important relating to the Roman defences. Here only those in the northern suburb and defences are considered.

Summary
Most of the finds relate to the defences and road system in this area. The finds from the Roman bank have previously been considered by Cunliffe (1962), but it is not clear from his report precisely where each group comes from or how sure is its stratification. The groups are republished here in full. Two observations relate to the Roman road system, F3 and L13. Unfortunately neither is informative. F3 is presumably the Cirencester road, which should belong to the Claudian period, but this particular surface is presumably later and there is evidence from K. Qualmann's excavations that this road was realigned. The deposits L13 which lie in the actual gateway of the North Gate tell us little other than when material started to accumulate. Recent work on the North Gate by Mr F. Aldsworth has helped to elucidate the plan, and has demonstrated that the arches of the bridge over the City Ditch still survive. Our evidence shows that the landscaping of this area, notably the infilling of the City Ditch west of the North Gate was already completed by the late seventeenth century, as L14, 15, and 16 are all presumably from the upper filling of the Ditch. Of the two medieval pits F1 and F2, that from Hyde Street is of interest, as such early pits have been notably lacking in the recent excavations.

Topographically the finds fall into three groups:

     North Walls: F1, L5, 6, 7, 8, 9, 10, 11, 12
     Hyde Street: F2, L13, 14, 15, 16
     Swan Lane: F3

The positions of the observations are marked on Figure 45, except some which are too far east. These have been referred to L10 in the text. The chronological division is shown in Table 10.

Table 10. Telephone Cable Trench: age of features and layers (x=later finds also present)

Period	Features	Layers
Early Roman	3	5, 6, 7, 8, 9, 10, 11, 12, 13
Late Roman	2(x)	
Early medieval	1, 2	14(x)
Post-medieval		14, 15, 16

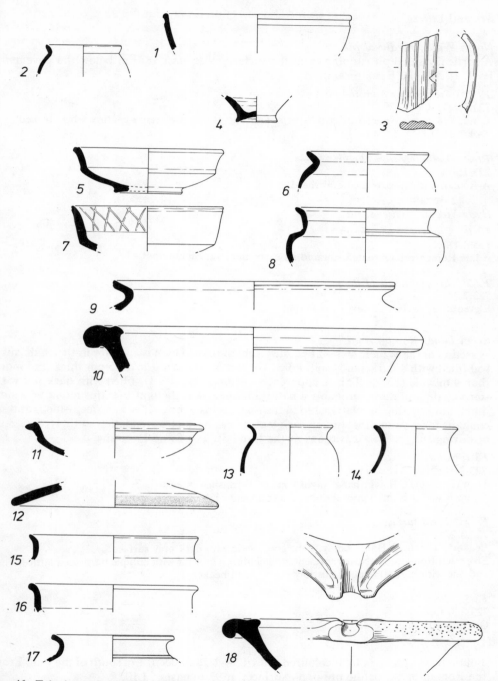

Fig. 46. Telephone Cable Trench: pottery from the Roman road F3/1(1), F3/2(2) and the Roman defences L7(3), L8(4), L10(5—10), L11(11—17), and L12(18) (scale ¼).

Features and Layers

F1: North Walls, medieval pit
A vertically-sided pit running from the surface to at least 1·70 m below the pavement level. It cuts the Roman rampart.

F1-1: Presumably from the pit
723.1.1/1.
Contains five early medieval gritty sherds and one from an eleventh-century wheel-turned cooking pot.

F1-2: Definitely from the pit
723.1.2/1.
A Roman and an early medieval sherd.

F2: Hyde Street, medieval pit

F2-1: Probably from the pit
723.2.1/1.
A late Roman colour-coated rim and an early medieval cooking pot.

F2-2: From the side of the pit
723.2.2/1.
Eleventh- or twelfth-century cooking-pot rim.

F3: Swan Lane, Roman road
A section of the Winchester—Silchester Roman road. There is a hollow in the chalk sub-soil filled with a dark sandy soil, F3-3. On top is a layer up to 12·5 cm thick and more than 4 m wide (F3-2). This is apparently cut by a slot (F3-1), filled with dark soil with some chalk and flints, probably a natural infill. It was thought that this might be a side ditch, but its siting in relationship to the road seems wrong. It is also steep-sided, and so could be for a water pipe, but no such feature has been observed either at 82 Hyde Street or during the recent excavations at the Hyde Street—Swan Lane site.

F3-1: Slot
723.3.1/1.
Dish (Fig. 46:1). Black, hard, slightly gritty. Burnished interior.
There is also a Roman grey sherd and a fragment of Antonine samian.

F3:2: Road surface
723.3.2/1.
Beaker (Fig. 46:2). Hard, sandy, light grey fabric with dark grey surface.
Five other Roman vessels are represented, including a grey jar with oblique burnished lattice, and one with barbotine dots, possibly poppy-head beaker.

F3-3: Below the road
723.3.3/1.
One small Roman sherd.

L5: North Walls
Found by workmen in light coloured soil 1·05—1·20 m deep, 1 m south of the wall. From the Roman bank, or the pre-bank surface, at 93 m east of L10.
723.00.5/1.
Two Roman sherds.
Samian sherd, possibly pre-Flavian.

L6: North Walls
In sand and clay, possibly the Roman bank, at 90 m east of L10.

L7: North Walls, Roman Bank
From low in the trench, with sandy clay adhering, at 47 m east of L10.
723.00.7/1.
Flagon handle (Fig. 46:3). Fine, cream ware.

L8: North Walls, Roman Bank
As L7, 45 m east of L10.
723.00.8/1.
Beaker (Fig. 46:4). Hard, grey, sandy ware.
A dupondius of Claudius.

L9: North Walls
From the dump. Probably from low in the trench, where there is a mixed sandy clay.

L10: North Walls, Roman Bank
Dark soil between layers of clay and sand, dipping to the west, 1·30 m down.
723.00.10/1.
Dish (Fig. 46:5). Dull brown, sandy fabric, with black surface.
Jar (Fig. 46:6). Soft, reddish-brown core, dull brown-black surface.
Dish (Fig. 46:7). Hard, sandy, off-white to black fabric, burnished internal decoration.
Jar (Fig. 46:8). Grey, sandy core, red-brown skin, and dull brown surface. 'Fur' deposit on the inside from boiling water.
Jar (Fig. 46:9). Hard, dark grey fabric with sandy, black temper; grey surface.
Mortarium (Fig. 46:10). Soft, buff fabric. Burnt.
Fragment of 8 other vessels, including a platter base and a sherd joining with one from L12. The samian is Flavian-Trajanic.

L11: North Walls, Roman Bank
From dump near L10.
723.00.11/1.
Dish (Fig. 46:11). Dark-brown, sandy fabric, dull surface. Abraded.
Lid (Fig. 46:12). Hard, harsh, light grey fabric, black, partly burnished surface.
Jar (Fig. 46:13). Fine, brown, sandy fabric, black burnished surface.
Jar (Fig. 46:14). Sandy, black fabric, grey core, light brown surface.
Jar (Fig. 46:15). Light grey to brown fabric with some mica.
Dish (Fig. 46:16). Soft, dark brown fabric. Light-brown, burnished surface.
Jar (Fig. 46:17). Light brown, sandy fabric, grey core and surface.
There are fragments of 22 other vessels, including the rims of three jars, a dish, and a lid. There are two samian sherds, one first century, the other Flavian.

L12: North Walls, Roman Bank
Tip of greyish-brown, sandy clay with tip lines of different material sloping south beneath yellow clay with flints. It lies on the original top-soil, 2·20 m below road level, 21 m east of L10.
723.00.12/1.
Mortarium (Fig. 46:18). Soft pink to reddish buff fabric.

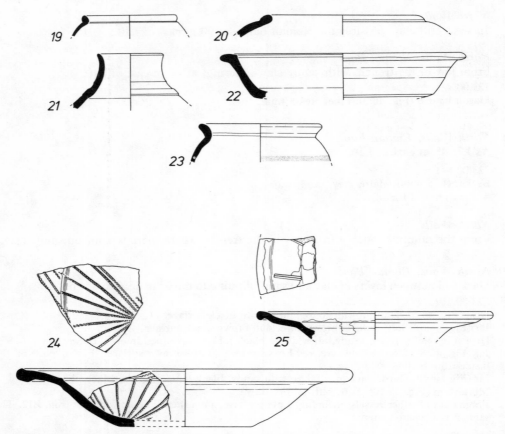

Fig. 47. Telephone Cable Trench: pottery from the Roman road L13(19—23) and the City Ditch L16(25—26) (scale ¼).

L13: Hyde Street, North Gate

Grey sandy fill, with a black streak, some sherds were derived from the dump. The deposit is just above natural chalk on the line of the Roman road coming through the North Gate.

723.00.13/1.

Bead-rim jar (Fig. 47:19). Grey-brown core, dark grey-brown surface, fine white grit.

Bead rim (Fig. 47:20). Hard, light grey, sandy fabric, black surface.

Cordoned flask (Fig. 47:21). Hard, light grey, sandy fabric, black-brown surface.

Pie dish (Fig. 47:22). Hard, light grey fabric, dark grey, smoothed surface.

Jar (Fig. 47:23). Light brown, sandy fabric, grey core and black burnished surface.

There are some 20 sherds of samian, mainly of Antonine date.

L14: Hyde Street, upper fill of City Ditch (?)

About 1 m down in the trench.

723.00.14/1.

A late seventeenth-century group, mostly of good quality, and one fragment of a spout and base similar to Winchester Ware. Also clay pipes and glass.

L15: Hyde Street, upper fill of City Ditch (?)

Found near L14, but no details are given. Perhaps the same deposit.

723.00.15/1.

Flanged dish (Fig. 47:24) in a dull, creamy grey fabric, of which a flange from the same dish occurs in L16. It is well thrown, fettled on the lower half, and decorated on the inside only with radial lines made with a pastry cutting wheel with wavy edges. The complete pattern cannot be seen. Probably a product of the Surrey kilns.

There is also a piece of fine red earthenware with white-slip decoration, trailed wet or blobbed on the pot, resulting in a fine red and yellow decoration.

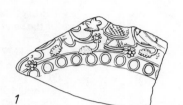
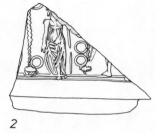

1

2

Fig. 48. Telephone Cable Trench: samian (scale ½).

L16: Hyde Street

Found between City Road and Swan Lane, perhaps the same as L14 and L15.

723.00.16/1.

Flanged-rim dish (Fig. 47:25) in a very dark, coarse-fabric earthenware covered internally only with a white slip. This slip is cut through with a two-pronged tool. The whole glaze is a clear lead glaze. A product of the Donyatt, Somerset kilns.

The Finds

Roman Coin by R. Reece

A Roman coin (C 1828) of Claudius I (A.D. 43—54) was found in L9 (RIC 67).

The Samian by G. Dannell

Provenance	Museum Accession Number	Form	Date	Kiln	Comments
F3-1	723.3.1/1	33	Antonine	central Gaul	
L1	723.00.1/1	37	Antonine	probably Rheinzabern	footring
L2	723.00.2/1	18	1st century	southern Gaul	
L4	723.00.4/1	33	2nd century	central Gaul	
	723.00.4/2	mortarium	2nd century	central Gaul	
L6	723.00.6/1	18R	1st century	southern Gaul	
L10	723.00.10/1	37	Trajanic	Martres-de-Veyre	Fig. 48. Vine leaf scrolls flanking a compound ornament, perhaps a

Provenance	Museum Accession Number	Form	Date	Kiln	Comments
					trophy; below a wreath of circles. The style is that attributed to DONNACVS (c.f. Stanfield and Simpson 1958: Pl. 43,500; Pl. 46, 546). I cannot identify the ornament for the small leaf, either in Terrisse (1968) or Rogers (1974), but c.f. that shown for QUINTILIANVS (Stanfield and Simpson 1958: Pl. 69, 11).
	723.00.10/3	18	late 1st century	southern Gaul	burnt
	723.00.10/4	27	late 1st century—early 2nd century	Montans	
	723.00.10/5	27	probably pre-Flavian	southern Gaul	
L11	723.00.11/1	18	Flavian	southern Gaul	
	723.00.11/2	35	1st century	southern Gaul	
L13	723.00.13/2	31	probably after		
	723.00.13/3	31R	c. A.D. 150 but not very late	central Gaul	
	723.00.13/4	33			
	723.00.13/5	38			
	723.00.13/6	33	Hadrianic—Antonine	central Gaul	stamped MALLIACI
	723.00.13/7	37	2nd century	central Gaul	
	723.00.13/8	30	Hadrianic—Antonine	central Gaul	Fig. 48:2 TETTVRVS style, his wavy line borders ending short in astragali (as Stanfield and Simpson 1958: Pl. 131, 1). The figure may be Minerva
L19	723.00.19/1	31	Antonine	central Gaul	
	723.00.19/2	chip	Antonine	central Gaul	

82 HYDE STREET (SCATS)
(82 HS, Site 720)

Winchester suffered little from wartime bombing, the one exception being the group of houses which stood on this site. The site was redeveloped in 1954—5 by SCATS for offices and a showroom, though the new building stands back from the street frontage, east of the filled-in cellars of the bombed houses. For the construction of the foundations a grid of 27 square holes was dug, and finds have been grouped according to the holes in which they were found (Fig. 49). The site was visited regularly by F. Cottrill between November 1954 and January 1955, to collect finds and record deposits, though the sections were often masked by timber shoring. Permission to visit the site was given by SCATS, and all finds have been donated to the City Museum, excepting the sarsen stone which has been placed in North Walls Recreation Ground, at the entrance to the Indoor Recreation Centre.

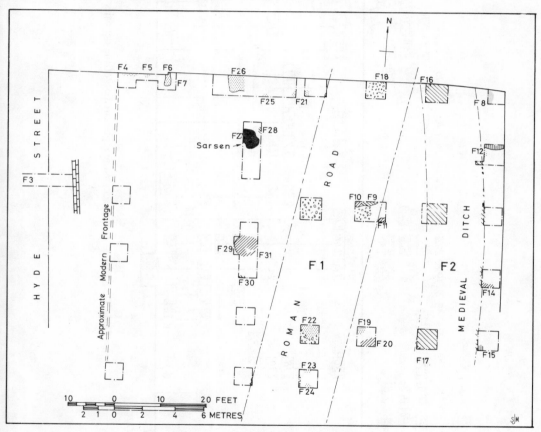

Fig. 49. 82 Hyde Street: site plan.

Summary

The site lies in the bottom of a small valley in which a stream, the Fulflood, used to run defining the northern edge of the Roman and early medieval city. However, no unambiguous evidence of the course of the stream was encountered, though the descriptions of the natural

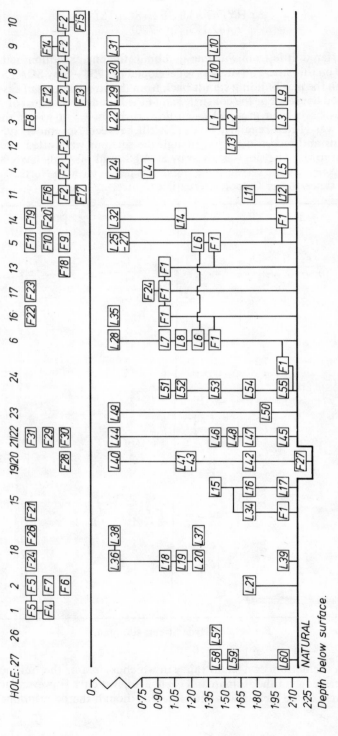

Table 11. 82 Hyde Street: schematic representation of the deposits

sub-soil often refer to 'clean sand'. This overlay a deposit of clay-with-flints, itself overlying decomposed chalk with many flints. Over much of the site the natural surface lay at a depth of just over 2 m (7 feet).

The earliest evidence of human activity found here is a pit (F27) of unknown dimensions, but about 1·36 m deep, filled with homogeneous brown silt. In the middle filling lay a large sarsen and beneath it a fragment of a Middle Bronze Age bucket urn. Otherwise occupation seems to start at the end of the first century A.D., but most of the Roman finds belong to the second and third centuries. The main feature is the Winchester—Silchester road (F1), which runs north—south across the site. The lowest level lies directly on the natural sand with a width of about 5 m. The final surface was probably considerably narrower. At their maximum the road deposits are about 1·20 m thick, though whether this represents a gradual build-up or a single construction for the agger is unclear. Due to this uncertainty it is impossible to give a date for its construction. If it started as a single layer of cobbles, then the Claudian samian — the only early sherds from the site — imply an early date. If the agger was all constructed at one time, it did not come into existence until Hadrianic times. Deposits had accumulated over its edge by the end of the second century, and a large part of the total build-up on the site belongs to this century, probably more than 1 m. It is mainly described as dirty sand or brownish clay (L3, 4, 6, 9, 10, 21, 42, 50, 53, and also L14, 16, and 45 though these last three are contaminated). There is no evidence for constructions or buildings within these layers.

On top of this deposit, and still probably within the second century, there is evidence for occupation in the form of chalk spreads, L41 and L43. The evidence is perhaps comparable with that from more recent excavations in Victoria Road, where light structures have been found lining the Winchester—Mildenhall road. Another parallel with that site is the lack of burials on the street frontage, and the cemeteries seem to have been set well back. On the SCATS site only one possible burial was encountered, the skull fragments in hole 25 (L56) on the western edge of the site. Later Roman occupation may have been removed by the medieval activity, but finds of this period are rare. Two features in the eastern part of the site, F13 and F15, both possibly wells, may be late Roman.

The major early medieval feature is a large north—south ditch (F2), perhaps of tenth- or eleventh-century date, but the finds are ambiguous. It is certainly on a different alignment

Table 12. 82 Hyde Street: age of features and layers (x=later finds also present).

Period	Features	Layers
Prehistoric	27	
Early Roman	1, 13(x), 17(x)	3, 4, 6, 9, 10(x), 15, 16(x), 21, 22(x), 29(x), 31(x), 41, 43, 44(x), 50, 53, 57, 58
Late Roman	2(x), 3(x), 13, 15, 17(x), 29(x)	14(x), 24(x), 34, 45(x), 49(x), 61(x)
Early medieval	2, 6, 9, 18, 28, 30	24(x), 25(x), 27(x), 32(x), 44(x), 45(x)
Late medieval	10, 11, 14, 17, 20, 29	14, 16, 18, 22, 24, 25, 26, 27(x), 28, 30(x), 31(x), 32, 35, 38, 39(x), 44, 45, 49(x), 61(x)
Early post-medieval		30, 31, 39, 49, 61(x)
Later post-medieval	3, 8	27, 29, 61

from the Roman road, running parallel instead with the medieval Hyde Street. A number of pits are also early medieval (F6, 9, 18, 28, and 30), but the most important medieval material is later, from a series of pits and wells, though unfortunately the associated floor levels could not be observed. All these pits avoid the street frontage as might be expected. After the wealth of fifteenth-century material, finds are notably lacking until the nineteenth, due perhaps to the removal of the later levels.

Features and Layers

The relationship of the features is shown in schematic form in Table 11. The age of features and layers is shown in Table 12.

F1:   *The Roman road*
The road from Silchester runs obliquely across the site, heading for the North Gate. It was recognized in seven trenches. The main sequence of deposits, starting from the latest was as follows:

F1-1:   *Flints and soil*

F1-2:   *A layer of gravel*

F1-3:   *Small flints and gravel*
720.1.3/1, 2.
Two samian sherds of Hadrianic-Antonine date.

F1-4:   *Small flints and powdered chalk*

F1-5:   *Clayey gravel*

F1-6:   *A layer of flints*
720.1.6/1.
A samian sherd of Claudian date. It lay at the base of the layer on top of a buried surface.

F2:   *The medieval ditch*
The ditch is apparently V-shaped, and it runs north—south across the site. The maximum depth is not recorded but it was noted in trench 11 at a depth of about 3·20 m (10 ft 5 in) below the modern surface. The highest surviving Roman surface, in Trench 16, is 1 m below the surface, so the ditch is over 2·20 m deep. Dating evidence is not plentiful, but the early medieval sherds in F1-2 seem securely stratified.

F2-1:   *The upper fill, a pale grey clean silt.*
720.2.1/1.
Two late Roman sherds.

F2-2:   *The lower fill of dark silt*
720.2.2/1.
Two late Roman sherds, one of early medieval gritty ware, and one of Winchester Ware.

F2-3:   *Dark fill, possibly F2*
720.2.3/1—5.
Internally flanged bowl (Fig. 50:1). Hard, off-white, sandy ware.
There are nine other Roman sherds including two piedishes and a first-century jar, decorated as Bushe-Fox 1949: Pl. 89, No. 398.
There are also samian sherds of Hadrianic-Antonine date, and two late medieval sherds.

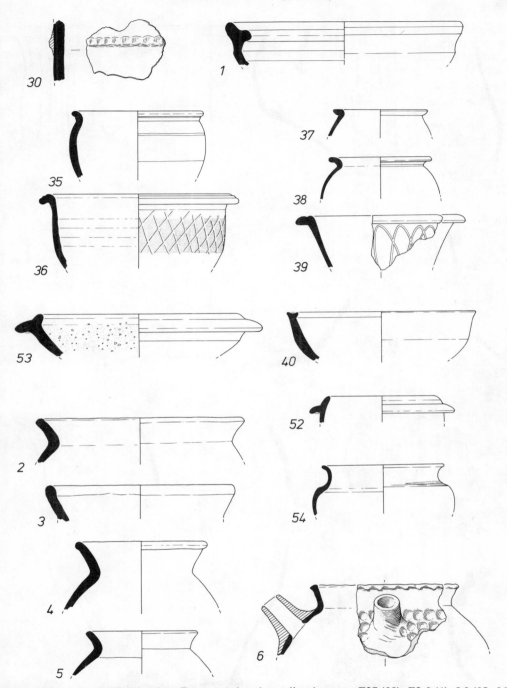

Fig. 50. 82 Hyde Street: Bronze Age, Roman and early medieval pottery F27 (30), F2-3 (1), L3 (35, 36), L10 (37—39), L43 (53), L21 (40), L41 (52), L57 (54), F6 (2—5), F9 (6) (scale ¼).

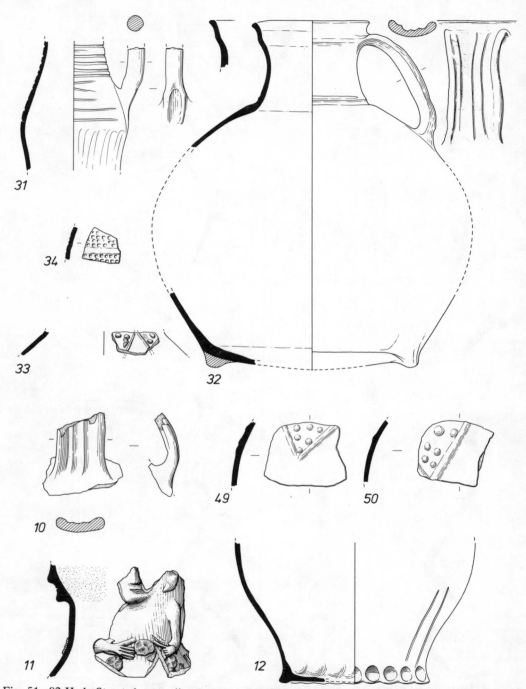

Fig. 51. 82 Hyde Street: late medieval pottery F29 (31—34), F14 (10), L32 (49—50), F20-2 (11—12) (scale ¼).

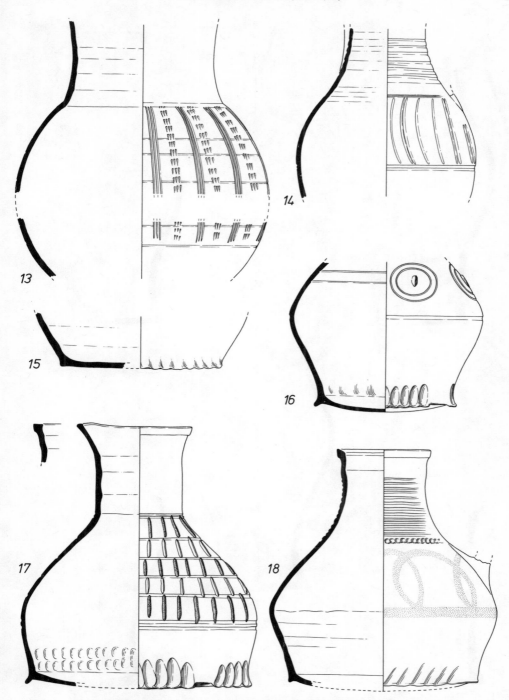

Fig. 52. 82 Hyde Street: late medieval pottery from F20-2 (scale ¼).

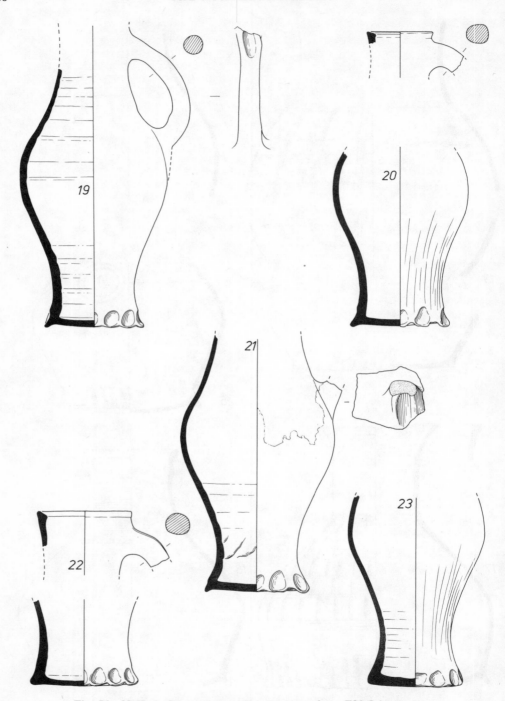

Fig. 53. 82 Hyde Street: late medieval pottery from F20-2 (scale ¼).

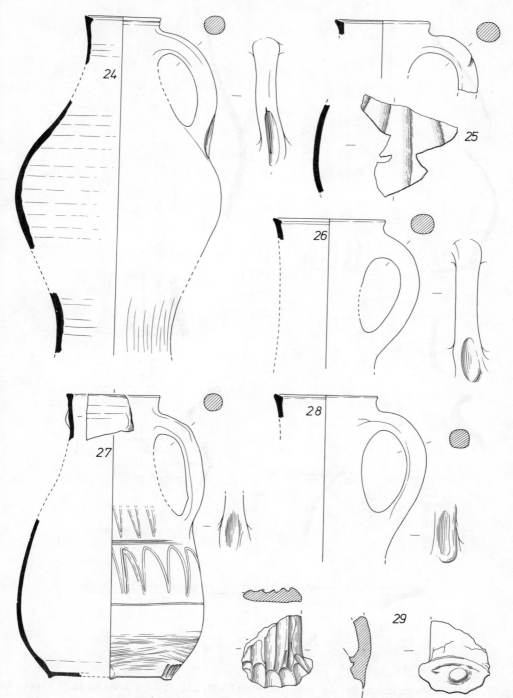

Fig. 54. 82 Hyde Street: late medieval pottery from F20-2 (scale ¼).

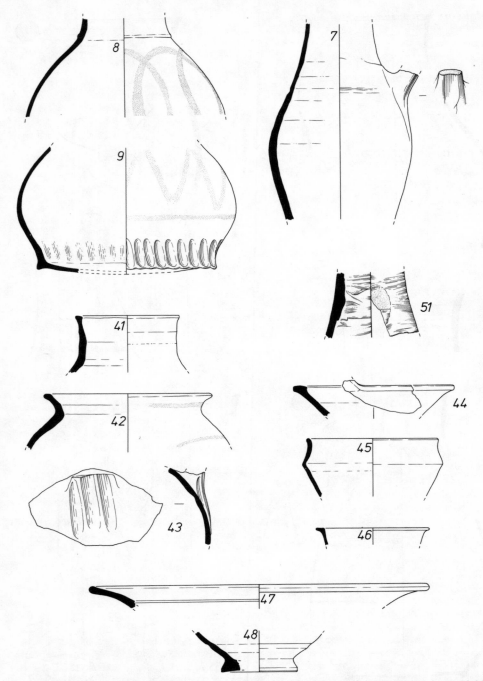

Fig. 55. 82 Hyde Street: late medieval pottery from F10 (7—9), L22 (41—43), L38 (51) and L30 (44—48) (scale ¼).

F3: **Make-up below the modern road**
720.3.2/1.
Late Roman sherds.

F4: **Pit**
Possibly post-medieval, cut by F5. No finds.

F5: **Cellar wall**
Two twelfth-century worked stones were built into this.

F6: **Medieval pit**
Subrectangular, 0·85 by 1·22 m.

720.6.0/1.
Cooking pots (Fig. 50:2—5) in standard type of gritty Saxo-Norman fabric.

F7: **Pit**
No finds.

F8: **Pit**
720.8.1/1.
Nineteenth-century finds.
720.8.1/2.
A creamer (Fig. 57:5) in hard, orange-yellow fabric with sparse thin internal glaze speckled with iron. Flush marks indicate it was fired on its side. Mid seventeenth to early eighteenth century probably a Poole/Hamworthy product.

F9: **Medieval pit**
At least 3·70 m deep.
720.9.0/1.
Pitcher spout (Fig. 50:6) from a globular vessel in gritty Saxo-Norman ware. It has a flared rim which has been crimped around the top, a spout set on the shoulder, and at this level are three bands of dimpled decoration spreading horizontally around the vessel. A good example of the combination of decoration and a spout. Similar to wares found and published from Chichester. It should be of eleventh-century date.

F10: **Medieval pit**
At least 3·70 m deep. Cuts F1.
F10-1: About 1·15—1·20 m deep
720.10.1/1—2.
Jug (Fig. 55:7) in reduced grey-brown, very hard, almost brittle fabric. The outside glaze is a dark dirty green colour. The base is fettled from the waist down.
There is also a white sherd with lustrous clear glaze, perhaps from northwest France.
F10-3: From 2·80 to 3·15 m deep
720.10.3/1—3.
Jugs (Fig. 55:8, 9) with slip under glaze decoration. The ware is hard and untempered, very smooth to the touch, the decoration is thin, brush-applied white slip, and the bases of the vessels are close thumbed in the West Sussex tradition. The decoration on both is, in the front, in the form of horseshoe-shaped loops terminating in a large horizontal band. The vessels have been fettled before crimping. These exactly parallel the jugs from Middleton-on-Sea which have been shown to be contemporary with the end of the West Sussex Ware production and preceding the black and white ware production, and therefore these pieces belong to the fifteenth century. This is not a common type in Winchester.
There is also three fragments of local fourteenth- to fifteenth-century jugs, and one fragment of Saxo-Norman pottery.

F11: Medieval pit
Pit at least 3·70 m deep.
720.11.0/1.
A mixed group of oxidized and reduced fine quality medieval wares, fourteenth century.

F12: Pit
No finds.

F13: Pit or well
Assumed to be medieval, though no medieval finds.
720.13.0/1.
An early Roman flagon and a late Roman bowl.
720.13.0/2.
A samian sherd of Late Antonine date.

F14: Pit or well
At least 3·40 m deep. Cuts F2.
720.14.0/1.
Strap handle of a large jug (Fig. 51:10) in a fine, buff to grey, sandy fabric found in globular grass-marked cooking pots. The handle is glazed to a very dark green colour.

F16: Pit cutting F2
No finds.

F17: Pit (?)
Perhaps cut by F2. No finds.

F18: Medieval pit
There is a layer of flints at the bottom, 3·40 m deep.
720.18.0/1.
An early medieval cooking pot.

F19: Pit
No finds.

F20: Medieval well
This group consists almost entirely of jugs, and there is also a lack of handles, which would confirm this is a well.

F20-1: Down to 3·70 m
720.20.1/1.
Sherds of a fourteenth-century pot.

F20-2: From 3·70 m to the bottom of the pit at 5·15 m
720.20.2/19.
Part of the front of one face and figure jug (Fig. 51:11) with black slip covering. Possibly of Bentley type. There is a white slip on the inside of the spout. Very hard, smooth, red fabric, reduced to blue-grey in places.
720.20.2/14.
Jug base (Fig. 51:12). Local buff coloured, hard fabric, with fine horizontal lines inside. Heavily fettled, no glaze.

720.20.2/2.
Jug (Fig. 51:13). Wholly oxidized fabric. Decorated with combing in vertical rows, and three prolonged jabs in-between. All under a lustrous olive-brown glaze.
720.20.2/15.
Jug similar to 27 (Fig. 52:14). It has curved decoration made with a double-pronged fork in the West Sussex tradition.
720.20.2/9.
Wide-bodied jug base (Fig. 52:15).
720.20.2/21.
Jug (Fig. 52:16) in a fabric similar to 19, but an oxidized buff colour. It has a decoration of incised circles and applied pieces in the centre of the circles, under a dark green glaze.
720.20.2/1.
White fabric jug (Fig. 52:17) with apple green glaze, iron-filled, applied strips alternating with self-coloured pieces, probably iron wash over the strips. It has a pulled spout, and the base is crimped all the way round.
720.20.2/22.
Painted jug (Fig. 52:18) in fabric as 8 and 9 above.
720.20.2/10.
Jug (Fig. 53:19). Hard, brittle fabric with a coarse, sandy texture, reduced outside but oxidized inside. Fettled from the waist downwards. The base is crudely and deeply thumbed. The glaze is dark brown and poor due to overfiring. The handle is rod sectioned and undecorated. The rims of this group of jugs (19—24, 26, 28) are plain with no spouts or other distinguishing features.
720.20.2/3.
Jug as 19 (Fig. 53:20).
720.20.2/6.
Jug as 19 (Fig. 53:21).
720.20.2/5.
Jug fragments as 19 (Fig. 53:22).
720.20.2/12.
Jug base as 19 (Fig. 53:23).
720.20.2/7.
Jug as 19 (Fig. 54:24).
720.20.2/13.
Jug (Fig. 54:25) with a rod handle in a sandy, red fabric with darker green glaze, and vertical applied strips.
720.20.2/4.
Jug as 19 (Fig. 54:26).
720.20.2/11.
Fragments of a jug (Fig. 54:27) in a white or creamy fabric with decoration comprising horizontal grooved band with grooved loops at regular intervals within the band. The handle is rod sectioned and fastened with an indentation at the base. The rim has traces of an ear, and therefore this is a 'face in front of collar' jug. The base has been pulled down in one place to make a lug foot which has subsequently broken off. A sparse frontal iron-green glaze only.
720.20.2/20.
Jug as 19 (Fig. 54:28).
720.20.2/24.
Wide strap handle (Fig. 54:29) of similar type to that seen on tripod pitchers. It has four grooves, each one terminating in depressions. The sides of the handle are wiped into waves. The tongue, which was inserted into the body of the vessel to fix the handle, is clearly visible.
720.20.2/8.
A base of a jug as 19.

720.20.2/16.
Fragments of another jug similar to 27, but plain.
720.20.2/17.
Jug base.
720.20.2/18.
Jug base.
720.20.2/23.
Two sherds from a jug similar to 25.
720.20.2/25.
Fragments of a rod handle and a strap handle, etc.
720.20.2/26.
Fragments from two Roman vessels, and three medieval cooking pots.

F21: *Well or cess-pit*
Perhaps recent. No finds.

F22: *Pit or well*
Circular, at least 3·70 m deep. No finds.

F23: *Well*
Lined with chalk and flint rubble. No finds.

F24: *Pit*
This is a cavity dug into the surface of the Roman road F1. It contained burnt sandstone slabs. There were no finds but it is apparently pre-medieval.

F25: *Pit, deeper than 4 m*
No finds.

F26: *Pit, deeper than 4·25 m*
No finds.

F27: *Sarsen and pit*
In holes 19 and 20 the natural subsoil was encountered at a depth of 2·72 m. Cut into it is a hole of unknown dimensions filled with dark sandy soil and flints, which goes down to 4·08 m, i.e. the feature is about 1·36 m deep. It is sealed by the Roman level L42. In the filling of the pit, though not projecting above the old ground surface, was a sarsen stone approximately 2·2 m by 1·4 m by *c.* 1·0 m high. Beneath it was the fragment of the bucket urn.
720.27.0/1.
Bucket urn (Fig. 50:30). Hard black fabric; coarsely gritted with flint or chert, some of which is calcined.

F28: *Medieval pit*
720.28.0/1.
A cooking pot with a pie-crust rim, possibly of fourteenth-century date.

F29: *Medieval well*
This is an interesting group as it seems to occur at the changeover from tripod pitchers to jugs. The jugs dominate, and the tripod pitcher is very worn. The life of both cannot be more than a couple of years, five at the most. The uniformity of the rims forms a

useful indication of a short period of time. This group should belong somewhere in the bracket 1275—1300.

F29-1: Down to 3·00 m

720.29.1/2.
Jug in red ware (Fig. 51:31). It is slightly more reduced than normal, thus giving a grey tinge to the fabric colour and making the fabric harder. Decoration is limited to the upper half, and that to scored lines. The rod handle has a deep indentation at its base. The glaze is a patchy green-brown colour.
720.29.1/1.
Two large fragments form a tripod pitcher (Fig. 51:32) of standard local form, similar in many ways to those made at Orchard Street, Chichester, though this one is not from that source. The fabric is very hard, almost untempered, with a dusted copper-rich lead glaze which gives a patchy green effect. The handle is a wide strap type with four pulling grooves. There is a pulled up lip, and one (presumably of three) foot, in the form of a roughly applied lump.
720.29.1/3.
Sherd (Fig. 51:33) with very fine fabric with a triangular applied strip with an iron-rich pellet set in it. The fabric is light grey and sandy, unlike south-coast fabrics.
Also exceptional is a sherd which appears to have a raised pellet of which only part remains, and this can be paralleled at Orchard Street, Chichester. There is a fragment of another vessel similar to 31, oxidized to a bright red colour, brown glazed, speckled with black; the body is grooved and the jug handle deeply indented at the base. There is also a base in soft red fabric which has regular and deep indentations around the foot ring. There is a wide variety of glazed wares, but two sherds are later, one an internally glazed late medieval bowl, and also one post-medieval which represent later contamination of the feature.
720.29.1/4.
Coarse wares, all in sandy reduced or oxidized fabrics. One appears to have some glaze on it which could be accidental. The bases are steep, the rims flaring and plain. Some pieces look as if they have been grass-wiped.
720.29.1/5.
Miscellaneous second- to third-century Roman sherds, and there are two fragments of samian.

F29-2: From 3·00—3·40 m
720.29.2/1.
Three fragments of a jug in cream fabric with brown glaze, and one fragment of the base of a cooking pot. All late thirteenth century.

F29-3: From 3·40—4·15 m
The flat bottom of the well lies at 4·15 m.
720.29.3/1.
Saxo-Norman rouletted sherd (Fig. 51:34) in hard, coarse, buff to grey fabric with square rouletting in bands of four, horizontally on the pot. Presumably eleventh century.
The rest of the finds include a late Roman 'knobbed rim bowl', presumably New Forest, and mixed medieval and Saxo-Norman sherds.

F30: Medieval pit
720.30.0/1.
Saxo-Norman rim in standard fabric, with pie-crusting.

F31: Pit
Post-Roman, no finds.

L3: Hole 3
Sand, some of it darkish, lying on natural, 2·25 m down.

720.00.3/1.
Jar (Fig. 50:35). Hard, dull brown fabric with fine sandy grit, smoothed black surface.
Piedish (Fig. 50:36). Hard, finely-gritted, dark brown fabric, red skin and black smoothed surface with burnished lattice.
Also a rusticated colour-coated sherd. All presumably second century.

L4: Hole 4

Dirty brown sand from 0·17 to 0·82 m above natural, and lying on clean sand. Natural is at 2·25—2:30 m.

L6: Holes 5 and 6

Coarse sand overlying the cobbling of the road F1, which lies on natural. A samian sherd is second-century in date.

L9: Hole 7

Dirty sand lying on clean sand, which may be natural, at 2·15 m down.
720.00.9/1.
Six early Roman grey sherds including a base, and a Hadrianic-Antonine samian sherd.

L10: Hole 8

Dark sandy fill, 0·60 m thick, lying on clean natural sand 2·25 m down.
720.00.10/1.
Jar (Fig. 50:37). Hard, sandy, light grey fabric, smoothed surface.
Jar (Fig. 50:38). Sandy, brown fabric with grey surface. Rim and shoulder smoothed.
Piedish (Fig. 50:39). Hard, grey-black fabric with grey-brown surface and burnished decoration.
Fragments of 19 other Roman vessels, mainly second to third century, but also two late medieval sherds. The samian is of Hadrianic date.

L14: Hole 14

Sand with root marks, 0·87 m thick, on natural, 2·10 m down.
720.00.14/1.
Two Roman sherds but also four late medieval.
Two samian sherds are Hadrianic and Antonine in date.

L15: Hole 15

Dirty sand between 0·30 and 0·70 m above natural at 7·20 m deep. It lies on clean sand (L16) which overlies the cobbles of F1.
720.00.15/1—2.
Two Roman, one medieval, and a second-century samian sherd.

L16: Hole 15

Clean sand underlying L15 and above F1.
720.00.16/1.
One Roman and one late medieval sherd.

L18: Hole 18

Medieval building rubbish, up to 1·40 m thick in places.
720.00.18/1.
Fourteenth-century pottery.

L21: Hole 2

Grey-brown clay with flints, lying on natural.

720.00.21/1.
Dish (Fig. 50:40). Hard, light grey, sandy ware, black to grey smoothed surface.

L22: Hole 3

Upper fill of hole.
720.00.22/1.
Jug (Fig. 55:41) in similar fabric to 42 with evidence of splashed glazing in a bright orange colour.
Cooking pot (Fig. 55:42) of black and white painted ware in a smooth, slightly sandy fabric oxidized on the surfaces with a pale grey sandwich, partially reduced on the outside.
Handle (Fig. 55:43) with deep fastening grooves at the base.
In association there is a fragment from a jug in Tudor Green pottery. The date is late fifteenth century.
Also a second-century rusticated sherd.

L24: Hole 4

Main fill.
720.00.24/1.
Late Roman colour-coated beaker and jar, early and late medieval cooking pot. One first-century samian sherd and one Hadrianic sherd.

L25: Hole 5

Main fill of hole.
720.00.25/1.
Five fragments of Saxo-Norman gritted ware and two glazed sherds, one fourteenth century.

L26: Hole 5

Main fill of western extension.
720.00.26/1.
Late medieval cooking pot.

L27: Hole 5

Main fill of eastern extension.
720.00.27/1.
A group of late medieval fragments of cooking pots and jugs, the latter without any decoration, together with some fragments of the base of a painted-ware jug. One fragment of Frechen ware would confirm a fifteenth-century date, but there is one intrusive sherd of eighteenth-century, brown, glazed ware. There is also a small piece of a decorated jug with white strip slips pierced with a small rod-sectioned tool of a type which also occurs on a vessel in L30.

L28: Hole 6

Main infill of hole.
720.00.28/1.
Fourteenth-century jug fragment.

L29: Hole 7

Main infill of hole.
720.00.29/1—3.
Second- to third-century dish, mortarium, and flagon. The samian is of Hadrianic-Antonine date, and there is a nineteenth-century child's mug.

L30: Hole 8, main fill

An apparently homogeneous group, dating to the end of the sixteenth century.

720.00.30/1.
Coarse-ware bowl (Fig. 53:44) with remains of a loop handle on the rim, in a hard, coarse, buff-coloured fabric, and dark green glaze. There is also a slashed handle in a similar fabric to 44; the vessel fragment adhering shows decoration in the form of an applied slip which has been pierced with a round tool (as in L27); the glaze is grey-buff.
Cup (Fig. 55:45) with a marked carination around the middle, in a hard, buff ware, glazed inside to a honey colour.
Well-thrown cup or bowl (Fig. 55:46) with a flanged rim, glazed, reduced copper-green to black outside.
Two fragments (Fig. 55:47) of a fine quality, yellow, glazed, flanged bowl in a white fabric.
Base (Fig. 55:48) in the same fabric as 47.
There is also a fragment of a Tudor Green cup with handle base, and the frilled base of a Raeren mug.

L31: *Main fill of Hole 9*
720.00.31.
Late medieval and Roman sherds, and the neck of a Surrey greenware costrel, of sixteenth- to seventeenth-century date.

L32: *Main fill, hole 14*
Most of this may be derived from F20.
720.00.32/1.
Two sherds (Fig. 51:49, 50) in a coarse, buff, sandy fabric with dark green external glaze, and decoration in the form of pendant(?) triangles of black slip infilled with raised dots in the same material. Some sign of wear on this vessel.
Other green-glazed wares mostly undecorated, a few with scored lines on them; 15 fragments of undecorated, red-ware jug sherds, three decorated with combing and two of these white slipped; three other pale green-white fabric wares decorated with white slip; one jug with sparse glaze, white slip, and fettling; two fragments from large, fettled, globular vessel; probably a jug with splash glaze and horizontal white slip around the middle. There is a small bowl with light brown internal glaze. One fragment of Saxo-Norman ware with a gritty fabric. The remaining sherds are reduced-buff or buff cooking pots, well thrown and fired, with some fettling. Everything points to a late fourteenth-century date.

L34: *Hole 11, in south corner, below L15, above F1*
720.00.34/1.
Two sherds of late Roman colour-coat beakers in soft fabric.

L35: *Hole 16, 7—8 cm above F1*
720.00.35/1.
Four thirteenth- to fourteenth-century jug fragments, one in soft red fabric.

L36: *Hole 18*
Infill of eastern extension.
Ridge tile.

L37: *Clean yellow sand, adjacent to L20, beneath L19 in hole 18*

L38: *Hole 18, fill of eastern extension*
720.00.38/1.
Jug neck (Fig. 55:51). Showing luting of the neck to the body.

L39: *Brownish silty soil, Hole 18*

L40: Holes 19—20, top fill
720.00.40/1.
Medieval in date are a Rouen jug handle, a spout and three body sherds of standard painted ware type, and other fifteenth-century sherds, but also a chamber pot and Norman stoneware of eighteenth-century date. There is also an Antonine samian stamp and a clay pipe.

L41: Hole 19—20, chalk and occupation soil beneath L40
720.00.41/1.
Flanged bowl (Fig. 50:52). Hard, light grey fabric with sand temper; roughly burnished surface. Also an Antonine samian sherd.

L42: Brown sandy clay, below L41, hole 19—20
Overlies F27.
720.00.42/1.
Fragment of a necked jar and a possible poppy-head beaker, and several bases, presumably all second century.
Two samian sherds are second century and a third post-A.D. 150.

L43: Hole 19—20
As L41, but perhaps contaminated by F28.
720.00.43/1.
Mortarium (Fig. 50:53). Hard, sandy, buff fabric with traces of a yellow to reddish surface. Fragments of amphora and of Antonine samian.

L44: Hole 21—22, top fill
720.00.44/1.
A second- to third-century beaker sherd, a first-century sherd, and thirteenth-century sherds, red-fabric jugs and grass-marked pottery.

L45: Hole 21—22
Brown sandy clay, beneath L47, c. 0·70 m thick.
720.00.45/1.
Three late Roman cavetto rims, one Saxo-Norman sherd, and late medieval jug fragments. There are Flavian and Antonine samian sherds.

L46: Hole 21—22
Dark soil beneath L44.
720.00.46/1.
Late Roman cavetto rim, and a Hadrianic samian sherd.

L47: Layer of chalk and sandstone, c. 0·15 m thick, below L46

L48: Brown clayey layer between L46 and L47
In northeast corner of hole 21—22.

L49: Hole 23, top fill to 1·65 m
720.00.49/1.
Late Roman flanged bowl, and 11 late medieval jug fragments.

L50: Below L49, in hole 21—22
Brown sandy clay, 0·60 m thick.
Two Antonine samian sherds.

L51: Dark soil 1·40 m thick, top fill of hole 24

L52: Chalk layer beneath L51, several centimetres thick
Fragments of quern.

L53: Sandy layer, c. 1 m thick of various colours, below L53
720.00.53/1.
Roman sherds including a piedish rim (second century), and quern fragments.

L54: Gravel, c. 0·30 m thick in southeast corner of Hole 24
Beneath L53 (Roman road ?).

L55: Clay layer, several centimetres thick, beneath L53 and L54

L56: Hole 25
Beneath the cellar floor. Fragments of human skull.

L57: Hole 26
Dark clayey soil 0·30 m thick below the cellar floor.
720.00.57/1.
Jar (Fig. 50:54). Hard, dark grey fabric, brown skin, dark grey, smoothed surface. There are fragments of 11 other early Roman vessels and an amphora. Three samian sherds are of Hadrianic date.

L58: Hole 27
Dark fill at 1·62 m.
720.00.58/1.
Two early Roman sherds.

L61: Unstratified finds
720.00.61/1—7.
Late Roman sherds and an Antonine samian stamp.
There is a large Siegburg jug, a spigot jug base, and rim of a large dish, all fifteenth to sixteenth century, a seventeenth- to eighteenth-century skillet handle, nineteenth-century jelly mould, a cream-ware drug jar, a fluted handleless cup, and transfer printed china. Other finds include Roman glass, a louvre fragment, and encaustic tile.

The Finds

The Samian by G. Dannell

Provenance	Museum Accession Number	Form	Date A.D.	Kiln	Comments
F1-3	720.1.3/1	37	Trajanic-Hadrianic	southern Gaul	
	720.1.3/2	18/31	Hadrianic-Antonine	central Gaul	
F1-6	720.1.6/1	24/25	Claudian	southern Gaul	2 fragments
F2-3	720.2.3/2	18/31	Hadrianic-Antonine	central Gaul	
	720.2.3/3	33	Hadrianic-Antonine	central Gaul	
	720.2.3/4	36	Hadrianic-Antonine	central Gaul	

Provenance	Museum Accession Number	Form	Date A.D.	Kiln	Comments
	720.2.3/5	37	Antonine	central Gaul	
F10-1	720.10.1/3	38	2nd century	central Gaul	
F13	720.13.0/2	31R	late Antonine	eastern Gaul(?)	
F29-1	720.29.1/6	chip	2nd century	central Gaul	
F29-2	720.29.2/2	45	late Antonine	central Gaul	
F29-3	720.29.3/2	chip	2nd century	central Gaul(?)	
L6	720.00.6/1	37	2nd century	southern Gaul	
L9	720.00.9/2	18/31	Hadrianic-Antonine	central Gaul	
L10	720.00.10/2	33	Hadrianic	central Gaul	
L14	720.00.14/2	18/31	Hadrianic	Martres-de-Veyre	
	720.00.14/3	37	Antonine	central Gaul	
L15	720.00.15/2	33	2nd century	central Gaul	
L24	720.00.24/2	18	1st century	southern Gaul	
	720.00.24/3	18/31	Hadrianic	eastern Gaul	
L29	720.00.29/3	33	Hadrianic-Antonine	central Gaul	
L40	720.00.40/2	31	Antonine	central Gaul	
L41	720.00.41/2	33	Antonine	central Gaul	
L42	720.00.42/2	79	Antonine (after 150)	eastern Gaul	
	720.00.42/3	37	2nd century	central Gaul	
	720.00.42/2	chip	2nd century	—	
L43	720.00.43/2	37	Antonine	central Gaul	Style of Cinnamus
L44	720.00.44/2	18	1st century	southern Gaul	
L45	720.00.45/2	18	Flavian	southern Gaul	
	720.00.45/3	45	late Antonine	central Gaul	
	720.00.45/4	31	Antonine	central Gaul	
L46	720.00.46/1	37	Hadrianic	eastern Gaul(?)	
L50	720.00.50/1	31R	late Antonine	central Gaul	
	720.00.50/2	37	Antonine	central Gaul	
L57	720.00.57/2	42	Hadrianic	central Gaul	2 fragments
	720.00.57/3	38	Hadrianic	central Gaul	
L61	720.00.61/7	31R	late Antonine		Stamped CENITI

The Roman Glass by D. Charlesworth

Part of a much abraded base ring (720.9) in green glass came from L61. It is of second-century date.

Medieval Iron Objects by I. Goodall

There is an iron blacksmith's punch (720.8, Fig. 56) from the late medieval pit F20-2.

Stone Objects

A fragment of rotary quern (720.6, Fig. 57:1) in green sandstone came from a second-century Roman level, L53.

A sandstone block (720.3, Fig. 57:2) was apparently part of a sculpture, but is too small to say of what. One side has been roughly hollowed (section 2b), another is convex with decorative tooling, and there is a second element which comes off this (section 2a). It could be part of a half capital/pilaster or part of a funeral monument. It was found in the early Roman level L15.

There is also a quern fragment (720.5) from L52, and squared blocks of green sandstone (720.4) from L47.

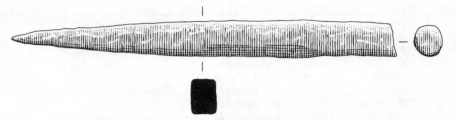

Fig. 56. 82 Hyde Street: iron punch from F20-2 (scale 1/1).

Architectural Fragments by J. C. Turquet

Both stones were found built into the nineteenth-century cellar wall, F5. Hyde Abbey, which was founded in 1119, lies close by. Much of the fabric was robbed in the sixteenth and in the eighteenth to nineteenth centuries, and these pieces presumably derive from it.

Stone 720.1 (Pl. IIIa, Figs. 56, 57:3). This has a rectangular carved face of three rows of overlapping fish scales, or scallops. The scales are defined by a double outline as well as drilled holes on the inside of the outline. The other sides of the stone have been damaged. The stone has been weathered, and this might suggest that it had originally been placed on the outside of a building.

This type of scallop decoration was used in the twelfth century to decorate internal and external wall surfaces, such as the spandrels of wall arcades and triforium arches. It was also carved on tympana, capitals, and columns, and occasionally on fonts and tombs. One of the earliest examples of scale patterning is seen on the abaci of the capitals of the north entrance to the crypt of Canterbury cathedral. Some of the capitals within the crypt have abaci decorated with fish scales, and one column is also covered with scales. Some of the faces of the capitals of the exterior arcades between the southeast transept and the southern ambulatory chapel have scale decoration. These examples may be dated to *c.* 1100—1105. Scale patterns were used not only on the tympana of small parish churches, but also of major ecclesiastical foundations, for example Ely and Peterborough cathedrals. Both have doorways in the north transepts with scale tympana, which date to before 1135. Scale decoration was also carved in the spandrels of arcades, for instance in the triforium arcade of Rochester cathedral, dating to *c.* 1130. It was used in a similar position at Christchurch Priory, Hampshire, and Chichester cathedral, both of which may be dated to the first half of the twelfth century. At Christchurch the spandrels of the interlocking wall arcade on the exterior of the north transept are carved with this pattern, and it also decorates the spandrels of the internal intersecting wall arcade of the chancels of the churches of St John and St Mary in Devizes, Wiltshire. Since these two churches have been connected with the masons of Roger of Salisbury, it may be that the fragments of scale decoration found at Old Sarum were used for the same purpose. The Old Sarum examples date to the 1130s and the Devizes churches to soon after Roger's death in 1139.

Of all these examples only the Old Sarum fragments have a double outline, but none have drilled holes as does 720.1. Drilled hole decoration is not frequent in the twelfth century, and suggests that this was meant to be an especially fine piece of carving. There is in Winchester a similar fragment of scale decoration, with double outline, drilled holes, and three rows of seven scales, built into a late sixteenth- or early seventeenth-century chimney-stack in a passage off the High Street. The two pieces may belong together. There is also a piece in the boundary wall at Hyde Barn, which strengthens the proposed link with the abbey.

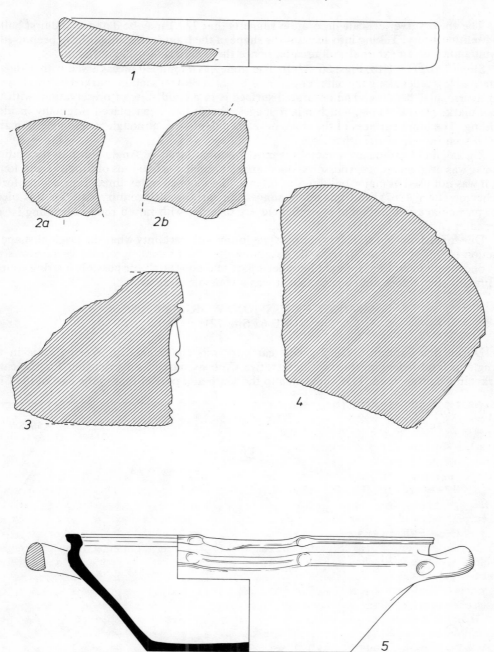

Fig. 57. 82 Hyde Street: cross sections of stone objects, and pottery from F8 (scale ¼).

The above survey of scale decoration suggests that 720.1 may be dated to the first half of the twelfth century. Taking into account the shape of the fragment, it might have been used in a tympanum, or an external wall arcade, hence the weathering it has suffered.

Stone 720.2 (Pl. IIIb, Figs. 56, 57:4). The stone has a rounded face, carved with a zig-zag pattern in low relief along the outer edges, and a raised central section marked by two rows of slightly irregular beading. The decorated surface is in a good state of preservation, with the chisel marks clearly visible, which might suggest that it had been placed originally inside a building. The other surfaces of the stone have been damaged, although coarse tooling marks can be seen on one of the other sides.

Zig-zag and beading are some of the most common forms of Anglo-Norman decoration. Zig-zag was used on arches, voussoirs, door jambs, tympana, surrounds of windows and fonts, but it was not used in major buildings as often as the more complex three-dimensional forms of chevron (Borg 1967), and this might suggest an early twelfth-century date for this piece. This particular combination of low relief zig-zag together with raised rows of beading is very unusual.

Due to its damaged state it is not possible to say with certainty what the original shape or function of this stone may have been. Assuming that the present decorated surface was the only one meant to be seen, it might have been part of a door jamb, or possibly a string course. Its present shape does not suggest that it was a voussoir of an arch.

MARKET EXTENSION, WORTHY LANE
(ME 62 Site 721)

During the autumn of 1962 a new car park was constructed in Worthy Lane in the triangle of land belonging to the Conservative Club as part of an extension for the cattle market in Andover Road. The whole area to the south and part of that to the east of the Club

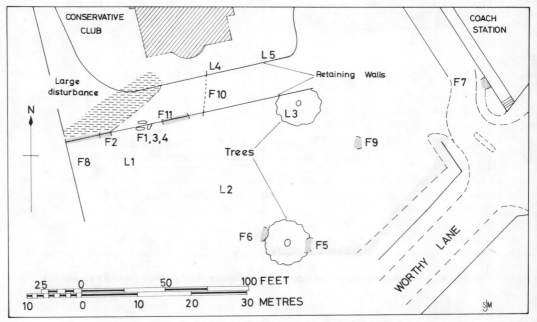

Fig. 58. Market Extension: general plan.

House was involved (Fig. 58). For the western part there was only limited terracing which entailed little new disturbance of the subsoil, but on the east a terrace was cut several feet into the underlying chalk. This latter operation was not observed, and only one feature, F7, was noticed in the sides of the excavation; another pit, F9, was located in subsequent trenching.

Most of the discoveries described here were found during trenching for terrace walls in the western part of the site. The trenches were cut about two feet into the chalk with a J. C. B. mechanical excavator. All the features were found subsequent to the trenching, though work was observed in progress. In fact on my first visit to the site, I talked to the driver of the excavator at the time when he was cutting through the burials, but these were not noted until two weeks later while I was recording the medieval pits! The burials F1—4, pits F5—8, and groups L1—2 were excavated in November 1962, the rest in March 1963.

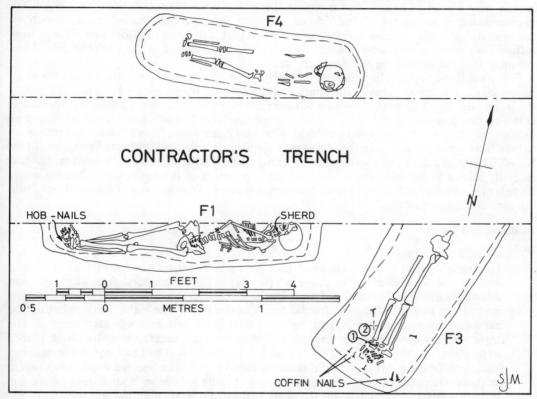

Fig. 59. Market Extension: plan of burials.

Work was limited not only by time and the contractors' requirements, but also by the presence of dumps on the sides of the cuttings. There were doubtless more burials, as only those cut by the trench were excavated, and no stripping of the soil in either direction was possible. I would like to thank Miss Sarah Slater for braving the November frosts and winds to help excavate the burials, and Miss Louise Millard, then secretary of the Winchester Excavation Committee, who took record photographs.

Summary

The northern side of the Iron Age, Roman, and early medieval Winchester was delimited by a small valley in which ran an intermittent stream, the Fulflood. The site described here lies on the lower part of the northern slope of that valley, looking towards the city defences.

The subsoil over the whole site is chalk, though of a very broken and friable nature. This was covered in places by a fine brown loam, which, it is suggested below, represents medieval cultivation. The site had undergone considerable landscaping probably in the 1930s, for tennis courts in the northwestern corner of the site. Overlooking Worthy Lane there was a very steep bank some 2 m in height, through which the access road to the Club House cut like a hollow-way. This scarp slope is probably the result of erosion caused by traffic passing along Worthy Lane in the post-Roman period. It is noteworthy that in the Middle Ages Worthy Lane was known as 'Bone Street', presumably because of the frequent exposure of Roman inhumations.

The finds fall into two major groups: Roman inhumation burials and medieval pits. Four burials were identified *in situ,* but mixed in the grave filling or on the contractors' spoil tip were remains of another 4—5 individuals. All were inhumations, buried north—south or east—west, but without grave goods, though Burial F1 had hobnail boots and F3 was in a coffin. They were concentrated in a tight group at the western end of the site (Fig. 59). They are apparently of second- to third-century date.

The medieval deposits both in the pits and lying on natural chalk consisted of a uniformly brown loam. The break between the chalk and the soil was sharp, with a layer of 'split peas', suggesting the area had been cultivated but later left fallow. One area of extensive disturbance in the northeast corner of the site could be a small marl pit. The other pits, dotted at random around the site do not appear to be rubbish pits, and again some form of chalk quarry seems to be a likely interpretation. In the eighteenth century an adjacent field was known as 'Lime Kilns'. There are one or two sherds which possibly date as early as the twelfth century, but the majority belong to the end of the thirteenth and beginning of the fourteenth centuries when there is evidence that there were a few houses on this side of Worthy Lane. Post-medieval finds are almost entirely lacking.

Features and Layers

F1:   Burial 1 (Fig. 59)
The burial is that of a female aged 19—20 years, but there are bones from a second woman and two children. The grave ran parallel to the contractors' excavation and one side of the grave had been sliced away by the mechanical excavator, damaging the right innominate and smashing the frontal bones of the skull. The right arm, excepting the hand had been ripped away, and the lower part of the left arm was also missing. The grave was just over 2 m long, but only about 30 cm wide, and the body had been placed on its right side, the right hand tucked under the stomach. The head was at the east end (magnetic bearing 261°), and the skeleton faced north. The legs were extended, again twisted on to the right side. The grave fill was of chalk rubble with some dirty brown soil and the bottom lay 0·35 m below the chalk surface. Skeletal condition was comparatively good. At the feet of the skeleton were some iron hobnails - at least 28 can be identified, and the total may be about 36. Mixed with them was a minute sherd of sandy grey ware. A second sherd was light brown and sandy. One surface is dark grey and burnished. There was also a small piece of brick.

F2:   Burial 2
This grave had been completely destroyed, and its presence was only indicated by bones on the spoil tip. Only the leg bones were found, suggesting that the skull had been removed by the medieval pit, i.e. the head would have been at the west end. It is an individual, possibly male aged about 18.

F3:   *Burial 3* (Fig. 59)

This was the burial of a woman aged 22—24, though there are fragments of a child and another individual. The upper part of the grave had been totally destroyed by the excavator, and only the legs, pelvis and lumbar vertebrae were in position. Some bones were found on the spoil tip, but generally the condition of the bones was so poor that most probably did not survive the disturbance. The body was apparently extended on its back, the head to the north (magnetic bearing 194°). The grave had vertical sides and a flat bottom which was 0·40 m below the chalk surface at the feet and 0·53 m at the pelvis.

Two pottery sherds were found with the burial. Sherd 1 is hard, grey, and sandy. The inner surface shows wheel marks, the outer is burnished. The edges are unabraded. Sherd 2 is thin, with external burnishing and internal wheel marks. This sherd, 1 cm², is the largest from any of the burials. Such thin grey sherds are especially characteristic of the second and early third centuries A.D.

Eight iron nails belonging to a coffin were found, as well as one or two odd iron fragments. The nails are generally about 55 mm long, with circular heads 15 mm in diameter. The coffin was made of planks 20 mm thick, identified by Mrs Ruth Morgan as oak and the tips of the nails were bent over on the inside. In two cases the nails were knocked in crookedly and had crumpled up. Two nails were found on either side of the body near the tibiae, the rest were in a line below the feet, 15 to 25 cm above the floor of the grave. The impression is of a hastily and poorly constructed wooden box.

F4:   *Burial 4* (Fig. 59)

One corner of the grave had been removed by the excavator but the skeleton, that of a child aged 5—6 years, was undisturbed. Generally its condition was poor. The head was at the east end, facing west (magnetic orientation 270°). The body was extended on its back, with arms parallel to the body. There were no grave goods.

F5:   *Medieval pit cut by the revetment wall around the tree*

The pit is probably oval, with a minimum width of 2 m, and of unknown depth. The fill is loamy brown soil with occasional lumps of chalk.

721.5.0/1.

There are twelve sherds of reduced cooking pot of which one is probably late Saxon. The rest are sand- or flint-tempered and represent a transitional state of development. This is borne out by the inclusion in this group of two strap handles. One has an orange glaze and a hard, sandy fabric with pulling grooves down the centre, and raised flanges at the edge. There are three fragments of body to go with this. These pieces are all reminiscent of the Orchard Street material 1250/1275. The other handle is cruder and has a D-shape section. The fabric is soft and sandy, it is decorated with two parallel slashes down the sides in-between which is a field of jabbing marks. The edges of the handle are notched. The decoration is similar to that found in Michelmersh and the piece should be twelfth to thirteenth century in date.

There is also a fragment of pre-Flavian samian.

F6:   *Pit similar to F5*

721.6.0/1.

The contents of this feature are very similar to that met with in L1, and include one piece of Saxo-Norman ware with incised decoration, probably from a pitcher (Cunliffe 1964, Fig. 34).

F7:   *Medieval pit*

The pit was only seen in section, but had a diameter greater than 1·5 m. Filled with fine

loam and chalk.
721.7.0/1.
Two fragments of a hard, black, flint-tempered fabric, probably from cooking pots. The hardness suggests a late date in the thirteenth century, and the ware is similar to that met with in L1.

F8:   *From the filling of a complex of pits*
In the northwest corner of the site. Generally it is just over 0·5 m deep, but it is deeper in places. The fill is of fine brown loam.

F8-1:   From low in the filling
721.8.1/1.
One fragment of black, glazed floor tile, fourteenth to sixteenth century in date, but probably medieval as the fabric is very soft and fired reduced.
One fragment of a rod-section jug handle with a central stick-end piercing sandy-buff fabric covered with thick apple-green glaze and other material which is similar to that met with in L1.

F8-2:   From the upper filling
721.8.2/1.
Two rim fragments of cooking pots which are similar to those in L1.

F9:   *A medieval pit with a diameter exceeding 2 m*
The fill is of fine brown loam with spreads of chalk, especially against the south side.
721.9.1/1.
Two rims similar to those in L1.

F10:   *A small V-sectioned gulley running north—south*
Its depth is 22·5 cm and the width 30 cm. It is filled with a reddish-brown clay soil. There are no finds, but the lack of a 'split pea' level sealing it suggests a medieval date.

F11:   *A pit filled with compact brown soil and chalk*
It is larger than the normal pits, and only 0·5 m deep. There is no dating evidence.

L1:   *Grey-brown loam, which overlies F1 and F3*
There is a 'split pea' level at its base.

720.00.1/1.
Four fragments of cream-coloured cooking pots in hard, thin, well-thrown fabrics which have been heavily fettled. Nine jug fragments of two types. One is in a very hard fabric oxidized outside but reduced within. Fragments of a wide jug in the same fabric. The other type is much sandier in tempering but quite hard. Sundry other pieces of earlier date occur in this layer. The nature of this selection points to a medieval date, probably going into the late fourteenth century.

L2:   *Unstratified, from the southwestern part of the site*
721.00.2/1.
Finds similar to those in L1.

L3:   *As L2*
721.00.3/1.
Finds similar to L1.

L4:   *As L1, immediately overlying F10*
721.00.4/1.
Unglazed jug handle, as L1.

L5: As L1, above the natural chalk
721.00.5/1.
The base of a wide strap handle in a soft, pink/grey fabric with a dull, apple-green glaze outside only. The handle is decorated with pull-grooves embellished with a central slash and stabbing along the edges. The handle is fastened from the inside suggesting that the mouth of the pot was wide enough to take a hand. The evidence for dating suggests a mid thirteenth-century date.

L6: Unstratified
A clay pipe stamped FT.

The Finds

The Samian by B. R. Hartley
A small fragment of a base of a cup (Drag. 27?) came from F5. The fabric suggests a pre-Flavian origin in southern Gaul.

The Burials by C. Wells
These burials are all incomplete and in extremely poor condition. The following brief notes are all that can usefully be said about them.

Burial 1. This is a collection of bones which is difficult to unravel owing to the defective state of what is present and the absence of many elements. Parts of two adults and two children are recognizable and, with some uncertainty, they may be defined as follows.

(*a*) Female, 19—20 years. This was an extremely lightly built individual with gracile slender limb bones and an overall lack of muscularity. A damaged cranial vault survives and has a maximum length of 178·5 mm and maximum breadth of 137·6 mm, giving a Cranial Index 77:1 (mesocranial). It is ovoid in norma verticalis. The frontal bone rises steeply from negligible brow ridges. All sutures are unfused and areas for attachment of nuchal muscles are poorly developed. In the lambdoid suture are four wormian bones (3 left, 1 right) and there is also a right asterionic ossicle. Damaged fragments of jaw are present. In all, 23 teeth are present, mostly loose, and they cannot with confidence be allotted between the individuals here. It is clear that the third molars were unerupted, attrition was light on all teeth and no caries was found.

Table 13. Measurements of human long bones.

| | Burial 1a | | Burial 3a | |
	left (mm)	right (mm)	left (mm)	right (mm)
HuL1	281·8	—	—	—
FeL1	397·2	397·0	409·3	—
FeD1	22·3	21·5	21·3	—
FeD2	30·1	29·8	29·1	—
TiL1	317·1	318·2	325·0	324·8
TiD1	29·7	30·0	30·0	29·1
TiD2	20·6	21·5	20·7	21·0
Meric Index	74·1	72·1	73·2	—
Cnemic Index	69·3	71·6	69·0	72·1

Post-cranial remains of this person include fragments of the vertebrae: C2—4, T? 5—7 and 10—12, L1—5. A typical, but broken, female pelvis has survived and many rib fragments. Shafts of long bones are present and the left humerus and both femora and tibiae are complete.

They give length and diameter measurements as shown in Table 13. This shows platymeric flattening of the femora; the left tibia is mesocnemic, the right tibia is eurycnemic. Stature as calculated from the above figures would be about 1525·0 mm (5 ft 0 in). A well-marked lateral flange is present on both femoral shafts. Moderate sized squatting facets are present at the distal articular surfaces of both tibiae. A few carpal, metacarpal, tarsal, metatarsal, and phalangeal elements are present and show that this woman had small hands and feet.

(b) A second adult, also probably female, is identifiable from some slight duplication of vault and mandibular fragments, together with teeth; from the presence of vertebral fragments, including part of an axis and the S1 segment; and from a left and right talus and calcaneus. These, too, are small, lightly built and lacking in well defined markings of muscle attachment.

(c) Child, aged 6—7 years. This is identifiable from some teeth and fragments of mandible, as well as from a left femoral shaft (diaphyseal length 229·7 mm) and a left tibial shaft (181·2 mm).

(d) Child, aged 11—12 years. This is identifiable from a mandibular fragment showing the second molar in the course of erupting.

Burial 2. This consists of 10 fragments of bone. They could all have come from one individual about 18 years of age. Present are a fragment of humeral shaft, a fragment of ulna, the head of a radius with unfused epiphysis, a femoral neck and head with recently fused epiphysis, two vertebral and two rib fragments. If they are all from one individual the epiphyseal fusion may be slightly anomalous.

The surviving femoral head shows that this person was of somewhat sturdier build than the woman in Burial 1 but it is nevertheless a light, non-muscular individual.

Burial 3. This burial contains fragments of three individuals.

(a) Female, 22—24 years. This is identifiable from a few much disintegrated fragments of cranial vault and from small fragments of vertebrae, pelvis, ribs, and a few small bones of hands and feet. The vertebrae include parts of all lumbars and the S1 segment. Some femoral and tibial elements are not greatly damaged. They show that this was a very lightly built woman. Muscle markings on all bones are weakly developed. Measurements of the left femur and the tibiae were obtained and are given in Table 13. This femur, too, is platymeric and, as with Burial 12, the left tibia is mesocnemic, the right eurycnemic. Stature can be estimated to be about 1553·0 mm (5 ft 1 in). A small squatting facet is present distally on both tibiae.

(b) With these bones is a duplicate fragment of femoral shaft. It is considerably more sturdy than that of 3a and may be from a male. The head and neck are missing but it can be seen that the epiphyses of the greater and lesser trochanters were unfused, so the age may be estimated as about 17 years.

(c) There is also a fragment of the right femoral shaft of a child, probably about 7—8 years old.

Burial 4. Child, age 5—6 years. This consists of a much broken cranial vault and damaged fragments of jaws. A few post-cranial fragments have also survived, including a tibial diaphysis. The dental condition is:

6										6
e	d	o	o	o		o	b	c	d	e
e	d	c	o	o		o	o	c	d	e
6										6

There is no caries. Attrition of the teeth is light. Tartar is present on the labial surface of the mandibular canines and on the lingual surface of the molars. Slight enamel hypoplasia is present on the canines and the erupting permanent molars. At least one wormian bone was present in the right half of the lambdoid suture. There is a trace of pitting in a fragment of the right orbital roof which is probably due to incipient cribra orbitalia. The tibial diaphysis measures 181·0 mm.

Summary. Nine individuals seem to be recognizable in these four burials, but the separation of the children from these defective fragments is somewhat uncertain: it is perhaps possible that 3c and 4 are the same child.

The likely sex and age of these nine persons is shown in Table 14. This shows a low age at death throughout the group, and this may be correlated with the lightness and apparent muscular weakness of their physique. They may have died young after years of chronic illness and malnutrition rather than as a result of some acute disease.

A notable feature is the extremely light attrition of all surviving teeth (which must come from a minimum of four individuals). In many Anglo-Saxon and medieval groups severe attrition is the rule, with pulp cavities opened after a few years of use and even the milk teeth

Table 14. Age and sex of Market Extension burials.

Burial	Sex	Age
1a	female	19—20
1b	female	25+
1c	—	6—7
1d	—	11—12
2	?	18
3a	female	22—24
3b	?	17
3c	—	7—8
4	—	5—6

heavily worn away before being shed. The absence of such features here must imply a relatively soft, non-abrasive diet. This is further supported by the weakness of muscle markings on jaw fragments. The absence of caries from such a small sample is not remarkable. The presence of slight defects in the dental enamel of Burial 4 (enamel hypoplasis) suggests illness or nutritional disorders during the first eighteen months of life. This may be connected with the appearance of cribra in its orbit.

Whenever a distal tibial articulation survives here, an unambiguous squatting facet is present. This suggests either that they practised some occupation which called for a crouched posture or else that they were a poverty-stricken group not much given to the luxury of chairs or benches.

NUNS' WALK, SAXON ROAD
(Site 722)

In the second week of January 1961 some employees of the Southern Electricity Board unearthed some pottery vessels while digging a trench for the erection of a small sub-station in Nuns' Walk, just east of Saxon Road in the northern suburbs of Winchester (Fig. 60). The

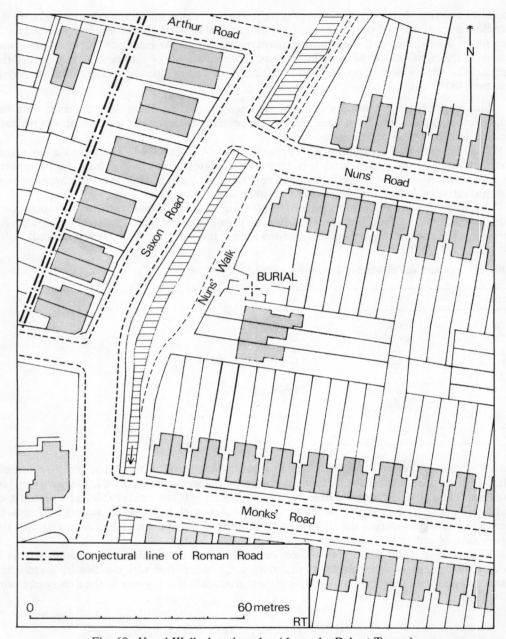

Fig. 60. Nuns' Walk: location plan (drawn by Robert Turner).

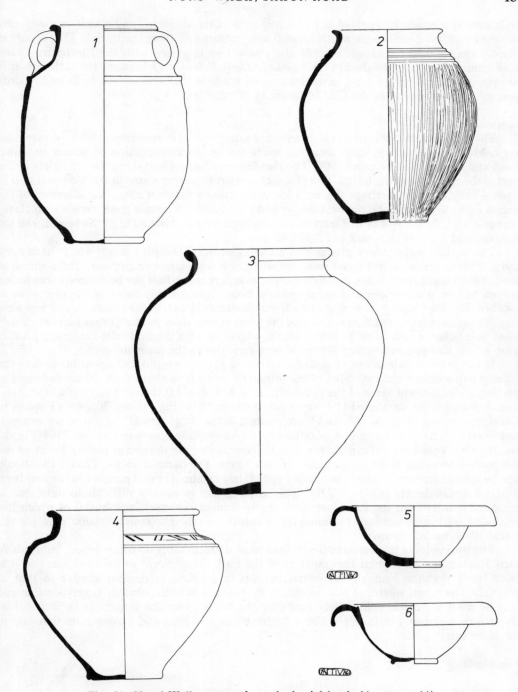

Fig. 61. Nuns' Walk: pottery from the burial (scale ¼, stamps ½).

finds were subsequently reported to F. Cottrill at the City Museum, and a visit to the site by museum staff produced more unstratified finds, presumably from the burial. This report is based on notes in the museum records and also on an interview with the Electricity Board workmen, which was published in the *Southern Daily Echo* for 13 January 1961, though it is now impossible to confirm some of the statements made in that article. The finds and records have all been deposited in the City Museum at Winchester.

Summary

The topography of the area in Roman times is impossible to reconstruct without extensive work. Much of the surrounding area was made up for the construction of houses in Nuns' Road and Monks' Road around 1900. The Headbourne Stream burial runs immediately to the west of the find-spot of the burial, in a channel created to supply water to the medieval mill in Hyde Abbey. The site perhaps lies on a low spur rising a few feet above the alluvium of the Itchen valley to the east. To the west the ground rises gently to form a river terrace with clayey orange gravel. At the foot of this terrace, and perhaps within about 30 m of the burial, ran the Roman road from Winchester to Silchester.

The burial itself was in a pit cut into a chalky subsoil. The pit's depth was 0·70 m deep and *c*. 0·50 m across, but it is not recorded whether it was square or circular. The position of none of the vessels is recorded, but the newspaper report states that the bone spoon was found broken in one of the dishes and some unburnt bones (presumably those of the pig) were in another. The four large pots were removed, with contents intact, to the museum, and two were found to contain cremated bones. Some of the other vessels show modern breaks and obviously some have been missed. Miss Brenda Capstick who dealt with the finds also remembers a clay lamp which disappeared before the finds were removed to the museum.

In our present state of knowledge of local coarse pottery it is not really possible to date the grave group within a century. Mr Cottrill originally dated it to about A.D. 50 on the basis of the Belgic character of some of the vessels (nos. 2, 3, 4, and 11). I would suggest a later date. Vessels 5 and 6 are paralleled at Jewry Wall (Kenyon 1948: Fig. 41 no. 30), with Flavian to Hadrianic samian. Vessels 7, 8, and 9 are platters in the Belgic tradition, but much evolved, and 9 certainly has no foot ring. A parallel with a concave base occurs in Cunliffe 1964 (Fig. 13 no. 26) with Vespasianic-Trajanic samian. In Winchester the dominant platter forms in the late second and early third century have convex bases. The flanged dishes, 12 and 13, should also be second century. Finally the smaller urn, 4, has an almost exact parallel in the urn from Burial 1 at Owslebury (Collis 1977b). This grave group is equally difficult to date, but is presumably later than the Late Iron Age—early Roman cemetery, one burial of which has produced Hadrianic samian. In summary, I suspect a late Flavian-Hadrianic date for the Nuns' Walk burial group.

The proximity of the burial to the Roman road is presumably no coincidence, but finds of early Roman burials suggest the cemetery of the town lay adjacent to the town, and so it is more likely that the Nuns' Walk burial belongs to a minor settlement similar to that at Winnall. The fabric of five of the vessels, 7, 8, 9, and two unillustrated, is very similar and may be a set of vessels deliberately made for the burial, like the larger set in Burial 1 at Owslebury, which was incidentally also a double burial of a man and a woman, in that case in the same urn.

The Finds

The Pottery

Double-handled urn (722.00.1/3, Fig. 61:1). The ware is buff, with occasional specks of red, perhaps grog. The surface is buff to yellow-buff, but some has flaked off, apparently in antiquity. The base is broken, but the fractures are not modern.

Jar (722.00.1/4, Fig. 61:2). The ware is sandy, and fairly hard, with a dull reddish-brown to brown surface. The decoration is of regular, vertical, burnished lines.

The larger urn (722.00.1/1, Fig. 61:3). The fabric is hard and sandy. The core of the pot is a light whitish grey, the surface light grey smoothed. The vessel is complete, excepting a few modern pick marks.

The smaller urn (722.00.1/2, Fig. 61:4). Hard fabric with some sand backing. The core is grey with a red-brown skin, the surface black and smoothed. There is a faintly visible decoration on the shoulder of lightly burnished lines. The breaks are modern.

Flanged bowl (722.00.1/8, Fig. 61:5). The core is red-buff, the surface off-white. The fabric is hard and fine, with occasional small red blobs. The vessel is complete excepting modern pick marks. The stamp perhaps reads AETIVM.

Flanged bowl (722.00.1/9, Fig. 61:6). Similar vessel with identical stamp. A piece of the flange is missing, the fracture being partly new, partly ancient.

Dish (722.00.1/6, Fig. 62:7). Fabric as vessel 9. Two fragments with modern fractures.

Dish (722.00.1/7, Fig. 62:8). Fabric as vessel 9. A quarter of the vessel is present, but the breaks are ancient.

Dish (722.00.1/5, Fig. 62:9). Soft, sandy ware with a grey-buff core and a dull orange-buff surface. The base has shallow rilling underneath. Almost complete, with modern fractures.

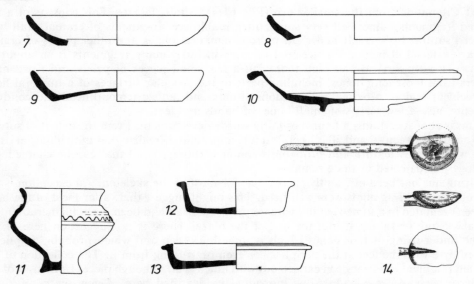

Fig. 62. Nuns' Walk: pottery and spoon from the burial (scale ¼, spoon ½).

Dish (722.00.1/10, Fig. 62:10). The fabric is sandy and fairly hard, and light orange-buff in colour. The surface is whitish-buff, especially internally. There is a trace of a rectangular stamp 19×5 mm. Two fragments representing half the vessel are preserved. All the fractures are ancient.

Cup (722.00.1/11, Fig. 62:11). Hard fabric with a little sand backing. The core is grey, the skin red-brown and the surface black and smoothed, with a slight burnish. The decoration is deeply incised. All breaks are modern.

Dish (722.00.1/13, Fig. 62:12). The surface is black and smoothed, and the fabric is quite sandy. The vessel is complete, excepting a modern chip on the rim.

Dish (722.00.1/10, Fig. 62:13). The ware is hard and sandy, with a grey core, reddish skin and fairly black surface. Half the pot is present, but the fracture is modern. It comes from the spoil tip.

Two small worn fragments (722.00.1/14) of a vessel 6 mm thick, perhaps with a beaded rim. The fabric is similar to vessel 9. Probably from a cup, perhaps imitating Dragendorff 27.

Wall sherds (722.00.1/15) of a vessel 2·5 mm thick. The fabric is as vessel 9, but lacks the grey core.

The Bone Spoon

The spoon (722.1, Fig. 62:14), carved from a single piece of bone, was found lying broken in one of the dishes. (Drawing by R. Moule.)

Tile

Two fragments of a brick 4 cm thick were found, one triangular 10×14×17 cm, the other rectangular 15×19 cm. The breaks are old and they do not join. There is also a triangular fragment of tegula, 18×18×20 cm (broken in half on discovery).

The Cremations by C. Wells

(a) Cremation from the smaller urn (Fig. 61:4). Adult, female. This consists of a few hundred fragments, almost all very small. Identifiable are: fragments of cranial vault with advanced sutural fusion, left and right petrous temporal bones and other pieces of cranial base; a few facial elements. Post-cranial remains include: many fragments from about 14 vertebrae (mostly cervical and high thoracic); a few small pieces of pelvis and ribs; many splinters from most long bones, including parts of the articular surfaces of a humeral head and trochlear region; proximal articulations of ulna and radius; femoral head and condylar fragments; also a few scraps of small bones of hands and feet.

This is almost certainly a female of fairly sturdy development. From the extent of sutural fusion an age between 40 and 50 is likely but it is important to realize that individual variation is very wide in this feature and probability, never certainty, is all that can be claimed. No pathology was detected in these remains.

Firing has not been efficiently carried out for most of the skeleton. An exception is the skull, of which all fragments were well fired. This might suggest that, after most of the body had been cremated in a somewhat inadequate pyre, the head had been given further attention by final stoking or raking it into the last of the blaze. There is no suggestion here of the extreme under-firing of foot bones which is sometimes seen and which probably implies a skimped pyre with the feet at the periphery or even protruding from it. The collection of the cremated fragments has not been carried out with much zeal, although pieces from most of the body have been recovered. Only one individual is identified here. A few pieces of sheep vertebrae and other small fragments of animal bone are also present.

(b) Cremation from the larger urn (Fig. 61:3). Adult, male. This consists of several hundred fragments, almost all very small. Identifiable are: pieces of cranial vault with early endocranial fusion of sutures, a left petrous temporal bone and other fragments of cranial base including both mastoid processes, a few facial elements, the left and right condyle of a mandible and a small piece of alveolus. Post-cranial remains include: many vertebral fragments from all levels of the column, a few pelvic and rib fragments, the bases of left and right scapular spines; many slivers from the shafts of all long bones (a few of these being fairly large — the biggest 105 mm long). Articular areas include fragments of the heads and trochlear surfaces of left and right humeri, proximal and distal ulnar and radial surfaces, pieces of the head and condyles of a femur, the distal articular surface of a tibia, and the distal extremities of left and right fibulae. A few fragments of hand and foot bones include metacarpals and phalanges, pieces of talus, cuboid, and metatarsal shafts.

It is probable, on the uncertain basis of sutural fusion, that this individual was less than 35 years old at the time of death. He was well built, with strongly developed areas of muscle attachment. No pathology was detected but a hint of a squatting facet was found at the distal end of a tibia. If this can be relied on (the bone is damaged here), it would perhaps suggest that this man was of somewhat humble status, accustomed to squatting in his hut rather than using chairs or benches. It might also reflect some occupation in which the squatting posture played a predominant part.

Most of the skeleton has been moderately well fired but a few deep structures (e.g. femoral head) are somewhat underfired. Only one individual is detectable here. Two small fragments of unfired animal bone are present.

The Animal Bones

In addition to those animal bones mixed with the human cremations, there is a group of bones which were apparently placed on one of the dishes. They represent the left hind quarter of a young pig. It may not have been in one piece when deposited, as the breaks on the femur are old, and do not join. The bones represented are the tibia (proximal unfused epiphysis), patella, femur (distal end and unfused epiphysis, proximal end and unfused epiphyses), pelvis (the ilium and pubis, unfused).

EASTON WATER-MAIN TRENCH (NORTH)
(EWT 55 Site 959)

The majority of observations from the cutting of the trench for this water pipe were made in the western suburb, and are discussed elsewhere in this volume (pp. 245-262). In the northern suburb it tended to skirt round the main areas of occupation, so observations and finds are few. The first discoveries were made in Edington Road which runs east from Worthy Lane just north of its junction with Hyde Street, but little was noted in Lankhills Road. Not all the field notes concerning these finds have survived.

Summary

There is a single worn sherd of Roman pot from Edington Road, and a fragment of tile. There are also a few fragments of twelfth-century pottery, but from both Edington Road and Lankhills Road the majority of material is thirteen to fourteenth century. The feature most worthy of note is the large sarsen (Plate IVa) which caused part of the trench to be diverted, when it proved impossible to break it up with a compressor. This sarsen is fairly certainly that shown on Godson's map of 1750, where it forms the northern limit of the boundary of the City Liberty, and the stone is also mentioned in earlier Tarrage surveys (Atkinson 1963:28). It is unfortunate that its significance was not recognised at the time of discovery. However its relationship to the pit F1 suggests the sarsen did not reach its present position before the thirteenth century.

Features and Layers

Edington Road
F1: *Pit and sarsen*
The sarsen was found a little under a metre below the modern road surface. It is about 2·50 m long east—west, and at least 1 m wide north—south, though its northern limit was not found; and it is about 0·60 m thick. It was overlain by a buried surface beneath the modern make-up. The sarsen partly overlies a pit filled with greyish soil from which came the pottery. The pit cut into the natural brown clayey sand. The centre of the sarsen lies 15·70 m from the eastern end of Edington Road, and 6·70 m from its southern fence.
959.1.0/1.
Late thirteenth-century pottery.

L1: *No details of discovery*
959.00.1/1.
Fragments of jugs with rod handles or grooved decoration of fourteenth-century date, and other contemporary sherds. There is also one uneroded rim sherd of a thirteenth-century cooking pot or dish, and one late Roman cooking pot sherd.

L2: *From the western part of the road*
959.00.2/1.
Cooking pot (Fig. 63:1). Fine, reduced fabric slightly tempered.
Rim and strap handle of a jug (Fig. 63:2) in sparse, green, glazed ware similar to Winchester Spouted Pitchers.
Bowl (Fig. 63:3), in oxidized Saxo-Norman ware.
Lid (Fig. 63:4). Hard red, late medieval fabric.

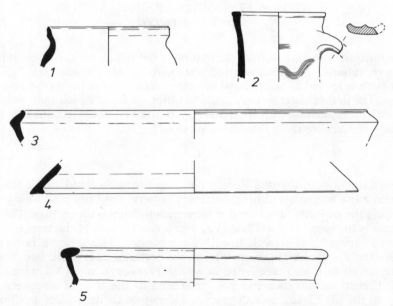

Fig. 63. Easton Water-Main Trench (North): pottery from Edington Road (scale ¼).

There are two other sherds in oxidized Saxo-Norman ware and a fragment of a tripod pitcher. The bulk of the material consists of jugs with grooved decoration and rod handles, and five have slightly tempered fabrics, mostly of fourteenth-century date.

L3: *Probably from the fill of a feature which goes to the bottom of the trench*
    959.00.3/1.
    Cooking pot (Fig. 63:5). Very coarse oxidized fabric, fine flint inclusions.

Lankhills Road
F2: *Pit*
    Details of position mislaid, filled with brown soil.
    959.2.0/1.
    Late thirteenth-century finds.

F3: *Pit*
    Adjacent to F2. No finds.

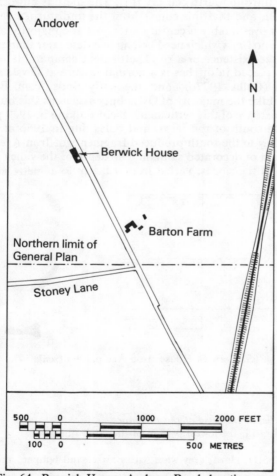

Fig. 64. Berwick House, Andover Road: location map.

BERWICK HOUSE, ANDOVER ROAD
(Site 1293)

The farm known as Berwick House lies just outside the boundary of the modern city, just west of Andover Road (Fig. 64). A certain amount of ribbon development took place in the earlier part of the century up to the city limits on the western side of the road, and more recently extensive housing development on the Weeke and Harestock Estates has enclosed the site to the west. At the time of writing the area where these discoveries were made is still open. The main discoveries occurred during the digging of a service trench in 1949, and the finds were reported to F. Cottrill on whose field notes this report is based.

Summary

Two features were discovered, a ditch and a burial apparently inserted into it. The finds from below the skeleton show a mixture of Iron Age and early Roman material. The earliest sherd (3) comes from a situlate jar comparable with finds from the earliest phase at Owslebury, presumably third to fourth century B.C. The sherd is unworn and implies we are dealing with a recut ditch, and that this comes from the undisturbed earlier phase. The one sherd of saucepan pot is presumably a century later, but the majority of finds belong to the Late Iron Age. There are no finds which need belong to a date later than the first century A.D.

These finds imply the existence of a rural settlement comparable with that of Winnall. The presence of burials placed in ditches is a normal feature at Owslebury from the second century A.D. onwards (Collis 1977b), and the early finds from Berwick House need not imply an early date. Like the majority of Owslebury skeletons this burial is male. There is other evidence for the existence of this settlement. Field walking in 1960 produced a fragment of samian from the field south of the farm, and holes dug in 1956 at the southern end of 1 Stoney Lane in the valley to the south produced fragments of Iron Age and Roman pottery including a worn fragment of decorated samian. The depth of the valley silt, presumably hill-wash due to cultivation of the slopes, varied from a metre to a metre and a half.

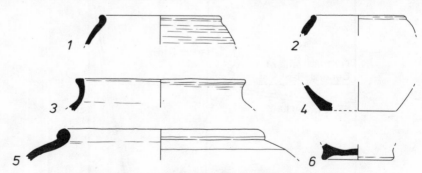

Fig. 65. Berwick House: Iron Age pottery (scale ¼).

The Features

F1: The ditch
    F1-1: Finds from below the level of the skeleton
    Excavated by Mr Cottrill, the lowest 0·45 m of the ditch filling.
    1293.1.1/1.
    Bead-rim jar (Fig. 65:1). Hard, grey ware with coarse sand temper, and brown burnished surface.

Bead-rim jar (Fig. 65:2). Identical fabric to vessel 1, but black surface. The shoulder has been burnished hard producing a faceted appearance, but the body of the vessel is plain (though it may have had vertical elements as on Fig. 72:20).

These two are typical of the century before the Roman conquest. This group also contains three earlier Iron Age sherds, one with a coarse, rusticated surface and hard, black fabric with sporadic shell (?) and organic temper comparable with vessel 3; one shell-tempered sherd, and one soft sherd with chert and burnt flint temper, typical of the saucepan pot series. There is a coarse burnt-flint-tempered sherd from a storage jar, and nine fragments comparable with vessels 1 and 2.

F1-2:   Excavated by the workmen c. 0·15—0·20 m below the skeleton, above F1-1
1293.1.2/1.
Situlate jar (Fig. 65:3). Hard, black, laminated fabric, coarse handmade. Coarse chert and burnt flint temper.
Base (Fig. 65:4) with band of burnishing, identical to and perhaps from 2.
Bead rim (Fig. 65:5). Hard, grey fabric with coarse, burnt flint temper, orange surface.
Base (Fig. 65:6). Hard, black to grey-brown, sand-tempered fabric, black inside, reddish-brown outside, well-burnished on both surfaces.
There are two sherds as no. 2, and also a very coarse, very hard sherd, dull red outside but reduced inside. It has coarse chert temper, and the exterior is roughly rusticated and wiped. This sherd and no. 3 belong to the fourth-third centuries B.C., no. 6 probably to the second half of the first century B.C.; the others to c. 50 B.C.—A.D. 50.

F2:   The burial
F2-1:   Found near the skeleton
1293.2.1/1.
A body sherd of a jar (probably the straight-necked series) broken off just below the shoulder, where there is a burnished wavy line decoration. Hard, grey, sandy ware with black surface and coarse sand temper. Presumably late first century A.D.

F2-2:   Collected with the bones
1293.2.1/1.
A hard, sandy sherd comparable with F1-1 and a black, burnished sherd, probably Late Iron Age.

The Finds

The Samian by B. R. Hartley
A small south Gaulish scrap (1293.0.1/1) of samian was found during field walking. It is of first-century date.

The human bones by C. Wells
The skeleton from the burial is male, aged 19—22 years. This consists of a damaged and incomplete skull; the T10 and L5 vertebrae; the sacrum and a few other pieces of pelvis; the right radius intact; most of the right humerus; fragments of clavicle, scapula, ulna; and the right femur lacking its head. The skull is rather lightly built with poorly developed muscle markings. It is ovoid in norma verticalis with no occipital tuber. The mandible is moderately heavy with slight gonial eversion. The dental condition is:

8	7	6	5	0	0	0	0		0	0	3	4	5	6	7	0
8	7	0	0	0	0	0	0		0	0	0	0	0	6	7	0

Dental attrition is moderate. There is no caries, but slight enamel hypoplasia is visible on the canine and first and second molars. The maximum bi-parietal breadth of the skull is 142·2 mm; the basion-bregma height is 129·8 mm.

The sacrum is composed normally of 5 segments: S4—5 are fused, the first three are unfused. Muscle markings on the limb bones are moderately strong. The right humerus was at least 340·0 mm long; the right radius is 255·8 mm. This corresponds to a stature of about 1764 mm (5 ft 9½ in).

Eight pieces of animal bone are present with this assemblage.

CHAPTER 6

THE WESTERN SUBURB
AND THE
WESTERN PART OF THE TOWN

The area outside the West Gate was defined by the pre-existing Iron Age defences, and they formed in part an important boundary, the limits of the City Liberty, in the medieval period. They were doubtless a marked feature on the Roman landscape as well. There had been a scatter of earlier prehistoric occupation along the gravel terrace which runs north—south along the hillside. From St James' Terrace comes a Beaker burial with two beakers of Clarke's Wessex/Middle Rhine 2 and Barbed Wire groups (Clarke 1970, nos. 352 and 353, and p. 70 note 40), and Middle Bronze Age pottery has been found on Oram's Arbour (Biddle 1966). The Late Bronze Age is represented by a cremation burial in Tower Street (Biddle 1965) and scattered sherds on the Westgate Car Park site. Both sites have also produced early Iron Age material including fragments of haematite bowls, but no features can definitely be assigned to this period.

Throughout the area within the defences there is evidence of occupation with saucepan-pot material belonging to the Middle Iron Age, including ditched enclosures and post-holes on the Westgate Car Park and Tower Street sites, but very few pits. West of the railway the old ground surface has been destroyed, and only the deeper features have survived, such as the pits and circular drainage gullies on Oram's Arbour. All this occupation seems to have had a very restricted chronological range. Later styles of decoration on the pottery including cross-hatching such as appears in the Assize Court ditch are totally absent, and purely burnished decoration, which seems to be an early feature, does not appear at all in Winchester, let alone the coarse saucepan pots which form the early phase at Owslebury. Sporadic Late Iron Age material has turned up in the Iron Age defensive ditch and in pits cut by the Easton Water-Main Trench, but there seems not to have been an extensive occupation.

There is little evidence for activity in this area during the first century before the construction of the Roman defences. Recent excavations in Crowder Terrace have produced a ditch which was filled in in the late first century with a large amount of waste from a bone-working industry, but the samian list from the Easton Water-Main Trench shows a marked dearth of early samian, and the western part of the town within the defences seems to have easily absorbed any expansion towards the west until the Antonine period. During the late second century ditches were being laid out within the area of the Iron Age earthwork around Oram's Arbour (Easton Water-Main Trench), though these may only be field boundaries. In St James' Terrace there is a substantial amount of Antonine samian though most of it occurs in later contexts, but it must mark the beginning of occupation in this area.

There are plentiful late Roman finds, including painted wall plaster from St James' Terrace (Easton Water-Main Trench) and pits on Crowder Terrace. During construction of the railway, traces of a substantial masonry building were found north of the Romsey Road (so

161

within the Iron Age earthwork), and hints of a second building south of the bridge, outside the enclosure (Haverfield 1900). Our evidence from St James' Terrace is also outside the enclosure. It suggests that domestic occupation went on here at least until the middle of the fourth century.

There is as yet no evidence for substantial cemeteries in the western suburb. Burials were found in the Iron Age ditch on the Ashley Terrace site (Biddle 1965) and on the adjacent site in Station Hill in 1975 (K. Qualmann), and these seem to belong to the first half of the fourth century. The child burial published here (p. 263) seems earlier, and isolated. Burials have also turned up in Clifton Road (K. Qualmann pers. comm.), and their hobnails demonstrate a Roman date, and burials from Oram's Arbour (Biddle 1968) and from Romsey Road (K. Qualmann pers. comm.) could likewise be Roman. Haverfield (1900) records burials from St James' Lane, one with a coin of Magnentius. These burials thus form a circle just outside the Iron Age earthwork, and no definite burials have been recorded from within the enclosure.

In the eleventh and twelfth centuries the western suburb was the wealthiest and most populous of those parts which lay outside the walls (Biddle, ed. 1977). Before the late ninth century, the West Gate seems to have been the main way into the walled area for traffic approaching the city from the north as well as from the west. This may account in part for the rapid development of this suburb which even before the Norman Conquest had a self-conscious social identity and played an important part in the religious life of the city. Already by the ninth century there was occupation on the Westgate Car Park site just inside the West Gate and similar evidence was found in 1975 on the New Road site and in Sussex Street. Otherwise finds of such early pottery are confined to the central areas of the town. The owners and/or occupiers of properties in the suburb in the eleventh and twelfth centuries included butchers, leather workers, and a bronze founder, for which tangible evidence was found on the Tower Street Rescue site (p. 195).

The pattern of pit digging within the suburb is much as one would expect. Most of those recorded here lie along the main street frontages of Romsey Road, Upper High Street, and Sussex Street, and also in Mews Lane. The varied ceramics including fine-ware imports perhaps reflect the wealth of the suburb especially in the eleventh and twelfth centuries. There were still some substantial houses here in the late thirteenth century, but the later economic and demographic decline affected this suburb with particular severity so that by the sixteenth century there were no more than a few houses huddled just outside the West Gate. The archaeological finds exactly reflect this pattern, and finds after the twelfth century are virtually non-existent.

The suburb was enclosed by a ditch which in part represented a recutting of the Iron Age defences, as on the western side of Oram's Arbour. This ditch was extended north on a new line to enclose the northern suburb, and in both areas it also formed the limit of the City Liberty. The entrances to the suburb were marked by churches, St James on Romsey Road and St Anastasius on the Stockbridge Road, and Biddle and Keene have noted this as a feature of the Winchester suburbs (Biddle, ed. 1977). Only one site has been tested by excavation, that of St Anastasius, which lies near the modern church of St Paul (p. 264).

FREDERICK PLACE, TOWER STREET
(FP 60 Site 484)

This site lies in Tower Street, just within the area enclosed by the city walls. In 1959 the terrace of nineteenth-century houses known as Frederick Place was demolished revealing gardens sloping steeply down from north to south, suggesting a bank over 1·5 m high. It seemed possible that this marked the line of the earliest Iron Age defences. The ground to the north and to the east had been terraced for the construction of houses fronting on to City Road and Jewry Street, including the Theatre Royal, and all archaeological deposits have long since disappeared. In Roman and medieval times the area lay in the angle formed by the main north-south route through the town, and by the City Wall west of the North Gate, though along this section both bank and wall have been totally removed (Figs. 45, 66).

The three trenches were dug by the writer during school vacations in 1960, primarily to

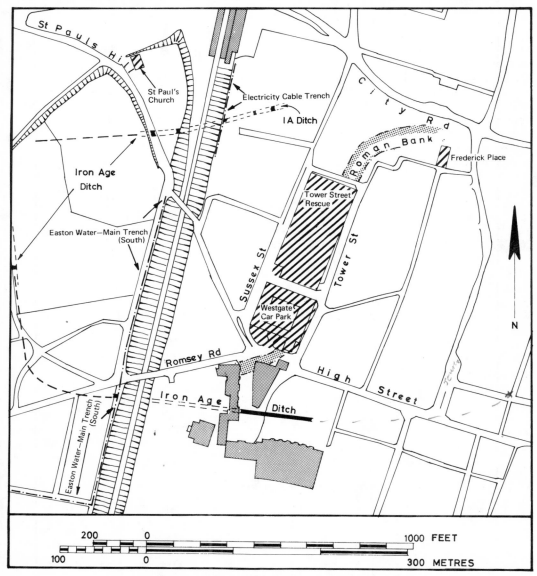

Fig. 66. The western suburb: general plan.

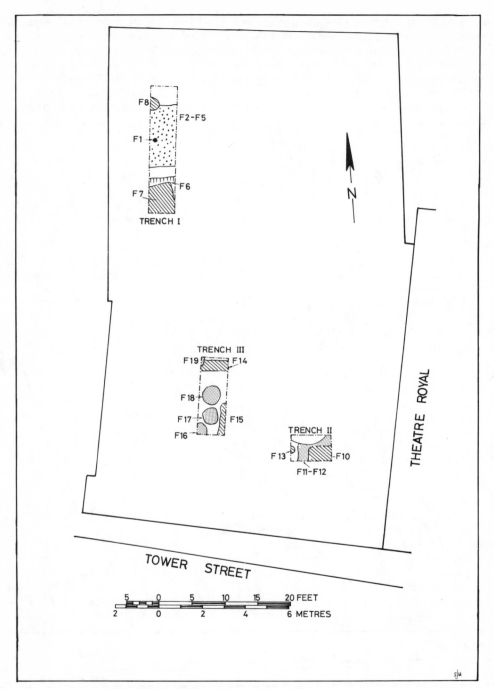

Fig. 67. Frederick Place: plan of Roman features.

find the Iron Age defences, and the Roman and medieval material were respectively considered of secondary and tertiary importance. In retrospect this judgement should have been reversed! The site has since been levelled as a car park for the premises recently occupied by Murray's shop, and thanks must be given to Mr Murray for permission to excavate. All finds are now in the City Museum, though a small number of small finds were mislaid during conservation.

Summary

No evidence of Iron Age occupation was encountered, at least helping to define the limits of the dense 'Saucepan pot'/Middle Iron Age occupation within the defences, which on recent evidence seem to coincide with the Roman defences at this point, on a line further north. The only Iron Age vessel, of local Late Iron Age type, came from a late Roman pit, which also contained a lot of residual early Roman finds. There is a little first-century material, all in later contexts, and occupation only starts in the second century (Fig. 67). Stratigraphically earliest is a small square post-hole, F1. Sealing this, and otherwise directly laid on the natural orange gravel was a cobbled trackway about 3 m wide running east—west through Trench I. This first phase was constructed of well-rammed small flint cobbles, but it was later reduced in size to about 1·5 m, using large flints and brick set in orange soil (section on Fig. 69). Parallel to this ran the gully F14, sealed by a deposit L11 which contained Hadrianic samian. The pit F13 is also probably of second-century date.

Sometime in the third or fourth centuries the cobbled track was resurfaced and widened, employing small cobbles (F4), before it was again reduced using large flints in loose black soil. The track went out of use before the end of the Roman period as an otherwise undated pit F8 cuts through it. The hollow F6 may represent a gully running parallel to the track at the end of the third century. Of similar date is the pit F7 with 12 radiate coins from Gordian III to the Tetrici in its lower filling. Further south four hearths F16—F19 produced evidence of metal working, including bronze and lead. Slightly later, probably of the early fourth century, is the large pit or pits F9 and F10 which had totally removed all earlier deposits in Trench II. Pit F10 had been deliberately filled up with soil containing much early Roman material as well as late third- and early fourth-century finds. It was sealed by two chalk floors F11 and F12 with fourth-century finds on them (L7 and L8) including a mint coin of Crispus. These apparently belong to a timber building (and the pit itself could be a cellar for it), but only one post-hole was located within the trench, F13, and that is probably later. All the Roman deposits were sealed by the 'Late Roman Black' deposit (L13) with its usual mass of late Roman coins and abraded pottery.

A single post-hole, F20, cut through this black post-Roman build-up. It is undated, but presumably pre-A.D. 900, as it was sealed with the Roman levels by a layer of small cobbles, compact and heavily rammed in Trenches I and III, but less continuous in Trench II. This could represent a northern continuation of the medieval *Brudenestret* (now Staple Gardens) which should date back to the original late Saxon lay-out of the street grid (Biddle and Hill 1971). Direct dating evidence was not obtained, but after some silt had been allowed to accumulate a shallow hollow (F33) was dug into the silt, and this produced a wheel-turned cooking pot of a type which seems to antedate the appearance of Winchester Ware (Biddle and Collis forthcoming). Sealing this was a layer of redeposited 'Late Roman Black', which was also noted in the section cut across Gar Street (Biddle 1964). Lying on this was a deposit containing much domestic rubbish (L17) and typical eleventh-century finds including Winchester Ware, though the top of this layer had been removed in the nineteenth-century levelling. In Trench I however there was evidence of patchy resurfacing into the twelfth century.

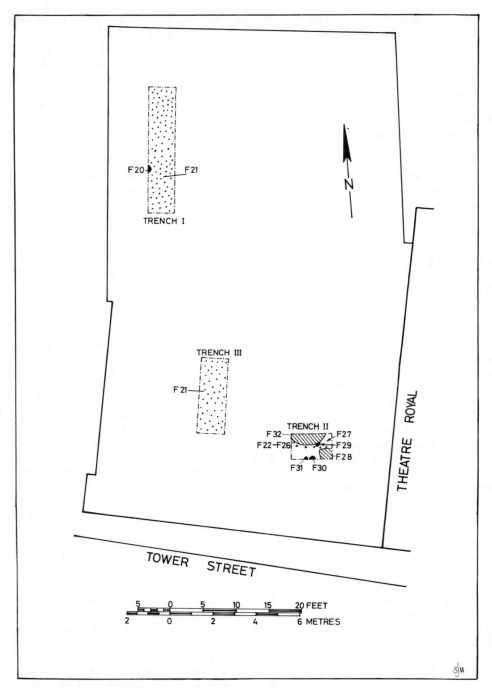

Fig. 68. Frederick Place: plan of medieval features.

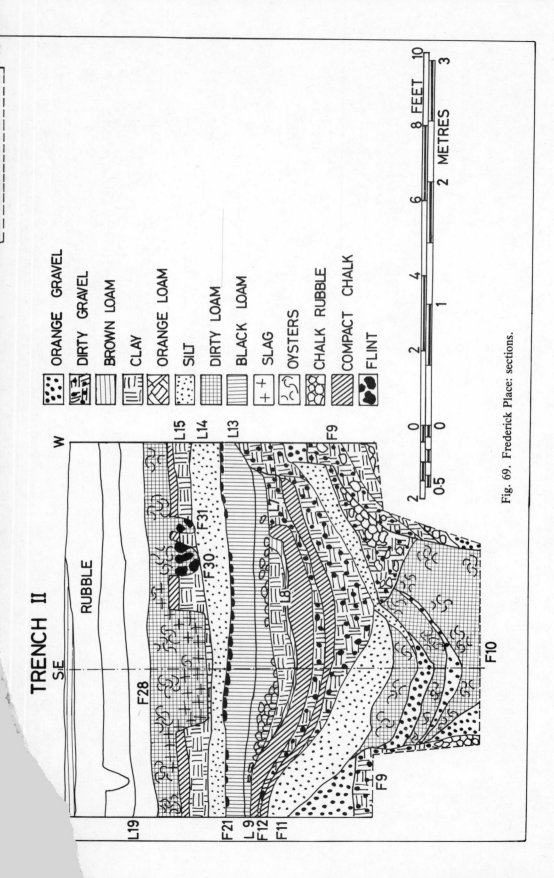

Fig. 69. Frederick Place: sections.

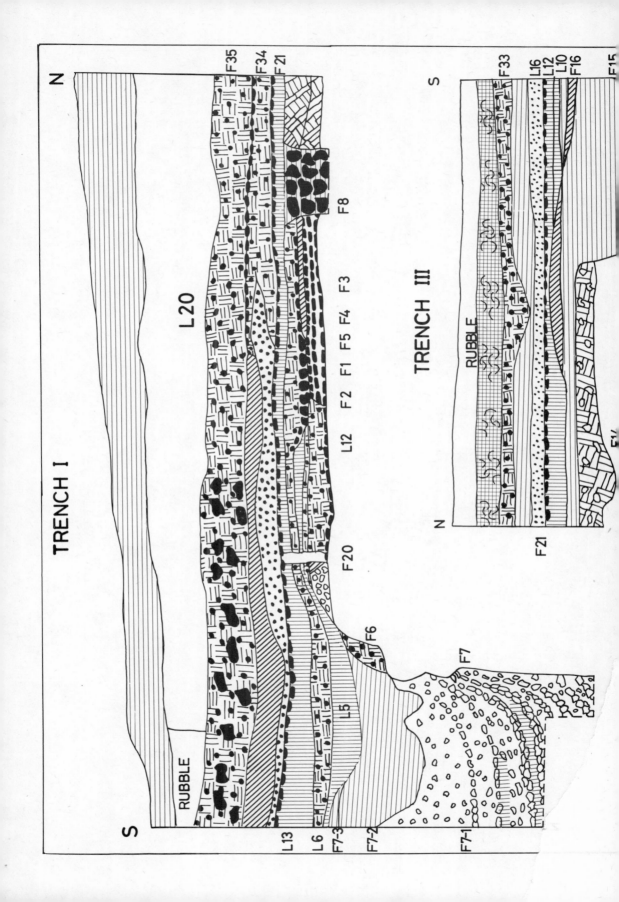

In Trench II (Fig. 68) occupation started to invade the road margin. After a build-up of silt a line of stake holes (F22—F26) was placed running east—west, then this was sealed by the chalk floor of a building. Cut into it were three post-holes (F29—F31) and a small pit (F28) which produced plentiful evidence of iron working, with slag which spread over the chalk floor. The finds again suggest an eleventh to twelfth century date, but the building had gone out of use by the thirteenth century when a pit (F32) was cut through it. Above was a build-up of medieval and post-medieval garden soil. Later medieval finds are almost totally lacking. It is not clear precisely when the street was blocked off, but no repairs are later than the twelfth century, and in the sixteenth or seventeenth a large deposit of brown soil containing one or two chalk spreads was deposited at the northern end of the site, forming the bank of soil which stimulated the excavation. The stratigraphic sequence is shown schematically in Table 15.

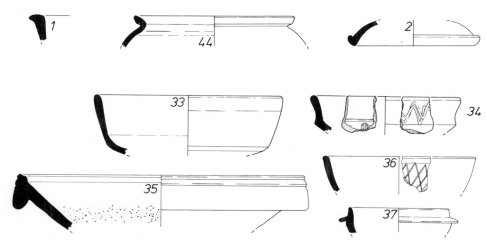

Fig. 70. Frederick Place: early Roman pottery from F2 (1), L1 (44), F6 (2), F15 (33—37) (scale ¼).

Features and Layers

F1:   Post-hole in Trench I
A square post-hole filled with grey silty soil, cutting into the natural gravel and sealed by the track F2.
484.1.0/1.
Three grey jar sherds, two decorated with burnished lattice.

F2:   First track surface, in Trench I
The surface consists of a single layer of small cobbles rammed into the natural gravel, and is about 3 m in width.
484.2.0/1.
Piedish (Fig. 70:1). Fine, grey fabric with black flecks and red grog; black surface; abraded. There is a sherd of a lid of second- or third-century type, and three sherds of second-century samian. Six vessels are represented.

F3:   Second road surface in Trench I
This is made of large flints and occasional lumps of brick set in ginger soil. It overlies the northern part of F2, but is only 1·5 m in width.

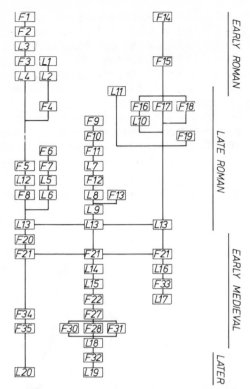

Table 15. Frederick Place: stratigraphic sequence.

484.3.0/1.
A piedish (cf. Cunliffe 1964, Fig. 18:5), a lid rim, an everted beaker rim, and a sherd with two bands of oblique burnished lines. With a single sherd of samian, perhaps of Trajanic date, six vessels are represented.

F4: *Third road surface, in Trench I*
This consists of a single layer of small cobbles overlying F3, 2 m in width. There are no finds.

F5: *Fourth road surface*
This is made of large flints in black soil, 1·5 m in width. No finds.

F6: *Gully or hollow in Trench I*
This could be a gully running east-west alongside the track F2—F5. It is filled with dark brown clayey gravel, and cut by F7.
484.6.0/1.
Bowl or lid (Fig. 70:2). Hard, light brown, slightly gritty fabric with black surface.
Five vessels are represented. There is a painted, internally flanged bowl, a black slipped, straight-sided dish, and a possible fragment of Ashley Rails parchment ware with purple slip.

F7: *A large pit in Trench I*
The dimensions were not recovered, but the one corner suggests a rectilinear pit. It cuts through the gravel into the underlying chalk. The finds are generally of late third-century date, and with eleven identifiable coins represents an important group, comparable with pit A (F20) on nearby Staple Gardens (Cunliffe 1964:176—182).

F7-1: *Layers of chalk rubble, the lowest filling excavated*
484.7.1/1.
Lid (Fig. 71:3). Hard, grey core, and orange skin with a matt purple-brown colour-coat.
Flanged dish (Fig. 71:4). Hard, fine, gritty black fabric, black burnished surface, with burnished decoration.
Jar (Fig. 71:5). Fine, gritty, grey fabric with reddish to grey-brown surface, slipped and burnished on the rim.
Straight-sided dish (Fig. 71:6). Soft, brown fabric with black burnished surface.
There is a second flanged dish identical to that illustrated, a handmade straight-sided dish, a piedish, and a very coarse storage jar with fingered hollows under the rim. Important is the presence of two sherds of parchment ware with a purple colour-coat from a flagon of Ashley Rails type.
Twelve vessels are represented.
There are five coins, one of Gordian III, one of Postumus, two of Tetricus I, and one of Tetricus II. Small finds include a fragment of a glass beaker and two iron objects.

F7-2: *Loose, light brown soil above F7-1*
484.7.2/1.
Folded beaker (Fig. 71:7). Steel-grey core and orange skin with a glossy dark brown colour-coat.
Beaker (Fig. 71:8). Hard, light brown fabric and dull brown surface, decorated with stamped patterns.
Beaker or flagon (Fig. 71:9). Soft, light brown fabric with brown colour-coat.
Cavetto jar (Fig. 71:10). Fine, light grey fabric with a black burnished slip on the rim and exterior.
Storage jar (Fig. 71:11). Fine, sandy fabric, light grey to brownish.
Jar (Fig. 71:12). Fine, slightly gritty fabric with brown, smoothed surface.
Dish (Fig. 71:13). Coarse, gritty, brown fabric with some grog, roughly burnished surface. Handmade.
Piedish (Fig. 71:14). Fine, hard, light grey fabric, black burnished internal slip and grey exterior with burnished decoration.
Storage jar (Fig. 71:15). Soft, brown fabric with much grit; black surface.
A total of 40 vessels are represented in the group. Other noteworthy fragments are two of New Forest colour-coat flagons, fifteen New Forest folded beakers, both hard and soft fabrics, four straight-sided dishes, a mortarium and an orange-coloured flanged bowl, not of New Forest fabric. There are six coins, one each of Gallienus, Salonina, Victorinus, Claudius II and Tetricus I, and a barbarous radiate.

F7-3: *Brown soil with no flints above F7-2 and underlying L5*
484.7.3/1.
Of the four vessels represented, there is one New Forest colour-coat flagon, the rim of an internally flanged bowl, and a vessel with bands of burnished squiggles.

F8: *A pit in Trench I*
Filled with large flints and black soil, it cuts F5, but is sealed by L13, and so is of late Roman date.

F9: *Pit in Trench II*
This gravel and chalk may be infill of pit F10, but if so, it represents earlier infill revetted in position.
484.9.0/1.
Nine vessels are present, including two fine burnished jars (probably cavetto-rim jars), one with fine oblique burnish, a New Forest beaker sherd in hard purple colour-coat, and two dishes and a beaker of second- or third-century date.

F10: A pit in Trench II

This is one corner of a large rectangular pit or cellar. The infill is loose brown soil with some gravel. It is possible that the pit had a timber lining and F9 is merely infill behind the revetment. It is sealed by the chalk floor fill. This large group is mainly of early fourth-century date, but it contains a considerable amount of residual material.

484.10.0/1.
Mortarium (Fig. 72:16). Hard, light buff fabric with sparse gritting.
There are fragments of two other mortaria.
484.10.0/2.
Folded beaker (Fig. 72:17). Buff fabric with dull brown colour-coat. New Forest.
Thirty-three vessels are present in this bag. There are fragments of fourteen 'hard' New Forest beakers or folded beakers and in soft wares two beakers and three folded beakers; one hard beaker with rouletted decoration; a parchment ware flagon with purple colour-coat, an internally flanged bowl, two beakers with brown colour-coating and rouletting, an unusual orange-brown folded bowl with red colour-coat, three thin orange sherds with red colour-coat, and one thin metallic sherd with rustication. There is a thin folded beaker with rouletting, perhaps Rhenish. The total number of colour-coat and related vessels is at least 33.
484.10.0/3.
Cooking pot (Fig. 72:18). Very hard, grey fabric with slightly gritted surface.
484.10.0/4.
A rope-rimmed storage jar in hard, sandy grey to brown fabric. The body sherds have been roughly grooved and frequently pierced with an iron point with a square section (c.f. Sumner 1927, Fig. 30:26) from Sloden.
484.10.0/3.
Jar, probably cavetto. Hard, fine, grey ware with a burnished black slip and oblique burnished lattice. Grafitto scratched on the shoulder.
484.10.0/6.
Cooking pot (Fig. 72:19). Soft, reddish-brown gritty fabric. Black interior, patchy black, reddish or grey exterior and burnished decoration. A Late Iron Age form.
484.10.0/7.
Jar (Fig. 72:20). Hard, dark grey fabric with fine grit, slightly micaceous, black surface.
Also a large handle in coarse gritty ware with much grog, and fragments of a gritty and of a sandy storage jar.
484.10.0/8.
Jar (Fig. 72:21). Hard, light grey with grey, slightly sandy fabric.
Jar (Fig. 72:22). Light grey fabric with dark grey burnished external slip.
Piedish (Fig. 72:23). Hard, grey fabric, burnished white to black internal slip.
Dish (Fig. 72:24). Light grey fabric, slightly sandy with black or dark grey burnished decoration.
Lid (Fig. 72:25). Light grey fabric with dull dark grey surface.
Flagon (Fig. 72:26). Harsh, grey fabric.
Piedish (Fig. 72:27). Hard, grey fabric with smoothed surface.
Not illustrated are a bead rim, a reeded-rim bowl, five straight-sided dishes, 21 jars or beakers, a lid, and a handle, in various grey wares. There is a minimum of 40 vessels.
484.10.0/9.
Jar (Fig. 72:28). Harsh, grey fabric with dark, smoothed surface.
Jar (Fig. 72:29). Soft, black fabric with burnished shoulder and rim. Possibly handmade.
Jar (Fig. 72:30). Hard, black fabric with black burnished rim and shoulder, and burnished lattice pattern.
Cavetto-rim jar (Fig. 72:31). Fine, grey ware, slightly sandy with black burnished slip.
Cavetto-rim jar (Fig. 72:32), as above.
There are five more cavetto-rim jars in similar fabric.

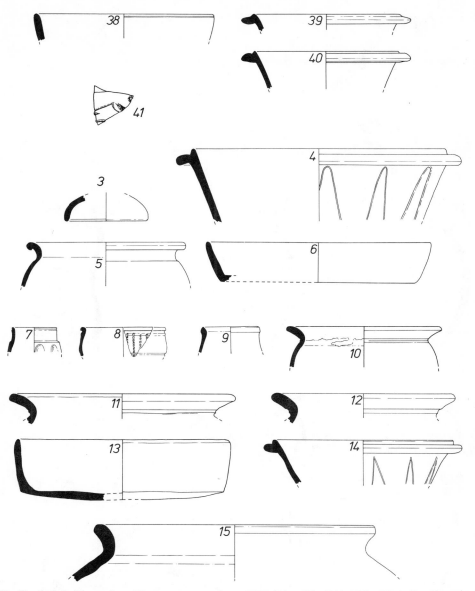

Fig. 71. Frederick Place: late Roman pottery from F17 (38—40), F18 (41), F7-1 (3—7); and F7-2 (8—15) (scale ¼).

There are six definite samian vessels, one first century and the rest second century, and a cup which could be samian or red colour-coat.

The minimum number of vessels from F10 is at least 100.

F11: Chalk floor sealing F10 in Trench II
No finds.

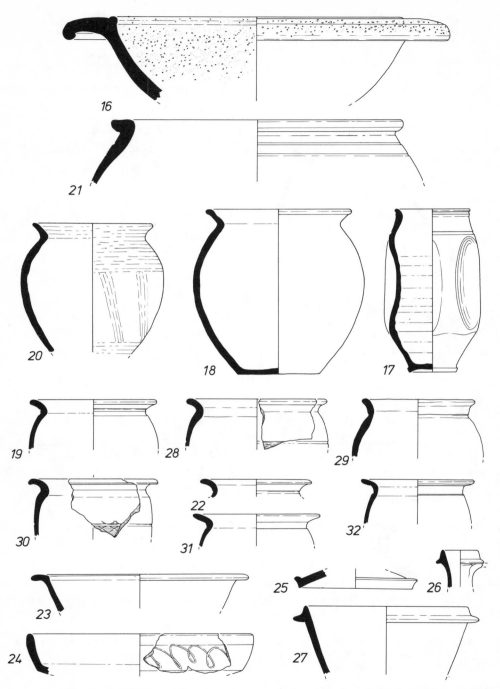

Fig. 72. Frederick Place: Iron Age (20) and Roman pottery from F10 (scale ¼).

F12: Chalk floor with clay patching, above F11 and L7, in Trench II
No finds.

F13: Post hole in Trench II, sealed by L13 and cutting F9
484.13.0/1.
Three vessels are present, including hard, purple colour-coat and a fourth-century cooking-pot rim.

F14: East—west gully in Trench III
It is cut into natural and is filled with ginger-brown soil. No finds.

F15: Pit in Trench III
Filled with ginger-brown soil; it is later than F14.
484.15.0/1.
Dish (Fig. 70:33). Hard, grey fabric with dark surface and black internal slip (at least two different vessels are represented).
Dish (Fig. 70:34). Harsh, black fabric with red skin and black surface, and burnished wavy-line pattern.
Mortarium (Fig. 70:35). Hard, off-white fabric, few internal grits.
Bowl (Fig. 70:36). Hard, slightly gritty, black ware, brownish-black surface, and burnished lattice.
Flanged bowl (Fig. 70:37). Fine, hard, light brown fabric with black to white slip.
At least 19 coarse-ware vessels are represented, including a rim and pierced base of lids, three pie-dishes, two other mortaria and a jar. There is one second-century samian fragment.

F16: Hearth resting on chalk, in Trench III
484.16.0/1.
Four vessels which include two straight-sided dishes, one with black internal slip.

F17: Hearth in Trench III
484.17.0/1.
Flanged dish (Fig. 71:38). Hard, light grey fabric, burnished surface.
Piedish (Fig. 71:39). Hard, black, slightly gritty surface with light brown, smoothed surface.
Flanged dish (Fig. 71:40). Hard, reddish-brown to grey fabric, grey smoothed surface.
Seven vessels represented include a grog-tempered storage jar, a straight-sided dish with internal black slip and burnished intersecting arcs. The hearth produced a lump of molten lead and a roughly worked stone block.

F18: Hearth in Trench III
484.18.0/1.
Castor-ware hunt cup (Fig. 71:41). Hard, creamy fabric with matt black slip.
Five vessels include a flanged bowl and a piedish with lattice burnishing.

F19: Hearth in Trench III
484.19.0/1.
Two non-descript sherds, and there is an iron hook.

F20: Circular post hole in Trench I
It cuts through L13, but is sealed by F21, so is presumably of Saxon date.

F21: Cobbled surface
This was found in all three trenches, though it was patchy in Trench II. It consists of

small flints rammed into L13, and is closely comparable with an early street surface in Gar Street (Biddle 1964). The only associated find in 484.21.0/1 is Roman, but it presumably is part of the street lay-out dating to around 900.

F22—F26: Stake holes
Row of five stake holes running east—west in Trench II. They appeared as voids beneath F27, cutting into L15, and so are of early medieval date.

F27: Chalk floor, in Trench II
Overlies L15, and cut by F28—F32. The floor is made of crushed chalk, and belongs to an early medieval building.

F28: Rectangular pit, in Trench II
This cuts into the floor F27, and is presumably contemporary.
484.28.0/1.
Six cooking-pot sherds including chalk-gritted pottery, probably of twelfth-century date. There was much iron slag and an iron object.

F29: Post-hole in Trench II
Filled with greyish soil and flints, it cuts F27.
484.29.0/1.
One early medieval gritty sherd.

F30, F31: Post-holes in Trench II
As F29, but no finds.

F32: Pit cutting F27, in Trench II
The infill is mainly brown soil.
484.32.0/1.
Eight medieval gritty sherds.
484.32.0/2.
Lightly stamped fragment (Fig. 74:42) in Saxo-Norman gritty fabric. Stamps are radial 'sunburst' patterns.
This is a very mixed group with medieval glazed-jug fragments, grass-wiped sherds, an imported thin, gritty sherd (cf.F35), and Tripod Pitcher Ware. There is also a lump of lead.

F33: Hollow in road silt, in Trench III
Cuts into L16, below L17, filled with loose greyish soil.
484.33.0/2.
Cooking pot (Fig. 74:43). Fine, black, sandy ware, made on a fast wheel. Late Saxon Sandy Ware (Biddle and Collis forthcoming).
Also two sherds of early medieval gritty ware.

F34: Middle street level, in Trench I
Gravel and chalk make-up above F21.
484.34.0/1.
Early medieval gritty sherds.

F35: Upper street level
Gravel, cobbling, and large flints F34, below L20.

484.35.0/1.
Early medieval gritty sherds including a thin imported sherd (cf. F32, and WCP F36, Fig. 98).

L1: *Dirty ginger soil in Trench I*
At the north end, overlying natural, and beneath L2.
484.00.1/1.
Bowl (Fig. 70:44). Harsh, grey to reddish-brown fabric, with grey surface; much fine grit.
Three other fragments, a lid, a jar and a flagon as well as a sherd of Antonine samian all suggest
a late second-century date.

L2: *Ginger soil with chalk in Trench I, overlying L1*
484.00.2/1.
Four vessels are present including a decorated lid and an unusual fine buff sherd with bands of
rouletting.

L3: *Light ginger soil above F2*
484.00.3/1.
There are six non-descript sherds (1 modern) and a piece of Antonine samian.

L4: *Dirty brown soil above L3*
484.00.4/1.
A mortarium, a piedish, and a jar fragment; and there is a worn, stamped samian base of
Antonine date, suggesting an early third-century date.

L5: *Brown soil with many flints, overlying F7, beneath L6, in Trench I*
484.00.5/1.
Internally flanged bowl (Fig. 73:45). Sandy, buff fabric with yellow-brown paint. Not like New
Forest examples.
Fourteen vessels are present, two red colour-coat vessels with grey core, and one in hard, buff ware
with an orange coat, four colour-coat flagons, a beaker, a late Roman cooking pot, a handmade
dish, a lid, a straight-sided dish, and a residual mortarium. There are seven coins, one each of
Victorinus, Claudius II, Tetricus I, Tetricus II, House of Constantine, two of House of
Valentinian, and a radiate minim.

L6: *Light brown soil with flints, overlying L5 and beneath L13, in Trench I*
484.00.6/1.
Seven vessels; a colour-coat flagon and beaker base (both New Forest), and residual material.
There are eleven coins, three of Tetricus I, one Helena, one Constantinopolis, three House of
Constantine, one House of Valentinian, and two illegible.

L7: *Occupation deposit between F11 and F12 in Trench I*
Patches of ash, charcoal and clay.
484.00.7/1.
Beaker (Fig. 73:46). Cream-buff fabric with matt red-brown colour-coat.
Folded beaker (Fig. 73:47). Dull cream fabric with matt brown to orange colour-coat.
Piedish (Fig. 73:48). Black, harsh fabric with sandy grit, black burnished surface with burnished
decoration.
Flagon (Fig. 73:49). Orange-buff fabric with matt brown external colour-coat decorated with
thick white paint. New Forest.
Mortarium (Fig. 73:50). White to pinkish fabric with grey core, flint and chert grits; incised
decoration.
Storage jar (Fig. 73:51). Dull grey-brown fabric, black surface, coarse gritty, with some grog.
There are fragments of 24 vessels; seven New Forest beakers, one incised (cf. Cunliffe 1964 Fig.

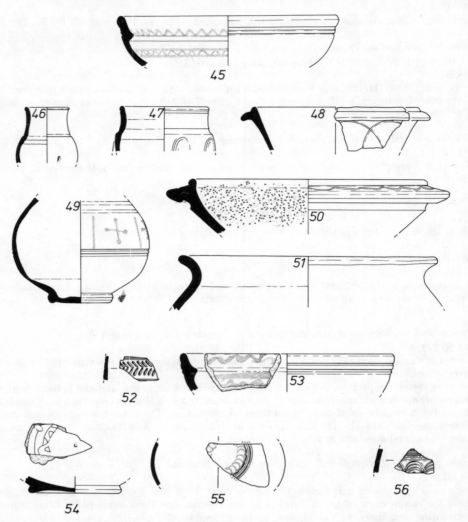

Fig. 73. Frederick Place: late Roman pottery from L5 (45), L7 (46—51), L8 (52—3), L9 (54—55) and L14 (56) (scale ¼).

61:26) and two flagons (one painted). In addition there are two fine rouletted beakers, and a rope-rimmed storage jar. Also a piece of limestone.

L8: *Ashy occupation and clayey gravel, above F12, beneath L9, in Trench I*
484.00.8/1.
Beaker (Fig. 73:52). Fine, hard, mauve fabric, black colour-coat, incised decoration.
Internally flanged bowl (Fig. 73:53). Fine, off-white, sandy ware, with red-brown paint.
Also a fragment of a storage jar, c.f. F10, 484.10.0/4. There is one coin, possibly radiate.

L9: *Dark soil above L8, and underlying L13*
There are oysters, roofing slabs and lumps of brick.

484.00.9/1.
Base of internally flanged bowl (Fig. 73:54). Off-white, sandy ware with dull brown paint.
Flagon (Fig. 73:55). Hard, dull mauve fabric, with matt brown external colour-coat, and white painted decoration. New Forest.
At least 23 pots are present. Of New Forest colour-coat wares there are three flagons (two painted), two folded beakers, and an incised beaker like L7. Not New Forest are an orange beaker and a buff sherd with brown painted decoration. Grey wares with white or grey slip are important, with one flagon neck and three or four jars with everted rims, which perhaps replace the black burnished jars which predominate in F10. There are two straight-sided dishes and a flagon in grey wares, and a storage jar with light burnished incised lattice made with an eight-toothed comb, a distinctive type which also occurs at Silchester (Collis forthcoming). The layer produced a mint coin of Crispus, a glass fragment, and second-century samian.

L10: A mortary level overlying F16 in Trench III
484.00.10/1.
Late Roman cooking-pot rims and a lid.

L11: Dirty brown soil above F15 in Trench III
484.00.11/1.
Mixed second- to fourth-century sherds (12 vessels), and there are three Hadrianic samian sherds.

L12: Light chalky soil over F5, and cut by F8, in Trench I
Only an iron object and a fragmentary bronze ring.

L13: 'Late Roman Black', in all trenches
This deposit, easily distinguished by its very black, sometimes greasy nature and its mass of abraded late Roman sherds and coins, is found throughout Winchester. It could represent post-Roman cultivation. At Frederick Place it is notably thin over the track, and thicker above the pits. None of the pots are illustrated, but a sherd count reveals the following statistics: red colour-coat wares nine vessels (one rouletted), five colour-coat flagons, twenty colour-coat beakers, two buff mortaria, three straight-sided dishes, four cavetto rim jars (two black burnished), two late Roman cooking pots with everted rims, and nineteen other vessels: a total of sixty-eight vessels. The high incidence of red colour-coat forms a contrast with the earlier deposits. There are thirty-eight coins, three Claudius II, one Constantine I, one Helena, three Constantinopolis, two Urbs Roma, four Constantine II, one Constans, one Constantius, four House of Constantine, two Valentinian I, two House of Valentinian, one Magnus Maximus, four minims and nine illegible. There is a glass bead, a fragment of bronze bracelet, and of bronze chain. Unusually from Trench III there are some pieces of daub.

L14: Clean mauve-coloured silt, overlying F21 in Trench II
484.00.14/1.
Sherd (Fig. 73:56). Light grey fabric, with fine, black, sandy grit, and combed decoration. Presumably Roman.
All the other nine sherds are residual Roman, including an internally flanged bowl.

L15: Mauve-brown silt with charcoal flecks, above L15, below F27, in Trench II
484.00.15/1.
Saxo-Norman cooking pots including three rims in gritty ware and one sandy sherd. Tenth to eleventh century.
There is a piece of Purbeck marble.

L16: Grey, gritty silt, lying on F21, in Trench III

484.00.16/1.
A Roman flagon base.

L17: Rubbish deposit in Trench III

The lower level is redeposited Late Roman Black, but most of the finds come from loose grey-brown soil with oysters. Despite being immediately below the surface the group seems uncontaminated.

484.00.17/1—2.
Cooking pot (Fig. 74:57), in hard, brown-black fabric with fine temper. Saxon type.
Sherd (Fig. 74:58). Hard, orange-buff fabric with a band of roller-stamp decoration round the rim. Fabric similar to Winchester Ware, but unglazed.
Winchester Ware sherd (Fig. 74:59). Hard, buff, sand-tempered fabric with glossy olive-green to orange glaze which overlies a spiral ornament consisting of a raised band and a roller stamp decoration.
Cooking pot (Fig. 73:60) in standard Saxo-Norman gritted fabric.
Spout or handle of a bowl (Fig. 73:61) in standard Saxo-Norman gritted fabric. There is a circular hole at the base of the handle, bored after firing.
Cooking pots (Fig. 73:62—64) in standard Saxo-Norman gritted fabric.
Cooking pot (Fig. 73:65) in light brown to grey, hard, sand-tempered fabric.
Cooking pots (Fig. 73:66, 67) in standard Saxo-Norman gritted fabric.

L18: Dirty black soil with oysters and iron slag lying on floor F27 in Trench II

484.00.18/1.
Early medieval, gritty-ware cooking pots including chalk-tempered wares, and two sandy sherds. Twelfth century.

L19: Dark brown soil above L18 in Trench II

Firm at the top, and looser beneath, it represents a garden soil.
484.00.19/1.
Finds extend from the twelfth century to post-medieval, and there are glazed roofing tiles.

L20: Grey-brown soil in Trench I

This was homogeneous throughout Trench I, and lay directly on the early medieval street surface. During levelling for the car park, tips of chalk were noted, implying this was a dumped deposit.
484.00.20/1.
Finds are mainly seventeenth century, and there are fragments of glazed ridge tiles. The iron objects were right at the base of the level lying on the street surface.

The Finds

The Roman Coins by R. Reece

Provenance	Museum Coin Number	Reference	Date A.D.
F7-1	C 1647	Gordian III, hybrid with reverse Uberitas Aug	238—44
F7-1	C 1648	Postumus, RIC 83	260—68
F7-1	C 1649	Tetricus I, RIC 123	270—73
F7-1	C 1650	Barbarous radiate, reverse from Invictus	270—90
F7-1	C 1651	Barbarous radiate, reverse Sacrificial Implements	270—90

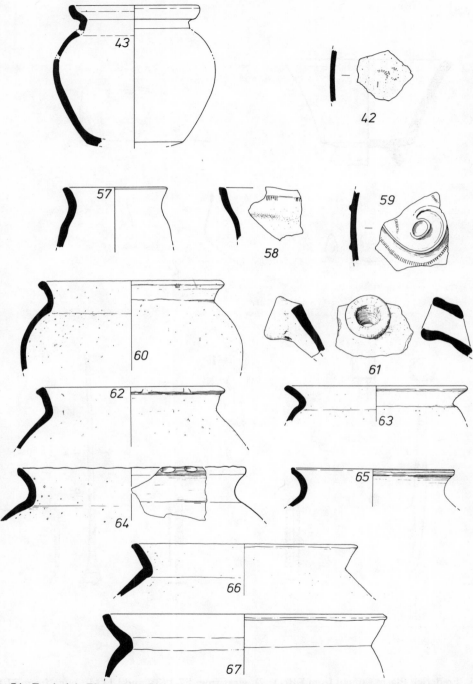

Fig. 74. Frederick Place: late Saxon and early medieval pottery from F33 (43), F32 (42) and L17 (57—67) (scale ¼).

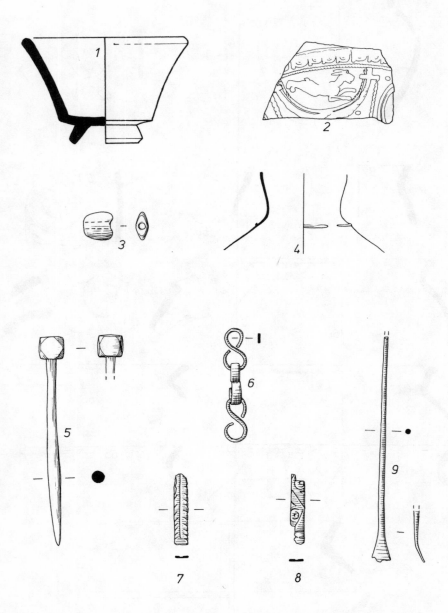

Fig. 75. Frederick Place: samian from F10 (1, 2), glass from F7-1 (3), and L13 (4), bone from F7-1 (5) and bronze objects from L13 (6—8) and F15 (9) (scale 1, 2, 4:¼; 3, 5—9: 1/1).

Provenance	Museum Coin Number	Reference	Date A.D.
F7-2	C 1652	Gallienus, RIC 280	260—68
F7-2	C 1653	Salonina, coin now lost	260—68
F7-2	C 1654	Barbarous radiate, reverse from Pax	270—90
F7-2	C 1655	Claudius II, reverse illegible	268—70
F7-2	C 1656	Tetricus II, as RIC 248	270—73
F7-2	C 1657	Barbarous radiate, reverse from Pax	270—90
L5	C 1658	Victorinus, RIC 118	268—70
L5	C 1659	Claudius II, RIC 266	268—70
L5	C 1660	Tetricus I, RIC 80	270—73
L5	C 1661	Tetricus II, RIC 272	270—73
L5	C 1662	Barbarous radiate, otherwise illegible	270—90
L5	C 1663	House of Constantine, copy as CK 25	350—60
L5	C 1664	House of Valentinian, as CK 275	364—78
L5	C 1665	House of Valentinian, as CK 96	364—78
L6	C 1666	Tetricus I, RIC 77	270—73
L6	C 1667	Tetricus I, RIC 86	270—73
L6	C 1668	Tetricus I, RIC 133	270—73
L6	C 1669	Constantinopolis, as HK 52	330—40
L6	C 1670	House of Constantine, as HK 137	345—48
L6	C 1671	House of Constantine, as CK 77	356—61
L6	C 1672	House of Constantine, copy as CK 25	350—60
L6	C 1673	House of Valentinian, as CK 96	364—78
L6	C 1674	Disintegrated	—
L6	C 1675	Helena, as HK 112	337—40
L6	C 1676	3rd-4th C illegible	—
L8	C 1677	Radiate, otherwise illegible	260—96
L9	C 1678	Crispus, RIC VII Trier 431	322—24
L13	C 1679	Claudius II, RIC 261	268—70
L13	C 1680	Claudius II, RIC 261	268—70
L13	C 1681	Claudius II, reverse illegible	268—70
L13	C 1682	Barbarous radiate, reverse from Spes	270—90
L13	C 1683	Barbarous radiate, reverse from Spes	270—90
L13	C 1684	Constantine I, RIC VI Trier 896	310—17
L13	C 1685	Helena, copy as HK 119	337—50
L13	C 1686	Constantinopolis, as HK 52	330—35
L13	C 1687	Constantinopolis, HK 52	330—35
L13	C 1689	House of Constantine, Hybrid HK 48/HK 51	330—45
L13	C 1690	Urbs Roma, copy as HK 51	330—45
L13	C 1691	Constantine II, HK 379	330—35
L13	C 1692	House of Constantine, copy as HK 49	330—45
L13	C 1693	House of Constantine, copy as HK 49	330—45
L13	C 1694	Constantine II, as HK 49	330—40
L13	C 1695	Constantine I, as HK 48	330—40
L13	C 1696	Constans, HK 142	345—48
L13	C 1697	Constantius II, CK 254	350—60
L13	C 1698	House of Constantine, otherwise illegible	330—45
L13	C 1699	House of Constantine, as HK 112	330—45
L13	C 1700	House of Constantine, as HK 137	345—48
L13	C 1701	Valentinian I, as CK 275	364—78
L13	C 1702	Valentinian I, as CK 275	364—78

Provenance	Museum Coin Number	Reference	Date A.D.
L13	C 1703	House of Valentinian, as CK 96	364—78
L13	C 1704	House of Valentinian, as CK 96	364—78
L13	C 1705	Magnus Maximus, CK 560	387—88
L13	C 1706	4th C, otherwise illegible	
L13	C 1707	4th C, otherwise illegible	
L13	C 1708	4th C, otherwise illegible	
L13	C 1709	4th C, otherwise illegible	
L13	C 1710	4th C, otherwise illegible	
L13	C 1711	4th C, otherwise illegible	
L13	C 1712	Completely illegible	
L13	C 1713	Lost	
L13	C 1714	Lost	
L13	C 1715	3rd—4th C, illegible	
L13	C 1716	3rd—4th C, illegible	

The Samian by G. Dannell

Provenance	Museum Accession Number	Form	Date A.D.	Kiln	Comments
F2	484.2.0/2	31	2nd century	—	
		18/31	2nd century	—	
		38	2nd century	—	
F3	484.3.0/2	36	Trajanic(?)	central Gaul	
F10	484.10.0/11	33	late 2nd century		Extremely poor and presumably late example. Profile exhibits external concavity closer to Drag. 46, and fabric is little better than earthenware. Difficult to decide in such cases whether or not vessel is true samian, but there does seem to be something better than a mere colour-coat, and complete foot is a good type. Unstamped. (Fig. 75:1).
	484.10.0/10	37	Antonine	eastern Gaul	Showing 0.1844 in a semi-circular wreath. Used by many potters of Rheinzabern, and this example may be of COBNERTUS (Fig. 75:2).

Provenance	Museum Accession Number	Form	Date A.D.	Kiln	Comments
	484.10.0/12	37	1st century	southern Gaul	
	484.10.0/13	27	Trajanic	central Gaul	
	484.10.0/14	31R	Hadrianic/ Antonine	central Gaul	
	484.10.0/15	31	Antonine	—	
	484.10.0/16	31	Antonine	—	Stamped]ICIM retrograde
F15	484.15.0/2	33	2nd century	—	
L1	484.00.1/2	31	Antonine	central Gaul	
L3	484.00.3/2	31	Antonine	central Gaul	
L4	484.00.4/2	31	Antonine	—	Stamped PA////IA/// PATRICIANUS (?)
L9	484.00.9/2	35/36	2nd century	central Gaul(?)	Burnt.
L11	484.00.11/2	31	Hadrianic	central Gaul	
	484.00.11/3	33	Hadrianic	central Gaul	
	484.00.11/4	79	Hadrianic	central Gaul	
L13	484.00.13/4	chip	2nd century	central Gaul(?)	Burnt.

The Glass by D. Charlesworth

Provenance	Museum Accession Number	Description
F7-1	484.4	Part of the neck and shoulder of a flask or jug in good colourless glass, trail round the base of the neck (Fig. 75:4). For possible shape see F. Fremersdorf, *Die Denkmäler des römischen Köln*, IV, Pl. 28-30.
L9	484.5	Two unidentifiable fragments of thin colourless glass.
L13	484.6	Emerald green glass bead, diamond-shaped section. A simple type, impossible to date (Fig. 75:3).

Miscellaneous Finds

Fig. No.	Provenance	Museum Accession Number	Description
Bone and Bronze Objects			
75:5	F7-1	484.39	Bone pin with octohedral head.
75:6	L13	484.24	Bronze chain with 3 interlocking links.
75:7	L13	484.23	Bronze strip with notched decoration and central groove, possibly from a bracelet.
75:8	L13	484.25	Bronze strip with incised ring-and-dot decoration, a common form of decoration on bracelets (e.g. Frere 1972, Fig. 32:33, 34).
75:9	F15	484.26	Bronze ointment spoon.
—	F10	484.40	Bone pin (mislaid).
—	F34	484.37	Bronze object with incised interlace (mislaid).

Fig. No.	Provenance	Museum Accession Number	Description
—	F7-3	484.29	Bracelet fragment with cog-like protruberances around its circumference (mislaid).

Roman Iron Objects by W. H. Manning

76:1	F7-1	484.30	Fragment of a figure-of-eight loop. Length 9·9 cm. Function uncertain, but not from a chain.
76:2	F7-1	484.31	Fragment consisting of broad tang, now broken, with a ferrule around one end. Tang tapers from edge of ferrule (where it is 2 cm wide) and is set to one side of ferrule with gap filled with lead to hold it in place. Ferrule is formed of a strip bent into a rectangle. Length 5·0 cm. Part of a tool or heavy knife.
76:3	F11	484.32	U-shaped staple or dog. Length 4·4 cm. May be compared to examples from Verulamium (Frere 1972: 184, Fig. 68, 84, 85, and examples cited there).

Medieval Iron Objects by I. Goodall

76:4	L17	484.47	Iron knife with incomplete whittle tang and blade.
76:5	F34	484.46	Horseshoe fragment with countersunk nailholes and plain edge.
76:6	F35	484.45	Horseshoe with countersunk nailholes, wavy edge and calkin to complete arm.

Stone Objects by F. R. Hodson and I. M. West

Small slab of stone (484.41, Fig. 77:1) with three smoothed sides from L15. From an early medieval level. This rock is Purbeck Marble. It is a limestone mainly composed of fossil pond-snail shells and it has been worked from the Upper Purbeck Beds of the Isle of Purbeck. It outcrops between Peveril Point, Swanage, and Stair Hole, Lulworth. In thin-section the rock is a biomicrudite in which the shell remains are mostly of *Viviparus cariniferus* and various pelecypods. The gastropods are uncrushed and unfilled with sediment except near the aperture and this indicates that the rock was lithified before any great overburden had caused compaction. The original shell material, probably mostly aragonite, has been replaced by cystalline calcite at fairly late stage. Some pleochroic calcite is present within the shell remains, and phosphatic fragments are probably of bone or scale. The reddish-brown colour of the rock is due to the oxidation of numerous sublenticular siderite crystals present in the micrite matrix. A green, moderately birefringent clay mineral is present within veins and shell fragments and has long been regarded as glauconite (*sensu lato*).

An irregular block of roughly shaped stone (484.43, Fig. 77:2) associated with the hearth F17. It is late Roman. This is a cherty limestone with some fine quartz sand and with much opaline silica and siliceous sponge spicules. Brown grains present may be oxidized glauconite. The rock is probably from the Malmstone of the Upper Greensand of Surrey, Hampshire, or other areas. A rather similar rock has been described from the Warminster area.

A rectangular block (484.44, Fig. 77:3) from which a groove has been roughly chipped. It has not been submitted for identification, but it is a shelly limestone (J.R.C.). From the 'Late Roman Black' L13.

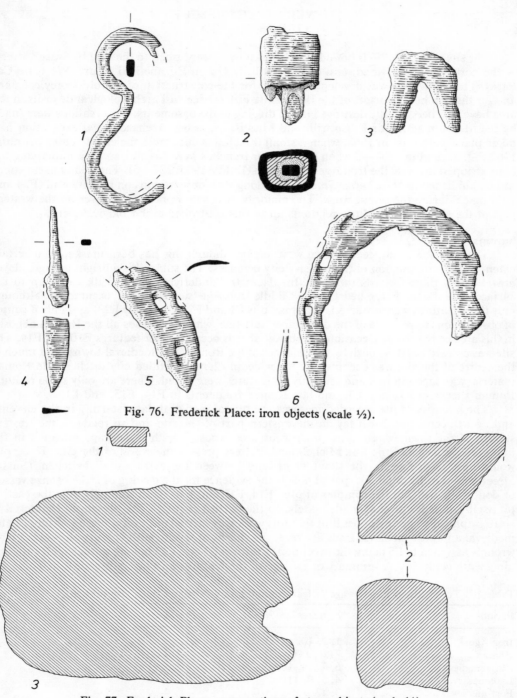

Fig. 76. Frederick Place: iron objects (scale ½).

Fig. 77. Frederick Place: cross sections of stone objects (scale ¼).

TOWER STREET RESCUE
(TSR 65, Site 724)

The site (Figs. 78, 79) is bounded to the east by Tower Street, to the west by Sussex Street, to the north by Tower Road, and to the south by Queen Elizabeth II Court (Westgate Car Park). The whole area was developed in 1965 for the construction of a multi-storey car park and for the new headquarters of the Hampshire Fire service. All archaeological deposits in the area have now been totally destroyed in the digging of the basements. Observations were made by the Museum staff, Mr F. Cottrill, and Miss B. Toogood. Archaeological excavation had taken place on the site in 1960, when a small trench was cut across the city defences (Cunliffe 1962 Fig. 3), and in 1964—5 when three larger trenches were cut and an area underlying the bank stripped to reveal the Iron Age occupation (Biddle 1965: 234—5). These later excavations will be published in *Winchester Studies* 3.i, along with observations on the city wall (F24 and F25) made during the rescue work. The majority of rescue work was however on the western part of the site and bears little relationship to this controlled archaeological work.

Summary

The land slopes noticeably from west to east, though this has been masked to a certain extent by the construction of the massive city defences. The sub-soil is a bright orange, clayey gravel which thins towards the west. In places the underlying solid chalk came up to the surface. The site lies in the heart of the Middle Iron Age 'saucepan-pot' occupation, although only three features were observed, two small pits F1 and F2 and a gully F23, and only a couple of observations were made of the distinctive 'turf-line' which underlies all the Roman deposits in this area of the town. Occasional Iron Age sherds occur in later features F10 and F14. The site was crossed north—south by the defences of the Roman and medieval towns, and much of the centre of the site was occupied by the wide and largely infilled city ditch. Little Roman material was encountered, and certainly no features were noted. There are only some residual Roman sherds in F16 and L1, and late Roman fragments in F14, F15, and L1.

The majority of the recorded features are pits of medieval date, starting in the eleventh and twelfth centuries. Most lay on the western part of the site and so relate to the western suburb of the town, a relatively prosperous area whose wealth is perhaps reflected in the imported pottery and the fine Michelmersh pottery present in several of the pits. These pits would have been dug on the shoulder of land between the extra-mural 'twitchen' (Sussex Street) and the city ditch. Of special note is the evidence for the casting of large bronze vessels or doubtfully bells, in the complex of pits, F14, F15 and F16. Unfortunately only the casting pit itself is dated, and that inadequately, to the twelfth century. The presence of material in stratigraphically later pits does hint that this work was carried out over a period of time. Later medieval and post-medieval finds are rare, the sherds of seventeenth century slip-ware plates wrongly assigned to F5 being the exception. Features F3 and F13 belong to the eighteenth and nineteenth centuries. A summary of the age of the features and layers is shown in Table 16.

Table 16. Tower Street Rescue: age of features and layers (x=later finds also present).

Period	Features	Layers
Iron Age	1, 2, 10, 14 (x), 23	
Roman	7 (x), 14 (x), 15, 16	1 (x)
Early medieval	6, 7, 14, 18, 19, 20, 21, 22	
Late medieval	4, 5, 9, 11(x)	
Post-medieval	3, 13	1

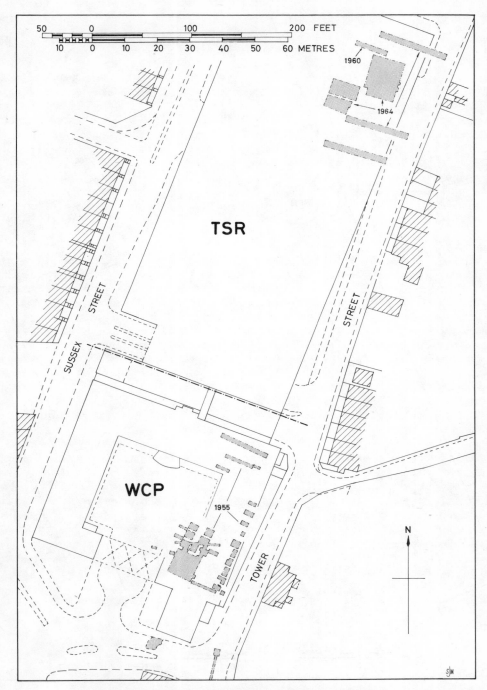

Fig. 78. Tower Street and Westgate Car Park: general plan.

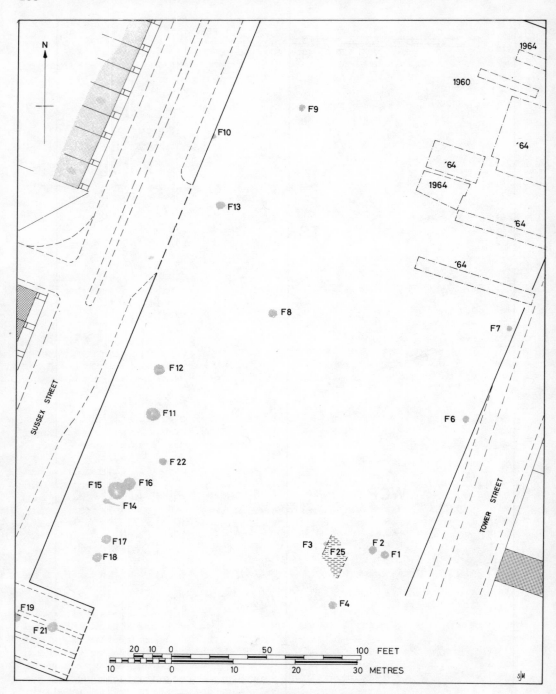

Fig. 79. Tower Street: plan of features.

Features and Layers

F1: *Iron Age pit A*

The pit is 0·80 m deep and 0·45 m wide, cut into natural. It is sealed by the Iron Age turf line, F1-1, which is 0·30 m thick. The infill is grey soil, F1-2.
724.1.2/1.
Thirteen fragments of a vessel in chert-tempered fabric and a small, sandy sherd.

F2: *Iron Age pit B*

The pit is 1·03 m across and 30 cm deep in natural. It is sealed by the turf line. The fill F2-2 is not described.
724.2.2/1.
A hard grey-black sherd with orange surface, with fine grits and occasional lumps of chert.

F3: *Pit C*

A nineteenth century pit cut into the footings of the City Wall.

F4: *Pit D*

A medieval pit just behind the City Wall, and cutting the Roman chalk foundations. It is 1·40 m in diameter. F4-1 is infill of flints and dark yellow mortar. It was dug by the mechanical excavator.

724.4.0/1.
Jug (Fig. 83:1). Fine, smooth, pink to buff fabric, with speckly iron-green glaze, and fine, combed decoration on the collar and shoulder. The base has a raised base and medium-sized, regular, deep indented foot ring impressions, and there are heavily scored trim marks at the base. It has a plain solid rod handle, and the body had been pierced through for it to be fastened at the base of the handle.
724.4.0/2.
Jug (Fig. 83:2). Sandy, pink-coloured fabric with an iron-green glaze. Only the stub of the rod-sectioned handle remains, fastened from the inside, and the resultant boss makes the handle stand proud; this bottom fixing is embellished by a teardrop-shaped, thumbed indentation.
724.4.0/3.
Fragment of a medium-sized jug (Fig. 83:3) in a very smooth, untempered, soft, red fabric, with a glaze in a coarse brown colour, heavily flecked with black specks. The outside is decorated with applied strips, iron-rich so they appear black, and this slip is very coarse to the touch. There are also circular pads of the same material which have been impressed with stamps in a group pattern. It has a pronounced foot ring with a deep indentation at regular intervals. There is a rim possibly from the same vessel from the Westgate Car Park, F37 (Fig. 102:74).
724.4.0/4.
Cooking pot (Fig. 83:4) as 5, but oxidized fabric.
Cooking pot (Fig. 83:5). Globular, grass-wiped vessel in hard, very black and sandy fabric. It has a simple everted rim, slightly bulbous at the top.
724.4.0/5.
This bag contains two rims of cooking pots as vessel 5 but simpler, and a piece with shallow flat strap decoration. There are also fragments of at least seven jugs: a rim in red fabric with a green glaze; the base of an over-fired jug with no foot ring and shallowly wiped indentations and with evidence of upside-down stacking in the kiln; a local form of handle with a double edged flange and slightly bulbous middle section in a pale grey, sandy fabric with iron-green glaze; a similar handle with the central portion decorated with a rouletted diamond pattern; three jugs in a fine, sandy fabric with decoration apparently with areas of panelling defined by vertical applied strips with pellets in between. The pellets may be boldly coloured or black slip. One has apple-green

glaze with pierced pellets at the top of each strip, another has orange glaze with black pellets in the centre of the panel, and the third an iron-rich slip wash in the panels leaving the strips green, the panels brown and the pellets black.

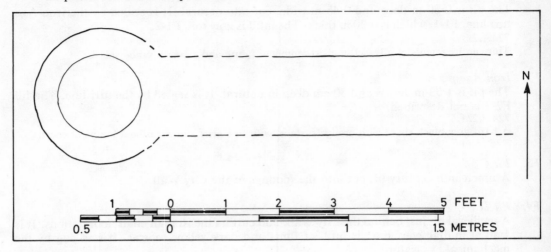

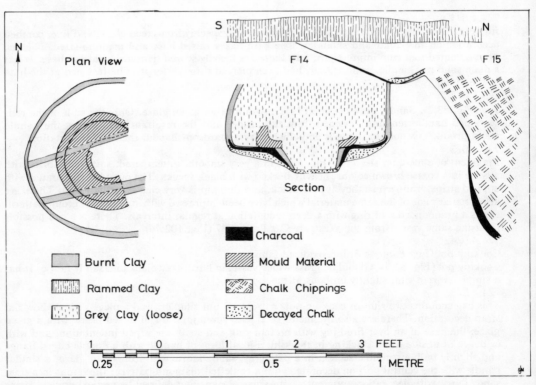

Fig. 80. Tower Street: bronze casting pit, F13. Top: plan, Bottom: plan and section.

F5:   *Pit E*

A pit cutting through the footings of the City Wall; it was excavated mechanically. Presumably of fifteenth-century date.

F5-1:   Possibly from this pit
724.5.1/1.
Two weathered rim sherds of eighteenth-century slip-ware bowls, and in view of the date of the definitely stratified finds, the field observation was obviously wrong.

F5-2:   Definitely from the pit
724.5.2/1.
A late fourteenth-century group including three standard undecorated jugs with rod handles and three fragments of cooking pot.

F6:   *Pit F*

Pit cut through the Roman city bank. Excavated mechanically.
724.6.0/1.
Small cooking pot (Fig. 82:6) with flint temper.
Cooking pot (Fig. 82:7) as 11 but heavily reduced.
Large cooking pot (Fig. 82:8) as 11, oxidized within.
Cooking pot (Fig. 82:9), fabric as 11, with a groove around the base of the collar.
Bowl (Fig. 82:10) in fabric as 11, with crude fettling around the base.
Cruzie lamp (Fig. 82:11). In partially oxidized, partially reduced fabric, coarse with burnt flint and chalk temper.
724.6.1/2.
Body sherds of similar vessels and also a completely reduced sherd with sandy fabric from a wheel-turned vessel. The quality of the wares is similar to normal Saxo-Norman wares, but more brittle, indicating firing control; most are wheel turned, and generally a late twelfth-century date should be considered.

F7:   *Pit G*

Pit in the east face of the contractors' excavation.
724.7.0/2.
A standard Saxo-Norman cooking-pot rim, and there is a chip of first-century samian.

F8:   *Medieval well*
Sectioned 9 m below the modern surface. No finds.

F9:   *Pit I*
Medieval pit mechanically excavated.
724.9.0/1.
Cooking pot (Fig. 83:12) in hard, semi-oxidized, semi-reduced fabric, of the bulbous grass-marked type.
724.9.0/2.
Cooking pot (Fig. 83:13) as 12 but with occasional quartz grits and some coloured stains on the outside, which were caused by a copper by-product, indicating that in the kiln it may have been in contact with other vessels glazed with copper.

F10: *Pit J*

A feature noted from 1·5 m to 3·2 m below the ground surface. It is 60 cm wide and cut at an angle.
F10-1: Loam and garden soil
F10-2: Chalk infill above the pit
F10-3: Loam with chalk fragments

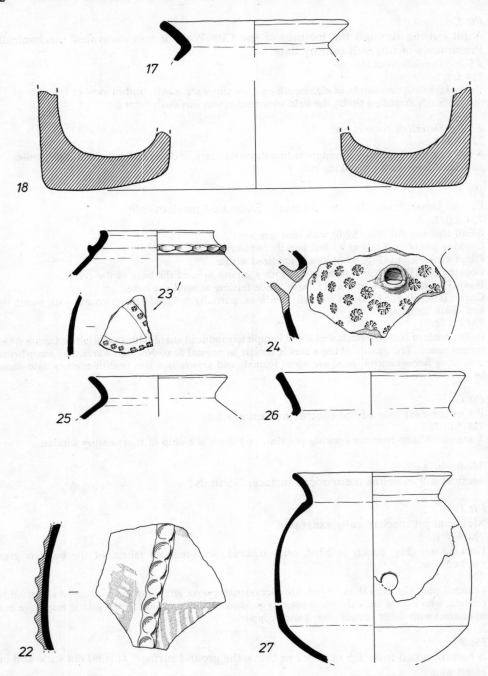

Fig. 81. Tower Street: medieval pottery and mould from F14 (17, 18) and medieval pottery from F21 (23—26), F20 (22) and F22 (27) (scale ¼).

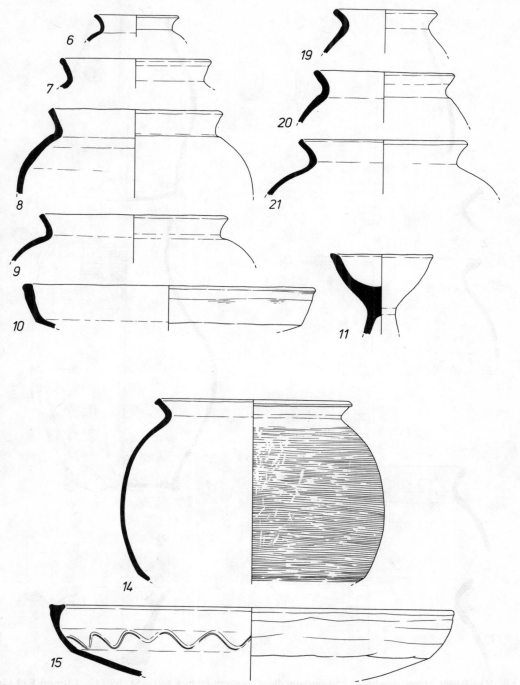

Fig. 82. Tower Street: medieval pottery from F6 (6—11), F19 (19—21) and F11 (14, 15) (scale ¼).

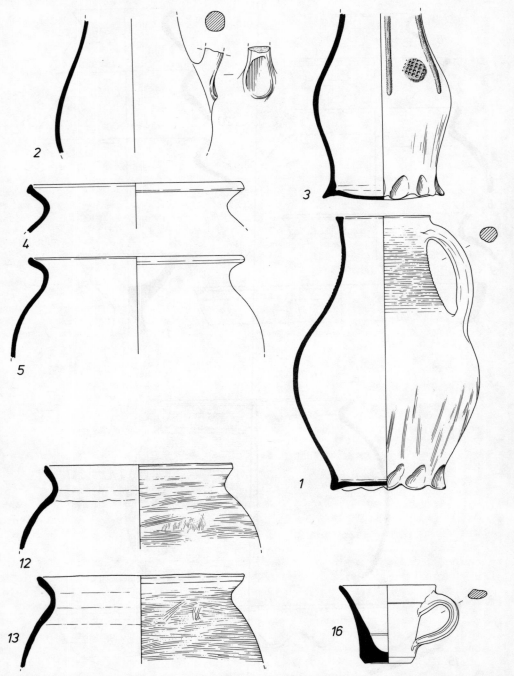

Fig. 83. Tower Street: medieval and post-medieval pottery from F4 (1—5), F9 (12, 13) and F13 (16) (scale ¼).

724.10.3/1.
A gritty Iron Age sherd, and a fragment of brick, perhaps modern.

F11: *Pit K*

Pit in the north face of the contractors' excavation, excavated mechanically.
724.11.0/1.
Cooking pot (Fig. 82:14). Fine, sandy, reduced ware with simple, flat-topped rim which has a slightly downward pointed flange. It is well thrown, and the whole outside surface has been horizontally wiped.
Large dish (Fig. 82:15) in pale grey fabric with brown oxidized surface. Incised wavy-line pattern on the inside. Well thrown.
724.11.0/2.
A fragment of a wide-based, deeply thumbed jug with slightly sagging base, and a tripod pitcher of identical characteristics, except that it does not have the indentations, but a foot lug which is set back from the edge. Associated are large wall sherds, perhaps from these vessels, with evidence of a light combed decoration on the glaze which resembles grass wiping, and this glaze has been partially oxidized. The fabric is pale grey and slightly sandy, with iron flecks probably from the sand tempering, and these show through the glaze as green flecks. There is also the base of a large open vessel with internal glazing (probably a dish which has seen a lot of wear) and this is in identical fabric. The fabric of 15 is not dissimilar.
724.11.0/3.
A globular cooking pot, very misshapen, but certainly of the grass-wiped series, and fragments of cooking pots with sandy ware as 14.
This group is very interesting in that it approximates to the pottery from Orchard Street, which is from a time when pottery styles in this area were changing. The jugs are new additions, the bowls are new additions, but the cooking pots are traditional. An important group which should date between 1260 and 1280.

F12: *Pit L*

Presumably medieval, but with no finds.

F13: *Pit M*

A well, lined with chalk blocks.
724.13.0/1.
A stoneware cup or mortar (Fig. 83:16). The handle is not English nor is the fastening. Although it is not immediately apparent what its origin was, it may possibly be German, eighteenth century. There was also two complete glass phials.

F14: *Pit N, a casting pit*

A length of the flue and the casting chamber (Fig. 80) were excavated by hand, but the intervening part was destroyed by the mechanical excavator. The pit was cut into the natural chalk which was highly disintegrated due to the effects of the heat.

The flue was 46 cm wide and 30 cm deep and ran for at least 2 m to the east from the casting pit, and also went through the pit to its back wall. The sides were partly lined with burnt clay about 3 cm thick. At the bottom were 2—3 cm of charcoal (F14-2) overlain by mixed clay, decomposed chalk, burnt clay, and charcoal (F14-1).

The field notes state that the layer of charcoal continued within the chamber itself with burnt clay above (F14-7) sealed by grey clay (F14-6), though the drawn section conflicts with this. The chamber produced the charcoal layer F14-5 sealed with a smear of clay (F14-4) apparently laid down at the time of use of the kiln, overlain by the grey clay F14-3. The chamber, preserved to a height of 23 cm above the chamber floor, was also lined with 2—3 cm of clay.

The circular mould for the bronze vessel had been placed across the flue in the centre of the chamber. Part of the base for the outer mould was preserved (Fig. 81:18), but there was no trace of the core. The inner part of the mould is eroded, and the original shape is not preserved. However, the angle seems wrong for a bell, and perhaps a mortar or a cauldron is more possible.

F14-1: Upper fill of the flue
724.14.1/1.
A residual Iron Age sherd, three Roman sherds, and a rim sherd of the large gritty cooking pot, vessel 17. There is one iron fragment.

F14-3: Grey clay in the firing chamber
724.14.3/1.
A fragment of the same medieval cooking pot, 17.

F14-6: Grey clay in the fill of the flue in the combustion chamber
724.14.6/1.
Another rim fragment of the medieval cooking pot, 17, and another early medieval gritty sherd. There is also a piece of bone, a lump of slag, and fragments of mould.
724.14.1/1, 724.14.3/1, 724.14.6/1.
Cooking pot (Fig. 81:17) in standard Saxo-Norman fabric.
Cross section of mould (Fig. 81:18).

F15: Pit O

This pit is adjacent to the casting pit F14. There is infill of broken chalk overlying charcoal.
724.15.0/1.
A fragment of a late Roman folded beaker.

F16: Pit P

The fill is similar to that in F15, with alternating layers of loam and broken chalk. Apparently the feature cuts both F14 and F15.
724.16.0/1.
A fragment of an early Roman jar.
A fragment of mould, for a vessel of larger diameter than that in F14.

F17: Pit Q

No finds or description.

F18: Pit R

Medieval pit. No description.
724.18.0/1.
Grass-marked sherds, including a rim. Mrs Ruth Morgan has identified charcoal from this pit as alder.

F19: Pit S

Medieval pit. No description.
724.19.0/1.
Cooking pot (Fig. 82:19), completely reduced fabric, tempered with chalk and fine calcined flints.
Cooking pot (Fig. 82:20) as 19.
Cooking pot (Fig. 82:21) as 19.

F20: Pit T

Medieval pit. No description.
724.20.0/1.
Sherd (Fig. 81:22), in hard white fabric, with an applied strip which has been thumbed. It is decorated with red paint. Presumably North French.

F21: Pit U
Medieval pit. No description.
724.21.0/1.
Fragments of Michelmersh ware (Fig. 81:23) in a very hard oxidized ware tempered with fine washed sand. One is decorated with applied strips which have been stamped over with diamond shaped quartered stamps. Two fragments are red due to being refired in an oxidizing fire. One is a rim fragment with an applied strip under it which has been carefully thumbed.
Spouted pitcher (Fig. 81:24) in very coarse, partially reduced fabric tempered with fine calcined flint, and with chalk which has washed out leaving a pitted surface. The rim is flared and the collar grooved at the base. The whole of the exterior is covered with wheel stamps.
Cooking pot (Fig. 81:25) in fabric as 24.
Cooking pot (Fig. 81:26) in fabric as 24 with partially reduced, partially oxidized exterior.
There is also a cat skull.

F22: Pit V
Medieval pit. No description.
724.22.0/1.
Cooking pot (Fig. 81:27) in reduced but partially oxidized fabric containing a high proportion of chalk and some calcined flint. The surface is pimply and feels smooth to the touch. At some time the vessel has had a hole pecked in its side.
There is also a plain body sherd from a largish vessel in fabric resembling Michelmersh.

F23: Feature W
An Iron Age gully sectioned by the mechanical excavator. It runs parallel to Tower Street between the city wall and the ditch.
724.23.1/1.
Saucepan pot (Fig. 93:28). Dull brown fabric with black burnished surface, and fine chert grit.
There is a base of a sherd in similar ware but in an oxidized fabric.

F24: Foundations of a tower
These will be discussed in *Winchester Studies* 3.i.

F25: City wall footings
As F24.

L1: Unstratified material
There are fragments of an early Roman buff flagon and a late Roman folded beaker in purple colour-coated ware. Of nineteenth-century date are a small Derbyshire salt-glaze casserole and an earthenware chamber pot.

The Finds

The Samian by G. Dannell
In F7 there was a first-century chip (724.7.0/2) from southern Gaul.

THE WESTGATE CAR PARK 1951—1955
(WCP, Site 483)

The circumstances of the excavation have been published previously, and are not repeated here (Cunliffe 1962:57; 1964:7). A general plan is shown in Figure 84 (see also Plate IVb). The Iron Age finds have been published, and many of the Roman, but none of the medieval. However there are a number of discrepancies in the reports, and most of the finds are republished here, giving the new catalogue number. Some of the finds were ascribed to the wrong features, and some of the Iron Age finds are no longer identifiable in the Museum. In passing it should be noted that the scales in Figure 4 of Cunliffe's 1962 report and in Figure 3

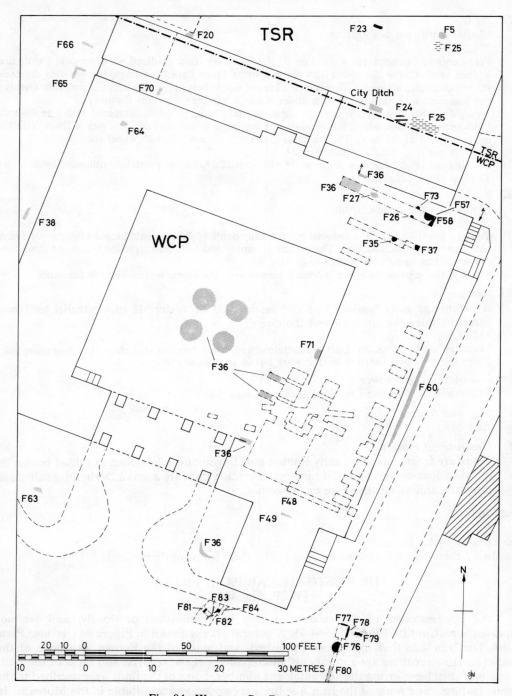

Fig. 84. Westgate Car Park: general plan.

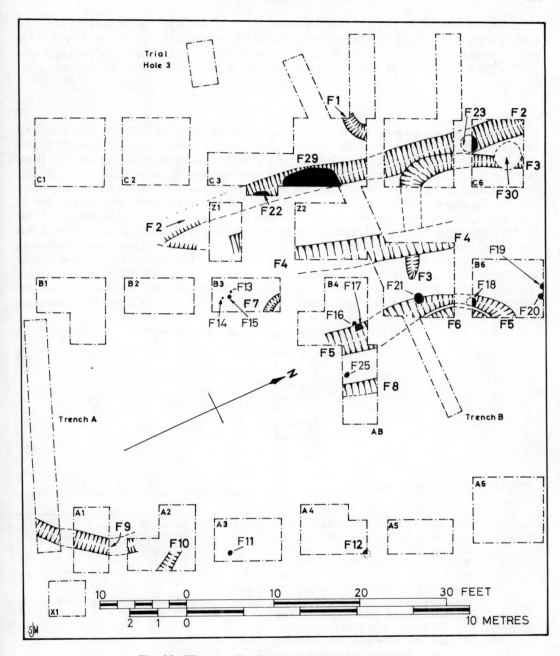

Fig. 85. Westgate Car Park: plan of Iron Age features.

of his 1964 report should be corrected as follows: for 10 ft read 8 ft, for 20 read 16, etc. The width given for the early bank that is shown should be a maximum of 38 ft, not 45—50. One 'post-hole' in trench A3, shown on Figure 3 in Cunliffe (1964), was caused by a leaking drain, and the pit post-hole in B4 was purely natural, and both have been left off this new plan (Fig. 85).

Summary

A few scraps of coarse pottery in the Iron Age levels may be of Late Bronze Age date, and are comparable with a pot containing a cremation found in Tower Street in 1964—5 (Biddle 1965: Pl. 48, Feature 71). The Lankhills cemetery has produced some similar sherds. There was also Early Iron Age activity, identifiable in a number of haematite-coated sherds, including angular furrowed bowls. The main period of occupation was in the Middle Iron Age, with the digging of a series of gullies and post-holes which have produced finds of the St Catharine's Hill saucepan-pot group. The stratigraphic sequence of features is shown in Table 17, the fabric types in Table 18, and the occurrence of finds in Table 19. Full analysis of this assemblage must await the publication of other groups from the city. Over these pre-Roman features there ran a homogeneous layer of dark gravelly clay (L2) containing almost only Iron Age sherds. The Late Iron Age is virtually unrepresented among the finds, and the area was certainly unoccupied in the later first century B.C., up to the time of the construction of the earliest Roman defences in the Flavian period. These run north—south across the site sealing

Table 17. Westgate Car Park: stratigraphic sequence of Iron Age features.

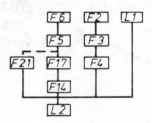

Table 18. Iron Age fabric types*.

Type	Description
1	Coarse, dark brown-black ware with large coarse flint inclusions.
2	Dark brown-black ware with bright red surface, sand tempered, haematite coated.
3	As Type 2 but thicker and coarser.
4	Brown or reddish sherds with coarse flint temper.
5	Black burnished, sand-tempered fabric.
6	Shell-tempered fabric, dull grey, or black wares.
7	Black sherds with reddish surface, much organic temper; possibly salt containers.
8	Black burnished wares with flint temper.
9	Oxidized wares with flint temper.
10	Black burnished wares with burnt flint temper.
11	Oxidized wares with burnt flint temper.
12	Black burnished wares with burnt flint and unburnt flint temper.
13	Oxidized wares with burnt flint and unburnt flint temper.
14	Black burnished wares with burnt and unburnt flint temper with grog.

*Fabric 1 is probably Late Bronze Age, 2—5 Early Iron Age, 5—14 Middle Iron Age.

Table 19. Number of sherds of each fabric type in each feature or layer.

Provenance	Fabric Type														
	1	2	3	4	5	6	7	8	9	10	11	12	13	14	R/B
F1					3		1	5		1		3	1		1
F2			6	3	6			8		2		22	7	2	
F3			1		7		2	12	4	3		28	4	2	
F4					8			7		1		4	1		1
F5/6	1		1		1			4	1	1		1			1
F7					3			7		1		1	1		
F9			3	2	28	16		20	2		8	3			3
F12					1							1			
F22				1		1		3		1	1		2	1	
F24				2								1		1	
F29		1		1	1			1					2	1	
F30												4			1
F35				1				2			1	2			1
Sub-total	1	1	11	8	60	17	3	69	7	11	9	70	17	8	8
L1				1	1								1		
L2	2	12	5	39	50	9	12	82	10	13	3	97	41	3	99
L3				2			1	8				8			7
Sub-total	2	12	5	40	53	9	13	90	10	13	3	105	42	3	106
F31			3		9			21	1			8	6	2	
F37		1	1		5			1					2		
Sub-total		1	4		14			22	1			8	8	2	
Total	3	14	20	48	127	26	16	181	18	24	12	183	67	13	106

the Iron Age level. The finds from these defences and the second-century addition are republished here to demonstrate better their stratigraphic context, but details of the defences in this area have already been discussed (Cunliffe 1962, Biddle 1965). Late Roman finds are notably absent, due in part at least to the planing down of the deposits in this area.

Of special note are two late Saxon pits. There is a group of pits under Tower Street itself (F76—80), but unfortunately only one of these, F79, produced any finds. These are probably ninth century, and this pit presumably pre-dates Tower Street, which at its south end overlies a medieval street that formed part of the late Saxon street system. Pit F71 is rather later to judge from the cooking-pot fabrics. But both these pits contain Late Saxon Sandy Ware datable to the ninth and tenth centuries. This pit presumably lay just behind the line of the City Wall.

As might be expected, the majority of the medieval pits (Fig. 86) are eleventh and twelfth century. Many of the pits listed as 'late' below are in fact twelfth century with tripod-pitcher wares and straw-marked cooking pots, or thirteenth century with decorated jugs. Fourteenth- and fifteenth-century and post-medieval finds are virtually confined to one or two pits in Tower Street, such as F51. This agrees with what we know of the economic decline in this area in the thirteenth century and later. The eleventh and twelfth century pits provide evidence of bronze and iron working in this area.

The majority of the site is covered by the City Ditch. Records of the finds are unfortunately slightly ambiguous, but the deposits on the eastern lip of the ditch (F36, bags 1—7) all contain eleventh-century finds, whereas bag 8 (find spot unknown) contains twelfth. It implies

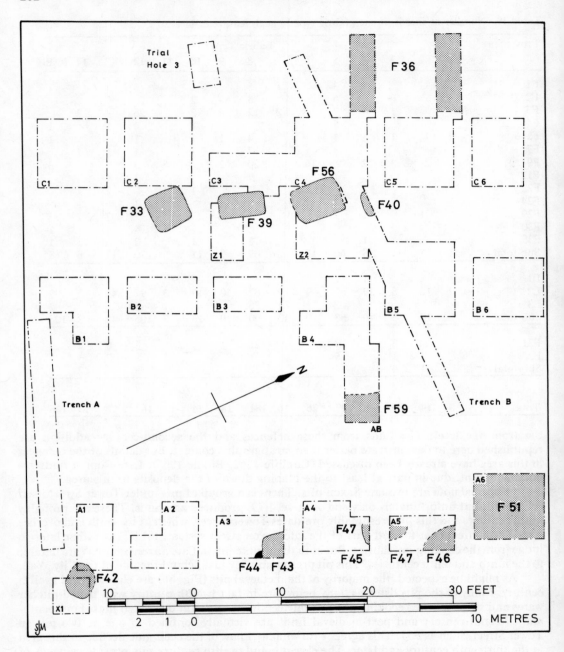

Fig. 86. Westgate Car Park: plan of medieval features.

that part at least of the ditch system was being allowed to fall into disrepair in the early medieval period, and there is evidence of this from City Road as well (Biddle 1975a).

Table 20 shows the age of features and levels in this site.

Table 20. Westgate Car Park: age of features and levels (x=later finds also present).

Period	Features	Layers
Prehistoric	1, 2, 3(x), 4(x), 5(x), 6(x), 7(x), 9(x), 12, 22, 24, 29, 30, 31(x), 32(x), 35(x), 36(x), 37(x), 38(x)	1, 2(x), 3(x), 4(x), 5(x), 6(x), 11(x)
Early Roman	4, 5, 6, 7, 9, 31, 32(x), 34(x), 35, 37(x), 38(x), 43(x), 47(x), 51(x), 58(x), 73	2, 3, 4(x), 5(x), 6(x), 7(x), 9(x), 10(x), 11(x)
Late Roman	4(x), 38(x), 40(x), 58(x), 63(x), 66(x)	4
Early medieval	32(x), 33, 34, 36(x), 37(x), 38(x), 39, 40, 41, 42, 43, 45, 46(x), 47(x), 56, 58, 61, 62, 63(x), 64, 65(x), 66, 67, 68, 69, 71, 75	6, 8, 10, 11
Late medieval	32(x), 36, 37(x), 38(x), 46, 47, 48, 49, 51(x), 60, 63, 65	
Post-medieval	32, 37, 50, 51, 53	5(x), 7

Features and Layers

F1: *Gully 1*
Trench C4, 9·45 m wide, and 0·15 m deep, filled with brown gravelly soil and sealed by a gritty lens.

483.1.0/1.
Saucepan pot (Fig. 87:1). Sparse chert and burnt flint temper, black burnished.
Base (Fig. 87:2). Chert temper, black burnished. Shallow groove above the base.
Jar or bowl (Fig. 87:3). Sand-tempered, black burnished ware.
Base (Fig. 87:4). Burnt flint and chert temper, black burnished.

F2: *Gully 2*
Trenches C3—C6. Gully 0·90—0·45 m wide, and 0·25—0·50 m deep. Filled with brown gravelly soil. Cut by F22 and F23.

483.2.0/2,4,5.
(The bag number of each piece is given in brackets following its description.)
Jar (Fig. 87:5). Black burnished with chert and burnt flint temper (/5).
Jar (?) (Fig. 87:6). Black burnished with sand temper (/5).
Jar (Fig. 87:7). Black burnished with chert temper (/4).
Sherd (Fig. 87:8) decorated with dots and shallow tooling. Black burnished with chert and burnt flint temper (/2).

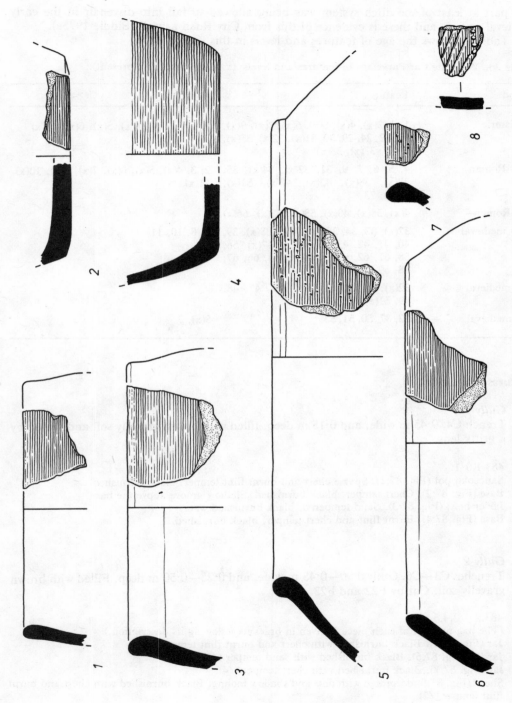

Fig. 87. Westgate Car Park: Iron Age pottery from F1 (1—4) and F2 (5—8) (scale ½).

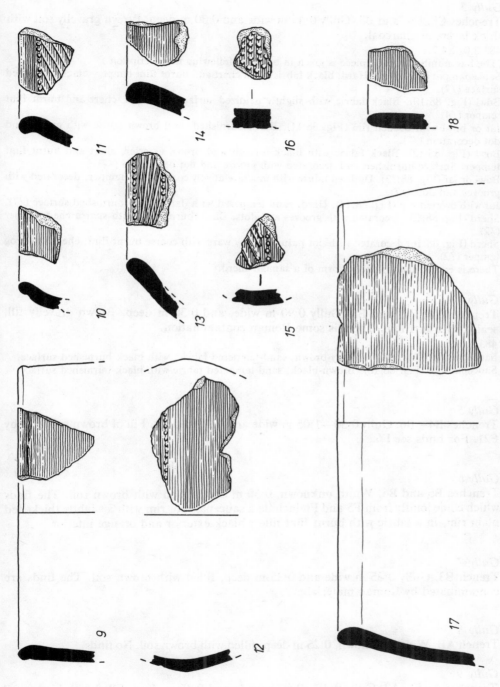

Fig. 88. Westgate Car Park: Iron Age pottery from F3 (9—16) and F4 (17, 18) (scale ½).

F3:   *Gully 3*

Trenches C5, C6, and B5. Gully 0·45 m wide and 0·30 m deep. Brown gravelly soil with thick layers of charcoal.

483.3.0/2,4,7.

(The bag number of each piece is given in brackets following its description.)

Saucepan pot (Fig. 88:9). Hard, black fabric, with chert and burnt flint temper, black burnished surface (/7).

Bowl (Fig. 88:10). Black fabric with slightly oxidized surface in places, chert and burnt flint temper (/4).

Jar or bowl with beaded rim (Fig. 88:11). Black burnished, dull brown fabric with groove and dot decoration (/7).

Bowl (Fig. 88:12). Black fabric with black interior and brown exterior, chert and burnt flint temper. Surface burnished and decorated with groove and dot decoration (/7).

Bowl or jar (Fig. 88:13). Dull red fabric with much relatively coarse chert temper, decorated with grooves and dots (/7).

Jar with everted rim (Fig. 88:14). Hard, sand tempered with dark brown burnished surface (/7).

Sherd (Fig. 88:15) decorated with grooves and dots. Black burnished, with sparse chert temper (/2).

Sherd (Fig. 88:16) decorated with dot pattern. Grey ware with coarse burnt flint, chert and grog temper (/2).

There is contamination in the form of a samian sherd.

F4:   *Gully 4*

Trenches Z1, Z2, and B5. Gully 0·90 m wide, and 0·30 m deep. Brown gravelly fill, sealed by a turf line. There is some Roman contamination.

483.4.0/2.

Saucepan pot (Fig. 88:17). Grey-brown, sand-tempered fabric, with black burnished surface.

Saucepan pot (Fig. 88:18). Brown-black, sand-tempered fabric with black burnished surface.

F5:   *Gully 5*

Trenches B4—B6. Gully 0·30—1·05 m wide and 0·30 m deep. Fill of brown soil. Cut by F21. For finds see F6.

F6:   *Gully 6*

Trenches B5 and B6. Width unknown, 0·30 m deep, filled with brown soil. The finds which come jointly from F5 and F6 include a saucepan-pot rim with a slightly thickened plain rim, in a fabric with burnt flint filler; black exterior and orange interior.

F7:   *Gully 7*

Trench B3. Gully 0·35 m wide and 0·25 m deep, filled with brown soil. The finds are contaminated by Roman material.

F8:   *Gully 8*

Trench AB. Width unknown, 0·25 m deep, filled with brown soil. No finds.

F9:   *Gully 9*

Trenches A, A1, A2. Gully 0·45—0·60 m wide and 0·45 m deep, filled with brown soil

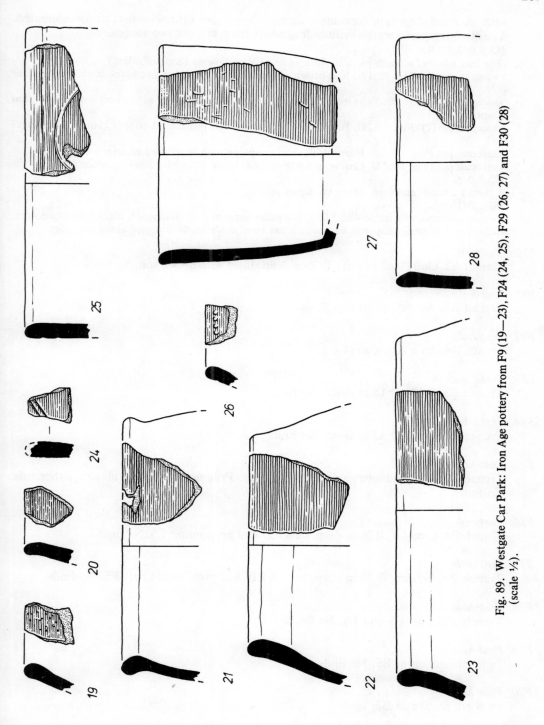

Fig. 89. Westgate Car Park: Iron Age pottery from F9 (19—23), F24 (24, 25), F29 (26, 27) and F30 (28) (scale ½).

with charcoal. One bag contains a Roman sherd, but otherwise it is uncontaminated. The shell-tempered wares include fragments from at least two vessels.
483.9.0/3,5,7,9.
(The bag number of each piece is given in brackets following its description.)
Saucepan pot(?) (Fig. 89:19). Red-brown fabric with chert temper and black burnished surface (/3).
Saucepan pot (Fig. 89:20). Grey ware with orange-grey surface, with chert and burnt flint temper (/7).
Saucepan pot(?) (Fig. 89:21). Black ware with chert and burnt flint temper, burnished surface (/9).
Saucepan pot (Fig. 89:22). Hard black sand tempered with burnished exterior (/5).
Saucepan pot (Fig. 89:23). Coarse, sand-tempered, black ware with brown surface (/3).
483.9.0/6.
A rim of a sand-tempered, black saucepan pot.
483.9.0/10.
Two sherds similar to that in 483.9.0/6, two plain bases in chert-tempered, black burnished ware, and a sherd of shell-tempered ware which has been deliberately trimmed along one edge.

F10: Gully 10
Trench A2. Gully 0·45 m wide, 0·30 m deep, filled with brown soil. No finds.

F11: Post-hole
Trench A3. No details and no finds.

F12: Post-hole
Trench A4. Iron Age sherds.

F13: Stake hole A
Trench B3, 0·12—0·15 m deep. No finds.

F14: Stake hole C
Trench B3, 0·12—0·15 m deep. No finds.

F15: Post-hole
Trench B3, 0·11 m diameter and 0·18 m deep. Fragments of burnt clay on either side. No finds.

F16: Post-hole
Trench B4. Circular, 0·30 m deep, cuts F17 and presumably F5. No finds.

F17: Post-hole
Trench B4. Square, 0·30 m deep, cut by F16 but presumably cuts F5. No finds.

F18: Post-hole
Trench B6. Cuts F5 and F6. No finds.

F19: Post-hole
In north section of B6. No finds.

F20: Post-hole
In north section of B6.

F21: Pit
In trench B5, cuts F5. No finds.

F22: Pit
Trench C3, cuts F2. Iron Age sherds, one chert gritted, with rusticated surface.

F24: Pit
In the north face of the contractors' excavation.
F24-1: Undifferentiated fill
483.24.1/1,2.
Saucepan pot (Fig. 89:24). Black with black burnished surface. Chert and burnt flint temper.
Saucepan pot (Fig. 89:25). Friable, sand-tempered ware with some organic temper. Black burnished with burnished line decoration.

F24-2: From the upper fill
483.24.2/1.
Several sherds of vessel 24.

F24-3: Not securely stratified
483.24.3/1.
Sherd in black ware with red surface, and chert, burnt flint, and grog temper.

F25: Post-hole
In trench AB. No finds or details.

F26: Pit
Trench N. There is charcoal in the fill and a layer of charcoal on the bottom which is burnt red beneath. Presumably sealed by L2. No finds.

F27: Hearth
Trench N. Oval, filled with a layer of grass, twig, and wood charcoal 1—2 cm thick. The ground is reddened beneath and the flints burnt. It is sealed by L2 but produced no finds.

F28: Post-hole
Trench N. Diameter of 4 cm and 6 cm deep.

F29: Pit
Trench C4. Cuts F2.

483.29.0/1,2.
(The bag number of each piece is given in brackets following its description.)
Saucepan pot (Fig. 89:26). Brown, chert-tempered fabric, with black to purple surface. Decorated with dots (/2).
Saucepan pot (Fig. 89:27). Black burnished fabric, tempered with sand and some organic material (/1).

F30: Hearth
Patch of burning in C6, overlying F3.
483.30.0/1.
Saucepan pot (Fig. 89:28). Black burnished ware with chert and burnt flint temper.

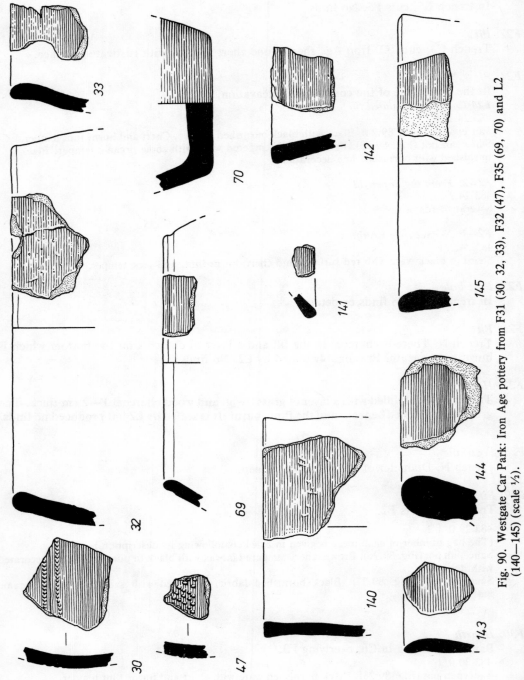

Fig. 90. Westgate Car Park: Iron Age pottery from F31 (30, 32, 33), F32 (47), F35 (69, 70) and L2 (140—145) (scale ½).

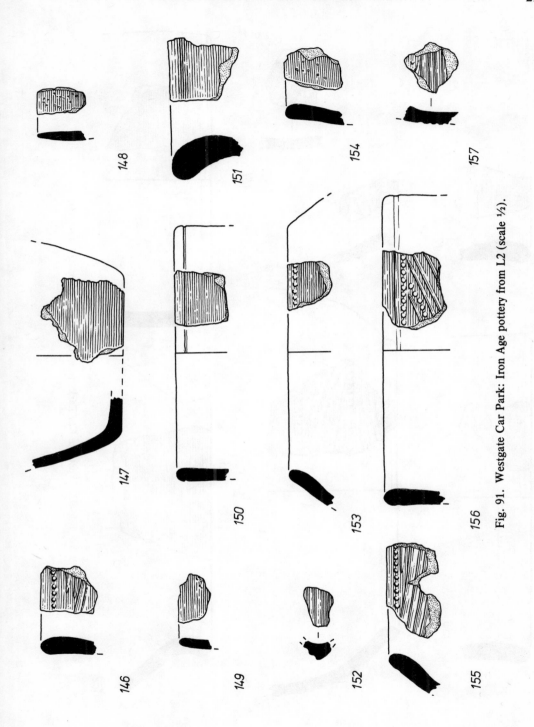

Fig. 91. Westgate Car Park: Iron Age pottery from L2 (scale ½).

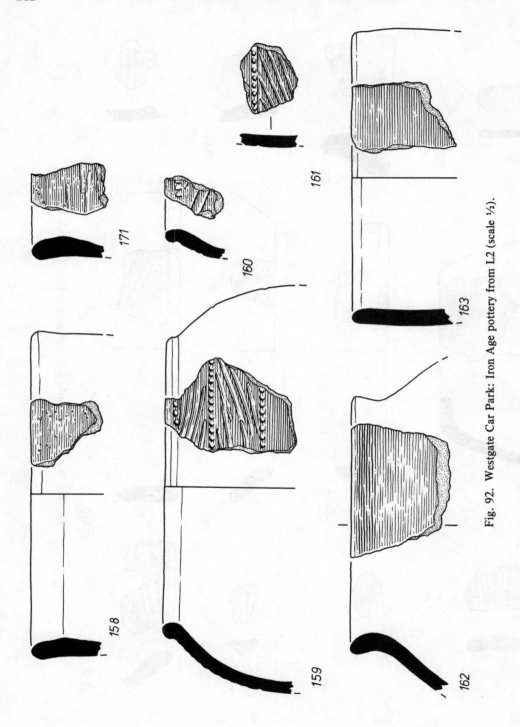

Fig. 92. Westgate Car Park: Iron Age pottery from L2 (scale ½).

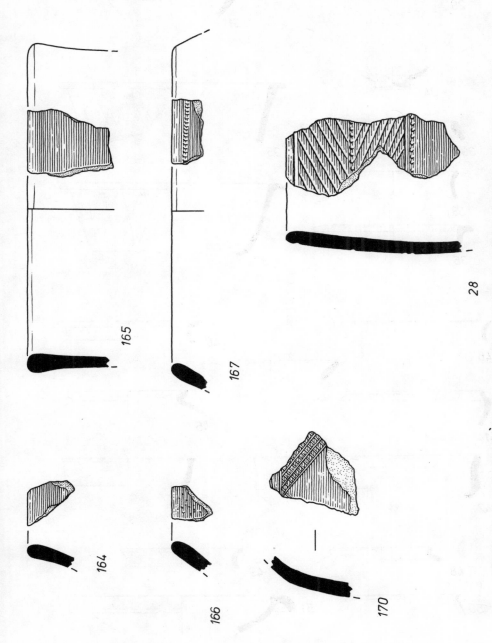

Fig. 93. Westgate Car Park: Iron Age pottery from L2 (164), L3 (165—6), L6 (167), L12 (170); and from Tower Street F23 (28) (scale ½).

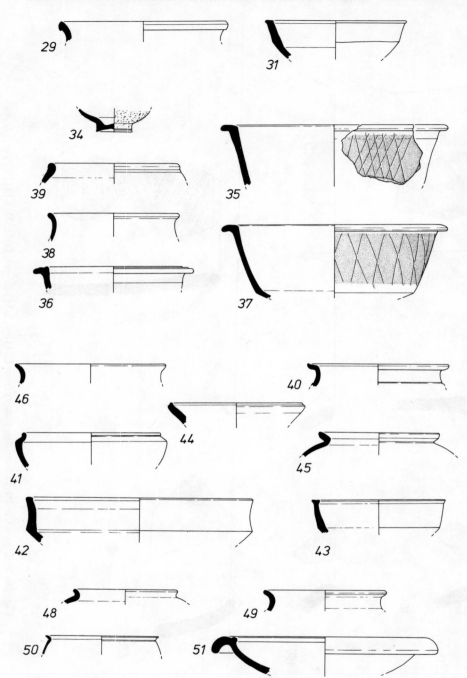

Fig. 94. Westgate Car Park: Roman pottery from the defences F31 (29, 31), F32-1 (34—39), F32-2 (40—46), F32-4 (48—51) (scale ¼).

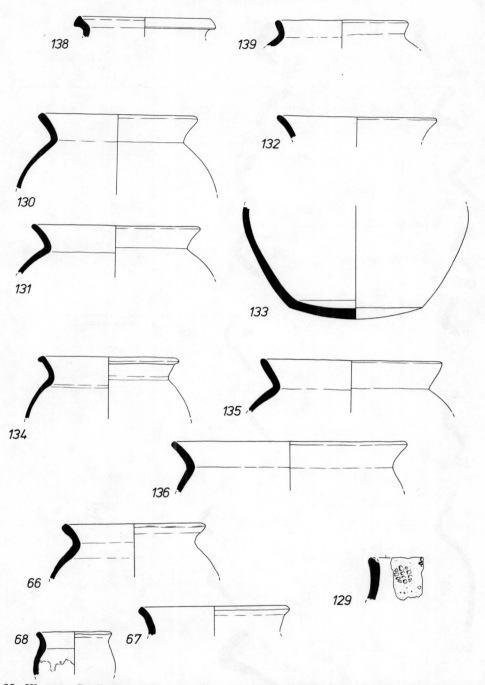

Fig. 95. Westgate Car Park: late Saxon and early medieval pottery from F79 (138, 139), F71 (130—136), F34 (66—68) and F69 (129) (scale ¼).

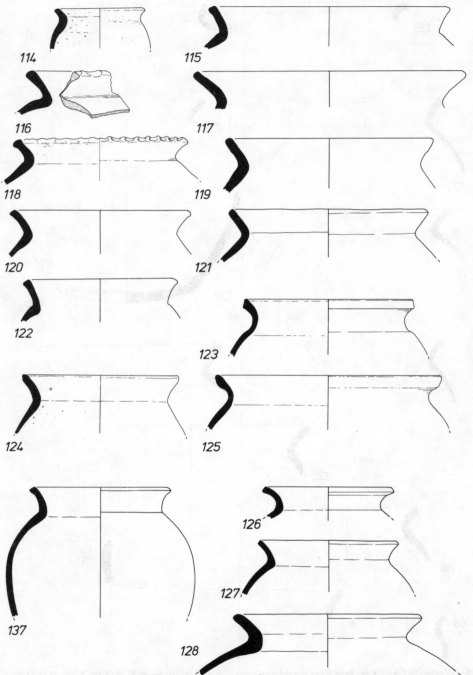

Fig. 96.   Westgate Car Park: early medieval pottery from F66 (114—125), F75 (137) and F67 (126—128) (scale ¼).

F31: The early Roman bank

The deposits in trench AB (F31-5) are almost certainly primary bank, as they are not the alternating turf and clay typical of the later addition. The deposits F31-1 to F31-5 represent a stratigraphic sequence, F31-1 being the latest.

F31-1: Definitely stratified in the early bank
483.31.1/3.
Jar with everted rim (two fragments) (Fig. 94:29). Hard, brown, sand-tempered ware with black burnished surface.
483.31.1/7.
Sherd (Fig. 90:30) decorated with a dot or comma pattern, possibly rouletted. Black burnished surface, dark grey fabric with chert temper. Harder than usual Iron Age sherds. There is a fragment of pre-Flavian samian.

F31-2: Probably from the bank
483.31.2/1.
Bowl (Fig. 94:31). Hard, light grey, sandy fabric, with light grey to grey-brown surface.

F31-3: From the primary core
483.31.3/3.
Saucepan pot (Fig. 90:32). Hard, light grey fabric with chert grit. Black burnished surface. Also a base (not grooved) in similar fabric.

F31-4: On the back of the primary core

F31-5: On the back of the primary bank, or just possibly from the addition (F32)
483.31.5/1.
Saucepan pot (Fig. 90:33). Soft, sand and organic temper. dark brown with brown surface.
483.31.5/2.
A rim possibly from a saucepan pot in brown fabric with chert and burnt flint temper, and a base in the soft sand-tempered fabric with black burnished surface.

F32: Addition to the Roman bank

As revealed in various excavations along this stretch of the defences, a considerable mound of soil was added to the defensive rampart sometime late in the second or early in the third century. It consisted of lenses of clay or gravel interspersed with many turves and patches of occupation soil, probably not derived from the immediate area in view of the general lack of Iron Age sherds among the finds. The layers F32-2 to F32-5 represent a stratigraphic sequence, F32-2 being the topmost level.

F32-1: Definitely stratified, but exact position unknown
483.32.1/1.
Beaker (Fig. 94:34) in fine, light grey fabric with buff surface and external rustication.
Piedish (Fig. 94:35). As 37, but surface shows some oxidation.
Piedish (Fig. 94:36). As 37, but with reeded rim.
Piedish (Fig. 94:37). Dark grey, sandy fabric with black burnished surface and burnished lattice. Several fragments. Also a large fragment in 483.32.4/19.
There is also a sherd with applied vertical ribs.
Of 45 miscellaneous other sherds, only two are Iron Age.
483.32.1/4.
One Roman and one sandy Iron Age sherd.
483.32.1/5.
Necked jar (Fig. 94:38). Light grey, sandy ware with grey surface.

483.32.1/6.
Bead rim jar (Fig. 94:39). Hard, light grey fabric with dark surface, sparse but coarse burnt flint grit.
From F32-1 there are four samian sherds, three of second-century date, and two amphora sherds.

F32-2: Brown loam, upper part of bank
483.32.2/3.
Necked jar (Fig. 94:40). Light brown, sand-tempered ware with grey core and black burnished surface.
Bead-rim jar (Fig. 94:41). Harsh, sand-tempered fabric with dark grey surface.
Dish (Fig. 94:42). Light grey fabric with grey-brown surface. Sand tempered.
Dish (Fig. 94:43). Similar to 42, but slightly finer fabric.
483.32.2/9.
Dish (Fig. 94:44). Light grey, sand-tempered fabric.
483.32.2/14.
Jar or beaker (Fig. 94:45). Brown, sand-tempered fabric with dull grey surface.
This group contains a cream-coloured sherd with external rustication and matt black slip. There is contamination from one medieval sherd.
483.32.2/15.
Bowl (Fig. 94:46). Harsh, sand-tempered, light grey fabric with grey surface.
Contamination from a late medieval sherd.
Information about unillustrated rim sherds is shown in Table 21. All the sherds tend to be small and much worn. There are two poorly dated samian sherds.

F32-3: Fine gravel and clay
Of the fifteen sherds in the three bags, there are three Iron Age and one jar rim. There is a fragment of quern and a piece of glass.

F32-4: A turf line of stiff clay
483.32.4/10.
A fine cream sherd with matt black slip.
483.32.4/13.
A dish rim with burnished zig-zag pattern.
483.32.4/15.
Iron Age sherd (Fig. 90:47), decorated with a curvilinear pattern infilled with stab marks. Brown to black ware with brown oxidized surface, chert and burnt flint temper.
483.32.4/16.
Jar (Fig. 94:48). Light grey ware with dull brown surface. Sand temper.
Beaker (Fig. 94:50). Hard, fine, orange fabric with purple colour-coat.
483.32.4/17.
Two saucepan-pot rims, sandy ware.
483.32.4/18.
Necked jar (Fig. 94:49). Reddish-brown fabric with grey core and black burnished surface. Fine sand temper.
483.32.4/19.
Flanged dish (Fig. 94:51). Hard, sand-tempered buff ware.
Also contains a fragment of vessel 37 and a storage jar with internal finger indentations.
483.32.4/22.
Two rim sherds including a lid. Also a fine grey-ware base.
Again sherds from this whole group are mostly very fragmented and worn, and bags containing only undescribed, unillustrated rim sherds are listed in Table 21.

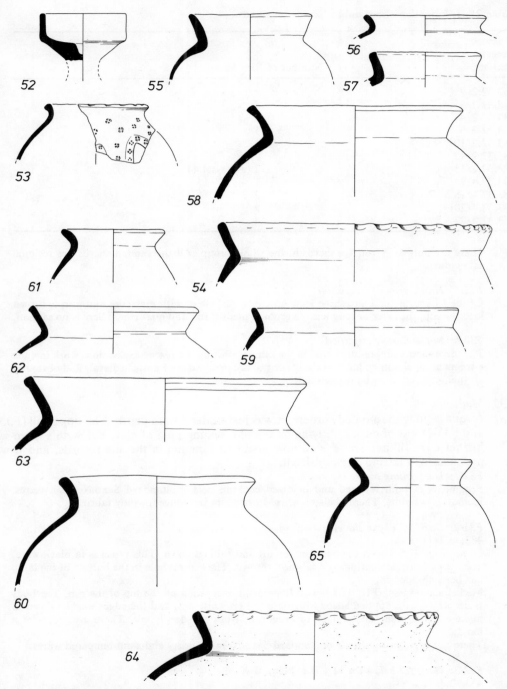

Fig. 97. Westgate Car Park: early medieval pottery from F33 (scale ¼).

Table 21. Information about unillustrated rim sherds.

Museum Accession Number	Number of Rim Sherds
483.32.2/2	1
483.32.2/3	4
483.32.2/4	1
483.32.2/5	1
483.32.2/10	1
483.32.2/12	2
483.32.2/15	1 (as vessel 44)
483.32.4/9	1
483.32.4/18	3
483.32.4/20	2
483.32.4/22	4

There are only 4—5 Iron Age sherds in the whole group. All the samian sherds are residual 1st century.

F32-5: Hard, brown, clayey soil
Of the 19 sherds there are three Iron Age, one buff sherd with grey core and purple-brown metallic slip, the exterior roughcast, a grooved piedish rim and a jar rim. There is no samian.

F32-6: Not definitely stratified
The three sherds supposedly found in the rampart during the rescue excavations work include a fragment of a Roman jar, but the other two are medieval and post-medieval, and obviously all this material must be discounted.

F33: Medieval pit
A square pit with rounded corners, it was just under 3 m in depth. The upper fill (F33-1 and F33-2) was of dark soil, lying on top of a sealing plug of clay. Below this there was further dark filling. There is no note about its function in the site records, and it was presumably a latrine or rubbish pit.

F33-1: Dark filling above the clay
Fragments of both reduced and oxidized cooking pots in standard Saxo-Norman wares, including two rims. There is also a wheel-turned rim in reduced, sandy fabric.

F33-2: Dark fill above the clay
483.33.2/1.
Lamp (Fig. 97:52) with the base broken off and rubbed down. This vessel is in black ware, and with a heavy tempering. It was wheel thrown. The central hole in the bottom of the lamp has been chipped in.
Michelmersh vessel (Fig. 97:53) with fingerprint decoration on the top of the rim. The body is decorated with applied strips which are put on while wet, and the edges washed down to make a low profile. The stamps of cruciform types are deeply cut. There are traces of a handle.
There are many body sherds of standard Saxo-Norman gritty and sand-tempered wares.

F33-3: Dark fill below the clay (i.e. below 0·90 m).
483.33.3/1.
Storage jar (Fig. 97:54) with thumbed rim in Saxo-Norman gritty fabric.

F33-4: Dark fill below the clay
483.33.4/2.
Cooking pot (Fig. 97:55). Simple plain vertical rim on a thickened shoulder. Very thin Saxo-Norman fabric.

F33-5: Dark fill below the clay
483.33.5/1,3.
Cooking pot (Fig. 97:56). Hard, sand-tempered, reduced fabric.
Cooking pot (Fig. 97:57). Saxo-Norman gritty fabric.
Storage jar (Fig. 97:58) with flaring rim, slightly thickened and flattened on top.
Cooking pot (Fig. 97:59). Saxo-Norman gritty fabric.
There is also a spout fragment from a Winchester Ware pitcher with yellow-green glaze.

F33-6: Dark fill deep in the pit, with slag and charcoal
483.33.6/1.
Cooking pot (Fig. 97:60), wheel thrown in a soft Saxo-Norman gritty fabric, reduced, but with some oxidation. The rim is flaring with a rounded top.

F33-7: Low in the filling at a depth of about 2·40 m
483.33.7/1, 2, 4
Cooking pot (Fig. 97:61) in reduced, Saxo-Norman gritty fabric.
Cooking pot (Fig. 97:62) in oxidized, Saxo-Norman gritty fabric.
Storage jar (Fig. 97:63) in reduced Saxo-Norman fabric.
Large storage jar (Fig. 97:64) with thumbed rim in Saxo-Norman gritty fabric.

F33-8: Lowest fill of pit, 2·40—2·75 m down
483.33.8/1.
Cooking pot in reduced, Saxo-Norman gritty fabric.
There are fragments of two other similar cooking pots.
Other finds from this pit include a stone lamp, bronze tweezers, crucible, and iron and bronze slag.

F34: Medieval pit

Cut into the natural chalk, on the corner of Upper High Street and Sussex Street.
F34-1: Probably from the pit
483.34.1/2,3.
Cooking pot (Fig. 95:66). Very dark and soapy texture, reduced right through. Filler of a variety of flints and sand.
Cooking pot (Fig. 95:67), similar ware but fabric oxidized.
Small cooking pot (Fig. 95:68). As 53, but reduced on the outside and grey to buff on the inside of the fracture. Handmade.
The decorated bone spoon was associated with this group.

F34-2: Definitely from the pit
A group of hard oxidized Saxo-Norman gritted wares, including three small fragments of cooking pot rims.

F35: Iron Age pit

In Trial Hole 1, a pocket of dark soil extending into the trench.
483.35.0/1.
Saucepan pot (Fig. 90:69). Purple-brown fabric with chert temper, black burnished surface. Slight burnished groove below the rim.
Base (Fig. 90:70). Black to brown fabric with coarse, burnt flint temper.

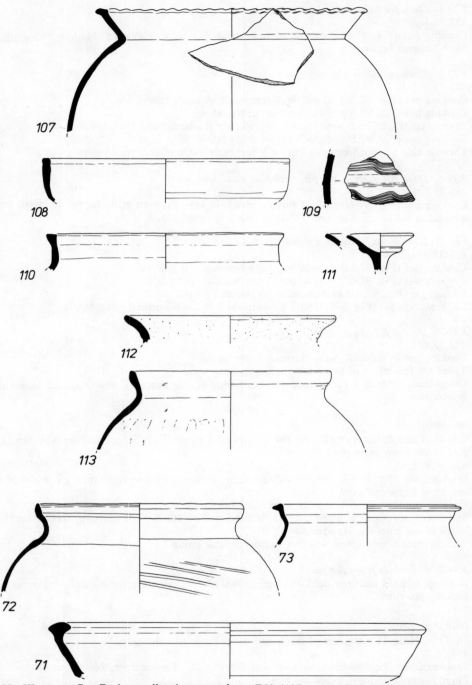

Fig. 98. Westgate Car Park: medieval pottery from F63 (107—111), F65 (112, 113), F36 (71—73) (scale ¼).

This pit also produced a fragment of a rotary quern.

F36: City ditch

The deposits have not been differentiated, and each bag of finds is a small group in its own right.

483.36.0/1. From Trial hole 3.

A mixed group of early medieval wares, including a rim of a totally reduced, pimply ware with coarse, squarish pieces in the temper.

483.36.0/2.

Inturned rim (Fig. 98:71) in a very hard, very coarse, sandy fabric with unselected flints in it. Grey all the way through.

With this is a plain rim of a cooking pot with slight thickening in slightly oxidized ware with fine selected or washed flint and sand temper. These two sherds should be early thirteenth century, but the group has later intrusions.

483.36.0/3,4,5.

All contain early medieval sherds with some Roman material in 483.36.0/5.

483.36.0/6.

Two rim sherds, one hard and fine with sandy temper, and grey in colour, reduced all through. It could be twelfth century.

483.36.0/7.

An Iron Age sherd.

483.36.0/8.

Hard, smooth, buff, globular pot (Fig. 98:72) with external grass wiping and heavily thumbed inside. These could have been caused by pummelling out the pot against a pad of straw held close to the body.

Cooking pot in 'thin ware' (Fig. 98:73). It is very hard and heavily tempered with a strong matrix. The clay has shrunk against it making the filler stick out. The fabric is very black right through, and extremely thin and brittle.

F37: Medieval pit

No details of the filling are recorded.

483.37.0/1.

A mixture of Iron Age sherds, including one of a haematite bowl, two early Roman bead rims and a second century bowl.

483.37.0/2.

Jug (Fig. 102:74), in soft, red fabric, decorated with vertical strips of iron-rich slip, with pads of the same slip stamped with a pronounced grid pattern. The glaze is brown and speckled with dark iron stains. The decoration is further embellished by horizontal grooves set at a distance. Fragments, possibly from the same jug come from Tower Street F4 (Fig. 83:3).

Jug (Fig. 102:75) in soft red fabric. The glaze is dirty, light brown with green flecks in it. The body is decorated with applied strips in self-colour making large panels. Up the centre of these panels are applied strips with thumbing up towards the rim of the vessel.

These two vessels are not well decorated. One has a rod handle, and they were presumably spoutless. The body is pear-shaped to a foot ringed flange, and therefore they should be of fourteenth-century date.

483.37.0/3.

Cooking pots (Fig. 102:76,77) in sandy, dark red fabric.

There are fragments of several glazed jugs and a skillet foot (?), with internal green glaze, as well as several sandy-ware cooking pots.

483.37.0/4.

Fragments of a skillet minus one leg and a handle, in a sandy, salmon-pink to red-buff fabric. The rim is flared and simple with a single barbed external flange. There is a reduced iron-green glaze around the inside of the rim and on the interior of the base, the legs are hollow, but pulled, not thrown. There is a large patch of glaze to one side of the vessel showing it had lain on its side when fired. This vessel with internal glazing and long legs should be fourteenth century.

F38: *Medieval pit*
No details of the filling are recorded.
483.38.0/1.
Two cooking-pot rims in gritty Saxo-Norman ware.
An Iron Age sherd, an unusual ribbed early Roman sherd, and a fragment of late Roman colour-coated beaker.
483.38.0/2.
Three cooking-pot rims in gritty Saxo-Norman ware.
Also a small fragment of the rim of a large storage jar with finger indenting, but this bag is contaminated by a post-medieval sherd.
483.38.0/3.
One cooking-pot rim in gritty Saxo-Norman ware.
483.38.0/4.
Two cooking-pot rims in gritty Saxo-Norman ware.
In this group there are also many small fragments of gritty Saxo-Norman ware and several fragments of sandy, grey cooking pots, including one with an incised wavy line pattern.

F39: *Medieval pit*
The top filling includes mortar and largish flints.
483.39.0/1.
An early medieval sandy sherd, and a lump of slag.

F40: *Medieval pit*
483.40.0/1.
Reduced Saxo-Norman wares including a cooking-pot rim, and a late Roman flanged bowl.

F41: *Medieval pit*
483.41.0/1.
An early medieval sandy sherd.

F42: *Medieval pit*
In Trenches XI and A1. Filled with loose, brown-grey soil with green stains, much charcoal, shell, small flint nodules, and small lumps of chalk.
483.42.0/1,2.
Fragments of Saxo-Norman pottery and a piece of glass.

F43: *Medieval pit*
In Trench A3, cuts F44.
F43-1: Upper fill of dirty yellow-brown soil with flints and charcoal
483.43.1/1—5.
Saxo-Norman sherds, and sandy cooking pot sherds in reduced fabric, including the rim of a large storage jar in off-white sandy ware in bag 483.43.1/4. There is one possible fragment of crucible and a number of late Roman residual sherds.

F43-2: Layer of mortar overlying sandy clay with flints and sandy grey soil with yellow flecks down to a depth of 2·40 m
483.43.2/1—4.
Bowl or jar (483.43.2/1, Fig. 99:79). Hard, grey-brown fabric with darker surface. A form

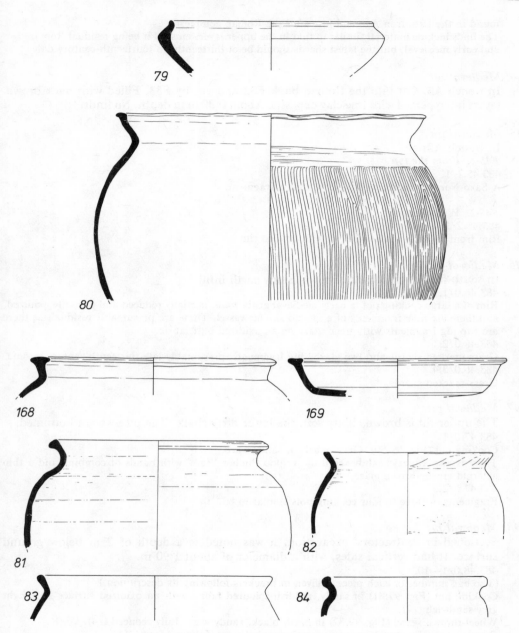

Fig. 99. Westgate Car Park: Roman pottery from F43 (79) and medieval pottery from F47 (80), L9 (168), L10 (169) and F48 (81—84) (scale ¼).

found in the Late Iron Age and just after the Roman conquest.

The finds include material similar to that in the upper layer, most of it being residual Roman and early medieval, but the latest sherds should be of thirteenth- to fourteenth-century date.

F44: Medieval pit

In trench A3. Cut into the Roman bank F32 and cut by F33. Filled with dark brown layers interspersed with fine clay deposits. About 0·30 m in depth. No finds.

F45: Medieval pit

In trench A3.

F45-1: From the top

483.45.1/1.

A Saxo-Norman sherd, and there is a glass fragment.

F45-2: Well stratified

483.45.2/1.

Rim from an early medieval bowl with beaded rim.

F46: Medieval pit

In south face of trench A5. Brown, stony earth infill.

483.46.0/1.

Rim of a large cooking pot in early medieval gritty ware, partially reduced and partially oxidized, and there are nine fragments of a second similar vessel. These are presumably residual, as there are two jug fragments with green glaze on an oxidized buff fabric.

483.46.0/2.

Grass-marked sherds and two glazed jug fragments, presumably late thirteenth century in date.

483.46.0/3,4.

Grass-marked sherds.

F47: Medieval pit

The upper fill is brown, flinty soil, the lower dirty chalk. The pit was not bottomed.

483.47.0/1.

Cooking pot (Fig. 99:80). Grass-marked, sandy ware.

There is also a black, sandy sherd of 'Tripod Pitcher Ware' with bands of combing and a thin external greeny-brown glaze.

483.47.0/2,3.

Fragments of three to four cooking pots similar to 80.

F48: Medieval pit

Sectioned in contractors' excavation, it was noted to a depth of 2 m below ground surface. It had vertical sides, with a diameter of about 1·90 m.

483.48.0/1—10.

(The bag number of each piece is given in brackets following its description.)

Cooking pot (Fig. 99:81) in sandy, reddish-coloured fabric with an oxidized surface in a light grey sandwich (/2).

Wheel-thrown vessel (Fig. 99:82) in hard, black, sandy ware, fully reduced (/4).

Cooking pot (Fig. 99:83) in hard, sand-tempered ware, fully reduced (/6).

Handmade vessel (Fig. 99:84) in reduced, soapy, sand-tempered ware (/4).

Cooking pot (Fig. 100:85) in a completely reduced, black, gritty fabric. This piece is presumably residual, indeed, at some point some unmarked sherds from F71 became mixed with this group, and this vessel may be from that feature (/9).

Glass lamp (483.34, Fig. 100:86). This most exceptional object will be fully described in a future volume.

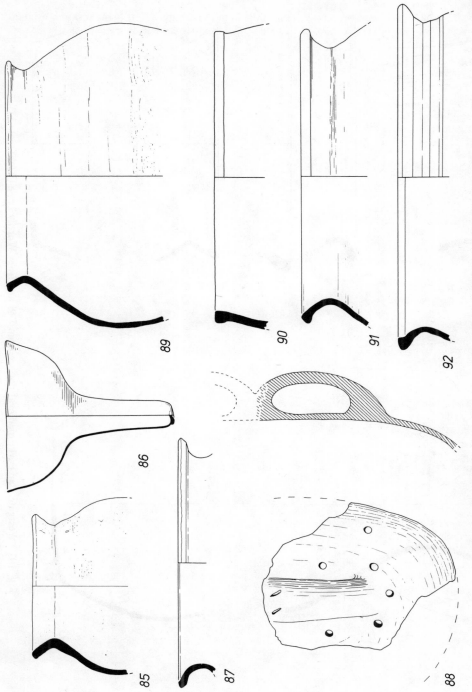

Fig. 100. Westgate Car Park: medieval pottery and glass from F48 (scale ¼).

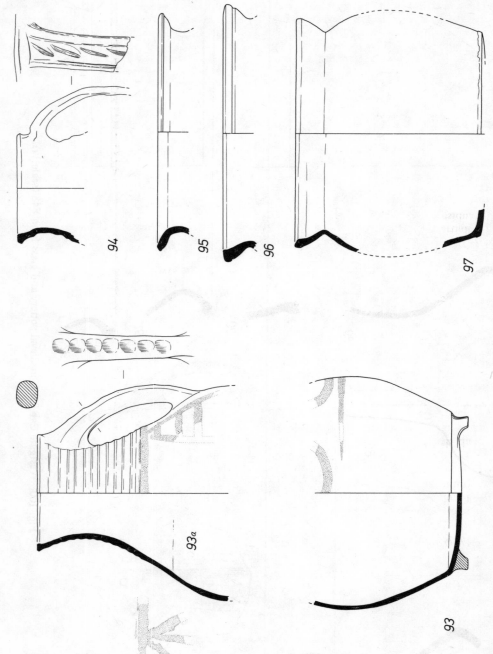

Fig. 101. Westgate Car Park: medieval pottery from F48 and from Worthy Lane (93a) (scale ¼).

Cooking pot (Fig. 100:87) in a smooth, sandy, grey-buff fabric. Wheel turned (/8).

Couvre-feu (Fig. 100:88) in a coarse, hard, sandy, reduced ware with two rows of holes pierced when the pot was very wet. The piece apparently had two handles springing from the middle of the top of the cover. The handle is decorated with a delta-pattern slashing (/1).

As 81 (Fig. 100:89) a late grass-marked vessel (/2).

Bowl or dish with squared rim (Fig. 100:90). Soft, dark brown to black fabric with flint filler (/8).

Cooking pot (Fig. 100:91) in a fine, creamy-buff, sandy fabric, similar to the tripod pitchers (/5).

Cooking pot (Fig. 100:92) as 85 (/8).

Base of a tripod pitcher (Fig. 101:93) in a fine, creamy-buff, biscuit-like fabric, the same colour all the way through. The exterior is decorated with an iron-rich, red slip thickly applied with a brush. The slip lies along a line around the belly on the pot and in loops above that. The upper body is covered with a yellow-green glaze (/12).

There are several fragments from a similar vessel, decorated with a zig-zag decoration and covered with a fine, shiny glaze. The type can be reconstructed using a handle and upper body found in Worthy Lane in 1933 (1231.0.1/1, Fig. 101:93a), where the decoration is in the form of upside-down shield patterns, plausibly the motifs on 93. The decoration is again in an iron-rich slip covered with a shiny yellow glaze, and the fabric is identical. It should be post 1250—1300. The Worthy Lane vessel was donated to the Museum by Mrs Maundrell.

Handle (Fig. 101:94) of an Orchard Street type jug in a hard, buff fabric with a dark green glaze. The neck is rilled and the handle grooved each side and thumbed down the middle (/13).

Cooking pot (Fig. 101:95), as 85 (/8).

Cooking pot (Fig. 101:96) in sandy, coarse fabric with pimply finish (/8).

Cooking pot (Fig. 101:97) in very hard, sandy fabric, buff coloured with a grey core (/10).

F49: *Medieval pit*

Pit cutting into natural observed in the contractors' excavation. The infill included a number of slates.

483.49.0/1.

Fragments of sandy, medieval cooking pots, and fragments of a tripod pitcher.

F50: *Post-medieval pit(s)*

This material is noted as coming from a feature found in the southern part of the site. The finds however fall into two distinct groups, one dating to about 1750—1770, the other late nineteenth century. The groups are separated here, though the material was mixed at the time of discovery.

F50A: *The eighteenth-century finds*

483.50.0/2,3,4,6,10.

(The bag number of each piece is given in brackets following its description.)

Bowl (Fig. 102:98) of white Staffordshire salt glaze (/6).

Brown, salt-glazed tankard fragment (Fig. 102:99) (/6).

White-coloured drug jar (Fig. 102:100), complete (/4).

Bowl (Fig. 102:101) of English polychrome Delft, *c.* 1730—1740 (/6,/10).

Bowl (Fig. 102:102) in plain white Delft (/6).

Westerwald mug (Fig. 102:103) (/2).

Neck of bottle-shaped vessel (Fig. 102:104) in a Spanish-type fabric (/10).

English slip-ware dish (Fig. 102:105) in an untempered fabric with a white slip underglaze radial pattern, brush applied with drops of copper on the slip, all under a fine, clear, lead glaze (/6).

English salt-glazed, stoneware mug (Fig. 102:106) (/3).

Bag 483.50.0/6 contains another fragment of English polychrome Delft.

Bag 483.50.0/10 has a second Spanish-type bottle neck, fragments of a polychrome Delft plate of fine quality, two fragments of a small fluted cup in Chinese porcelain decorated with blue pine trees, and the lower half of a Lambeth-type, salt-glazed, half-pint tankard.

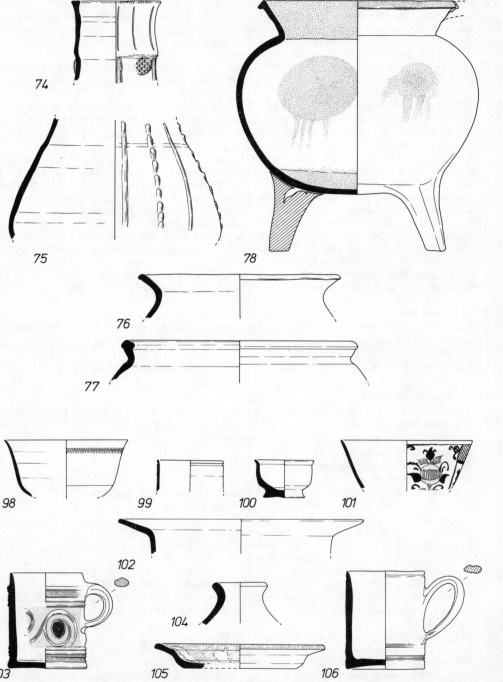

Fig. 102. Westgate Car Park: medieval and post-medieval pottery from F37 (74—78) and F50 (98—106) (scale ¼).

F50B: The nineteenth-century finds

The bulk of the finds are post-1850 and are comprised principally of transfer-printed and salt-glazed wares; there is also an enamelled candlestick holder.

F51: *Medieval pit*

A pit at least 3 m deep occupying the whole of trench A6.

483.51.0/1,2.

Fragments of fifteenth- and sixteenth-century pottery including painted wares (c.f. 82 Hyde Street), stoneware, and imitation Tudor Green. Other finds include a complete stone mortar, glass, and medieval tiles.

F52: *Medieval pit*

A pit in Trench A7, at least 2 m deep, but no finds are recorded.

F53: *Medieval pit*

In trench A8, excavated to 1 m, but at least 2 m deep. No finds.

F54: *Medieval pit*

In Trench A9. No finds.

F55: *Medieval pit*

In trench A10. No finds.

F56: *Medieval pit*

In trenches C4 and Z2. In C4 the fill was of dirty yellowish chalk, 0·45 m deep, and in Z2 of mortar and flint rubble.

483.56.0/1.

An early medieval sandy sherd.

Also the bones of a cat.

F57: *Chalk pit*

In trench N. No finds.

F58: *Medieval pit*

In trench N. It was excavated to a depth of 1·35 m. The upper fill was of dirty chalk, the lowest of brown earth, and between was a thin layer of burning.

483.58.0/1—5.

All contain early medieval gritty wares, including 2 cooking pot rims in /1 and one in /2, and a possible spout in /4. There is much late Roman residual pottery, including cooking-pot cavetto rims, colour-coat wares, and a Rhenish rim sherd. There is a samian fragment.

F59: *Medieval pit*

In trench AB, cuts F8. No finds.

F60: *Medieval filling*

A large deposit in the east face of the contractors' excavation.

483.60.0/1.

Sandy cooking pot in hard, sand-tempered fabric with fettled body; fragments of green-glazed jug, thirteenth to fourteenth century.

F61: Medieval pit
Filling in the east face of the contractors' excavation.
483.61.0/1.
Fragments of early medieval vessels in gritty fabric.

F63: Medieval pit
Sectioned in a circular soakaway in the southwest corner of the site.
483.63.0/1—4.
(The bag number of each piece is given in brackets following its description.)
Cooking pot (Fig. 98:107) with crimped rim in oxidized, biscuit fabric heavily charged with flints (/1).
Bowl (Fig. 98:108) in very hard, fully oxidized fabric with occasional small pieces of flint in the temper. The rim is rolled slightly and the base sags from the bottom edge which is fettled (/2).
Green-glazed jug fragment (Fig. 98:109). The fabric is heavily tempered with fine, angular-grained sand, very hard with a pale yellow interior. The coarse fabric gives an equally coarse texture to the glaze. The pattern consists of vertical combing between raised strips (?) (/4).
Cooking-pot rim (Fig. 98:110) in fine, sandy ware with an oxidized finish and a light grey sandwich (/4).
Cruzie lamp (Fig. 98:111). Heavily sand-tempered fabric with some spots of green glaze on the inside (/4).
Bag 683.63.0/4 contains a Roman sherd with burnished herring-bone pattern which can be paralleled at Mill Plain, Christchurch (Christchurch Museum).

F64: Medieval pit
Northeast corner of the site.
483.64.0/1.
A large fragment of a globular cooking pot very crudely made, of grass-wiped type. Very hard, sandy, grey, brittle ware with occasional pieces of thin flint.

F65: Medieval pit
Rubbish pit in the northwest corner of the site.
F65-1: Definitely stratified
483.65.1/2.
Flared rim of cooking pot (Fig. 98:112) in Saxo-Norman reduced gritty fabric.
Globular cooking pot (Fig. 98:113) in hard, oxidized fabric.
There are other sherds of early medieval gritty fabric, and a rim of a second globular cooking pot. It seems to be an early occurrence, and early form, of this type.

F66: Medieval pit
Rubbish pit in the northwest corner of the site.
483.66.0/2.
Some late Roman material, including a cooking pot and a lid in parchment ware, and one piece of amphora.
483.66.0/3.
Cooking pot (Fig. 96:114). This is a small cup which was probably a toy as it has a very poorly finished interior. Coarse, partially oxidized fabric, as 115.
Cooking pot (Fig. 96:115) in reduced, Saxo-Norman, gritty fabric with slightly oxidized surface.
Cooking pot (Fig. 96:116) as 118, but with more grit and a more oxidized surface.
Cooking pot (Fig. 96:117) as 115, but fabric more oxidized.
Cooking pot (Fig. 96:118), with slightly flared rim, the top of which has been dimpled with the finger. It has a marked collar groove and thickening where the pot is bent to make the collar. In hard, partially oxidized fabric producing a smooth blackish colour.
Cooking pot (Fig. 96:119) as 115.

Cooking pot (Fig. 96:120) as 115.
Cooking pot (Fig. 96:121) in smooth, slightly sandy ware with oxidized surface.
Cooking pot (Fig. 96:122) as 115.
483.66.0/4.
Globular cooking pot (Fig. 96:123) in a brittle, biscuit-like fabric, part oxidized on the outside and reduced within. Evidence for patting out the vessel to make it globular, which leads to considerable deformity of the wall of the vessel. The rim is short with virtually no collar, round topped and with a flat face on the outside.
Cooking pot (Fig. 96:124) as 123.
Cooking pot (Fig. 96:125) as 123.
These last three vessels were excavated on a different occasion from the first group, and the field notes themselves suggest that they may not in reality be the same group, as the forms would suggest.

F67: *Medieval pit*

In the western part of the site.
483.67.0/1.
Cooking pot (Fig. 96:126) with slightly flaring rim in reduced, Saxo-Norman gritty fabric.
Cooking pot (Fig. 96:127) as 126.
Cooking pot (Fig. 96:128) with flaring rim in oxidized, biscuit fabric charged with flints. It is plain, but closely resembles the series with crimped rims.

F68: *Medieval pit*

The pit impinged slightly on the north face of the contractors' excavation.
483.68.1/1,2.
None of the finds definitely comes from the pit, but probably from it are a cooking pot in early medieval gritty ware with a very marked collar groove ring and a rim more flaring than usual; and also a sherd of grass-marked pottery in hard, oxidized, sandy fabric.

F69: *Medieval pit*

This pit appears on the section of the north face of the contractors' excavation published by Cunliffe (1962, Fig. 3). It is the easternmost of the three pits shown. The upper fill is of dark soil lying on a plug of clay and flints, beneath which is a variegated soil with ash, animal bones, and oyster shells. It cuts pit F74 and the Roman bank F32.

F69-1: Definitely stratified
483.69.1/1.
A fragment of sand-tempered cooking pot with sparse grit, presumably twelfth century.

F69-2: Probably from the pit
483.69.2/1.
Rim of a large storage jar (Fig. 95:129). The fabric is most unusual for Winchester, almost tile-like, and is tempered with small water-worn black pebbles. It is apparently from a large jar with a flaring rim, with stamp decoration on the inside of the rim. The stamp is large and probably part of a series, as there is evidence of a second one adjacent to it. The ware is oxidized and should be developed Saxo-Norman ware.

F70: *Pit*

Presumably medieval. No finds, except an iron blade.

F71: *Medieval pit*

Pit in side of contractors' excavation.
F71-1: Definitely stratified

483.71.1/1.
Cooking pot (Fig. 95:130). Fabric pale cement-grey to black, tempered with chalk which has washed out, and occasional chips of flint.
Cooking pot (Fig. 95:131) as 130.
Cook pot (Fig. 95:132) in Saxo-Norman gritty fabric.
Cooking pot (Fig. 95:133) in hard, thick, sandy fabric thrown on a fast wheel, Late Saxon Sandy Ware (Biddle and Collis forthcoming).

F71-2: Probably from the pit
483.71.2/1.
Cooking pots (Fig. 95:134—6) in early medieval gritty fabric.

F72: Medieval pit
In the north side of the contractors' pit, westernmost on Figure 3 in Cunliffe (1962). The only find possibly from the pit is a fragment of crucible.

F73: Roman pit
Pit cut into natural, presumably behind the early rampart.
483.73.0/1.
A jar rim and fragment of a storage jar, presumably early Roman.

F74: Medieval pit
Pit in north section of contractors' excavation, middle one on Figure 3 in Cunliffe (1962) cut by F69. No finds.

F75: Medieval pit
In the eastern part of the site.
483.75.0/1.
Cooking pot (Fig. 96:137). Globular, with an almost vertical rim surmounted by a horizontal rim. The fabric is coarse and heavily filled with fine, selected calcined flints.

F76: Medieval pit
Beneath Tower Street. No finds.

F77: Medieval pit
Under Tower Street.
483.77.1/1.
Fragments of sandy globular cooking pots, one with straw marking.

F78: Medieval pit
Under Tower Street. No finds.

F79: Medieval pit
Under Tower Street. May contain some earlier material.
483.79.0/1.
Cooking pot rim (Fig. 95:138), probably Late Saxon Sandy Ware (Biddle and Collis forthcoming).
Cooking pot (Fig. 95:139) in hard, brown fabric with sparse grits.
This group is unusual. The fabric of 139 is closely comparable with early types which have turned up beneath the Wessex Hotel, though the angular base (not illustrated) is unusual. This pit should be tenth century in date at the latest.

F80: Medieval pit (?)
No finds.

F81: Gully
Running north—west, it is 0·35 m deep. See L3.

F82: Iron Age pit (?)
Depression in the gravel. For finds see L3.

F83: Iron Age gully (?)
Ledge-like depression in natural, *c.* 0·10 m deep, running north—south. See L3.

F84: Iron Age gully
Runs northeast from F82, *c.* 0·12 m deep. See L3.

L1:   *Top of natural gravel beneath L2*
       Probably merely staining from L2. For finds see Table 19.

L2:   *Dark clayey gravelly soil, with much burnt flint*
       Probably a plough soil, overlying natural and the Iron Age features, and underlying the Roman bank F31. The finds are summarised on Table 19.
       483.00.2/3—74.
       (The bag number of each piece is given in brackets following its description.)
       Saucepan pot (Fig. 90:140). Soft, sand tempered with some organic material. Black fabric and black burnished surface (/3).
       Lid (?) (Fig. 90:141). Black ware with fine chert grit (/10).
       Saucepan pot (Fig. 90:142). Grey-brown fabric with black burnished surface, and much fine chert temper (/30).
       Saucepan pot (Fig. 90:143), with slightly everted rim. Fabric as 142 (/3).
       Storage jar (Fig. 90:144). Hard, grey fabric with calcite and burnt flint grit. Black burnished. Could be Roman (/5, /69).
       Saucepan pot (Fig. 90:145). Dark brown and tempered fabric with black burnished surface (/7).
       Saucepan pot (Fig. 91:146). Red-brown fabric with black burnished surface, flint tempered. Decorated with groove and dot (/44).
       Base (Fig. 91:147) in black ware with black burnished surface. Sparse chert and burnt flint temper (/48).
       Lid (?) (Fig. 91:148). Soft, dull red fabric with orange surface, coarse chert and burnt flint temper (/57).
       Saucepan pot (Fig. 91:149). Dark brown ware with coarse chert and burnt flint temper (/48).
       Saucepan pot (Fig. 91:150). Black burnished ware with burnt flint temper and coarse chert and grog (/55).
       Storage jar (Fig. 91:151). Light grey, oxidized surface with chert and burnt flint temper. Very light clinker-like, over-fired (/58).
       Furrowed bowl (Fig. 91:152). Light grey, sandy ware with orange-red surface (/59).
       Saucepan pot (Fig. 91:153). Hard, light grey ware with dark grey to whitish surface. Chert and burnt flint temper. Decorated with groove and dot (/59).
       Saucepan pot (Fig. 91:154). Hard, black ware with burnished surface, chert tempered (/60).
       Jar (Fig. 91:155). Soft, brown-red fabric with chert temper. Dark brown to reddish burnished surface, decorated with groove and dot (/60).
       Saucepan pot (Fig. 91:156). Hard, grey-brown with chert and burnt flint temper and oxidized surface, decorated with groove and dot (/61).
       Jar (Fig. 91:157). Black ware with burnished surface with chert and burnt flint temper. Decorated

with groove and dot (/60).

Storage jar (Fig. 92:158). Grey fabric with coarse burnt flint and chert temper. Black-brown surface with external pattern burnishing (/61).

Storage jar (Fig. 92:171). Grey fabric with coarse burnt flint and chert temper. Black-brown surface with external pattern burnishing (/61).

Jar (Fig. 92:159). Hard, grey-brown fabric with coarse burnt flint and chert temper. Oxidized buff surface (/62).

Jar (Fig. 92:160). Black, coarse fabric with coarse chert and burnt flint temper, decorated with groove and dot decoration (/66).

Sherd (Fig. 92:161) decorated with groove and dot in dark brown-black burnished fabric with chert temper (/70).

Jar (Fig. 92:162). Sand tempered with dark brown burnished exterior (/66).

Saucepan pot (Fig. 92:163). Hard, red-brown fabric with much chert temper, black burnished surface (/71).

Saucepan pot (Fig. 93:164). Hard, brown-black fabric with much chert temper (/72).

Saucepan pot. Sand-tempered, grey-brown fabric with black burnished surface (/7).

Saucepan pot in black burnished fabric with chert temper, decorated with groove and dot (/9).

Saucepan pot rim in grey fabric with red surface, quartz grit (/9).

Saucepan pot (?). Purple-brown fabric with flint temper, and black burnished surface (/34).

Sherd decorated with groove and dot, black chert and burnt flint tempered fabric with burnished surface (/41).

Bowl. Hard, dark grey fabric with much burnt flint temper, decorated with grooves (/41).

Saucepan pot with plain rim. Black burnished fabric with burnt flint temper (/46).

Sherd with grooved decoration, black burnished with chert and burnt flint temper (/50).

Saucepan pot (?) with slight groove below the rim. Abraded sherd in dark grey fabric with oxidized surface, with chert and burnt flint temper (/51).

Decorated sherds, illustrated by Cunliffe (1964 in Fig. 6:16). These sherds are all missing.

Romano-British platter rim in hard, grey ware with dark brown burnished, sandy fabric (/68).

L3: *From road constructed around the West Gate in 1958*
The finds, from F81, 82, 83, and 84 and from L2 were all mixed and have been assigned to L3. The finds are listed on Table 10.
483.00.3/1.
Saucepan pot (Fig. 93:165). Black burnished fabric with chert and burnt flint temper.
Saucepan pot or jar (Fig. 93:166). Grey-brown fabric with chert temper and reddish-brown surface.

L4: *Unstratified*
From the extension of Trial Hole 4.
483.00.4/1—4.
Mixture of Iron Age sherds, and Roman and Saxo-Norman rims and sherds.

L5: *Unstratified*
From Trial Hole 1.
483.00.5/1—2.
Same mixture as L4, but also some post-medieval. There is one saucepan-pot rim in black ware with burnt flint temper. The coin of Commodus came from the dump in this trench.

L6: *Unstratified*
From the area excavation in 1951.
483.00.6/1—7.
Same mixture as L4, but in /3 there is a fragment of a *terra nigra* flanged bowl, as Winnall (Fig. 30). Also a fragment of crucible.

483.00.6/5.
Saucepan pot (Fig. 93:167). Hard, grey-brown fabric with sparse chert temper, and rouletted decoration. Presumably an import.

L7: Unstratified
From the 1955 excavation.
483.00.7/1—4.
Saxo-Norman wares, including cooking-pot rims and crucible. There is a token which has been mislaid.

L8: Unstratified
No details from the rescue work. Mainly Saxo-Norman, but also neck of green-glazed tripod pitcher, a bullet mould and five unmarked Iron Age sherds.

L9: Unstratified
From the rescue work on the eastern part of the site.
483.00.9/1—3.
Mainly late Saxo-Norman wares, and a sherd of samian.
483.00.9/3.
Cooking-pot rim (Fig. 99:168). Developed Saxo-Norman ware with very coarse fabric with burnt flint temper. An uncommon form for Winchester.

L10: Unstratified
From the northern part of the site.
483.00.10/1—6.
Mainly late Saxo-Norman wares, including a spout, a bowl, and a grass-marked (?) cooking-pot rim.
There is a fragment of crucible.
483.00.10/3.
Bowl (Fig. 99:169), in heavily tempered, coarse fabric, probably twelfth to thirteenth century.

L11: Unstratified
From the western part of the site.
483.00.11/1—7.
Mixture of Iron Age, Roman (including a piedish), Saxo-Norman (including to eleventh- to twelfth-century rims and a bowl), and painted wares of fifteenth-century date.

L12: Unstratified
No details recorded.
483.00.12/1.
Fragment of Glastonbury ware (Fig. 93:170) with burnished lattice pattern. Shell temper (Peacock 1969, Group 4), an import from Somerset.

The Finds

The Samian by G. Dannell

Provenance	Museum Accession Number	Form	Date A.D.	Kiln	Comments
F3	483.3.0/9	29	Nero-Vespasian	southern Gaul	

Provenance	Museum Accession Number	Form	Date A.D.	Kiln	Comments
F31-3	483.31.3/5	29	Pre-Flavian	southern Gaul	Fig. 103:7.
F32-1	483.32.1/10	18/31	2nd century	central Gaul	
	483.32.1/2	27	Trajanic/ Hadrianic	Martres-de-Veyre	
	483.32.1/9	18	Flavian	southern Gaul	
	483.32.1/8	31	2nd century	central Gaul	Heavily worn on the interior.
F32-2	483.32.2/13		2nd century (?)	central Gaul	Bowl.
	483.32.2/17		1st century (?)	southern Gaul	Chip.
	483.32.2/21	18/31	Flavian/ Trajanic	Montans	
	483.32.2/22	36	1st century	southern Gaul	
	483.32.2/23	29	c. 75—90	southern Gaul	Fragment showing torso of dog or hare running to right.
	483.32.2/24	18	Flavian	southern Gaul	
	483.32.2/25	37	Trajanic	Martres-de-Veyre	Style of DRVSVS. In panel decoration with bead rows; showing legs of Venus (0.28) and a portion of the branched ornament (Stanfield & Simpson 1958:156, Fig. 20).
	483.32.2/26	37	75—90	southern Gaul	Portion of wall showing arrowhead infill.
F32-4	483.32.4/14	18	1st century	southern Gaul	
	483.32.4/23	18	1st century	southern Gaul	
	483.32.4/24		1st century	southern Gaul	Flange.
	483.32.4/8		1st century	southern Gaul	Chip.
	483.32.4/10	18 or 11/31	Late 1st—early 2nd century	southern Gaul	Rivetted.
	483.32.4/12	30	Late 1st century	southern Gaul	4 sherds.
F36	483.36.0/9		2nd century	central Gaul	Chip.
F37	483.37.0/5	18	Flavian	southern Gaul	
F43-2	483.43.2/5	31 or 31R	Antonine	—	Burnt.
F58	483.58.0/6		2nd century	central Gaul	Chip.
L9	483.00.9/4	18/31	2nd century	central Gaul	
L2	483.00.2/74	29?	1st century	southern Gaul	

The sherd in the style of PATERCLUS published by Cunliffe (1962:72) cannot be found.

The Coins

Provenance	Museum	Emperor	Date	Identification
L2	C 1718	Ptolomey V	240—180 B.C.	Sovronos 1237
L5	C 1717	Commodus	A.D. 180—192	Alexandria: rev. Anibis

The Ptolemaic coin was identified by the Ashmolean Museum, and that of Commodus by Richard Reece.

I have discussed the authenticity of these two finds elsewhere (Collis 1975). The coin of Ptolemey was supposed to have been found in the base of the Iron Age level L2 (the measurement given in fact put it into the top 2—3 cm of the natural gravel) in a trial hole dug by schoolboys from Winchester College. The Roman one came from the dump of the same trench. It belongs to a group of coins well known to museum curators, but as Richard Reece comments, no example has yet been found in an authenticated archaeological context in this country. The occurrence of these two Egyptian coins, types not usually found in this country, both in the same trench, in a state of preservation unusual for the site indicates, I think conclusively, that they are modern 'plants', and certainly the coin of Commodus *cannot* 'safely be considered to belong to [the bank]' (Cunliffe 1962:58). Biddle (1975b) has however pointed to the relatively large number of Ptolemaic coins from the Winchester area, and to dismiss this one coin does not necessarily imply that all are modern losses.

The Roman Glass by D. Charlesworth

Both pieces of glass come from the addition to the Roman bank.

Provenance	Museum Accession Number	Description
F32-3	483.28	Possibly same vessel as 483.29.
F32-4	483.29	Fragments of an open base ring of a flagon or globular jar, in thin almost colourless glass, *c.* A.D. 70—130.

Miscellaneous Finds

Fig. No.	Provenance		Museum Accession Number	Description
Bone Objects				
103:6	F69	early medieval pit	483.57	Antler tine. The tip has been trimmed and polished smooth, the point cut off, and some of the core hollowed out. On body of tine there are several small cut marks and 3 to 4 heavy ones at thick end.
104	F34-1	medieval pit	483.56	Bone spoon, carved from a single piece of bone, and incised with a

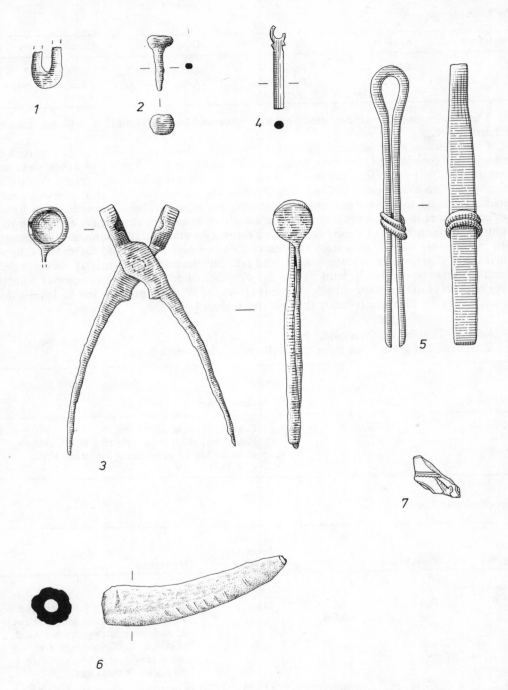

Fig. 103. Westgate Car Park: finds of samian, iron, bronze and antler (scale: 1—3, 6: ½; 4, 5, 7: 1/1).

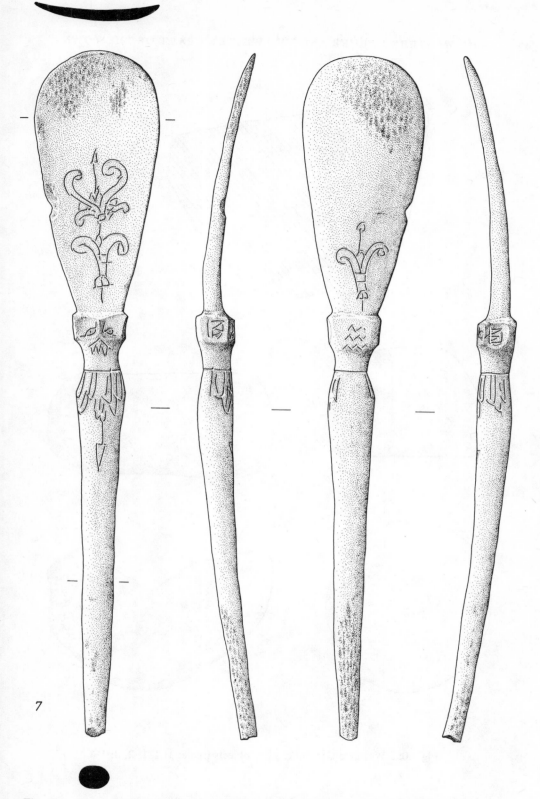

7

Fig. 104. Westgate Car Park: bone spoon from F34-1 (scale 1/1). *Drawing by David Hyde.*

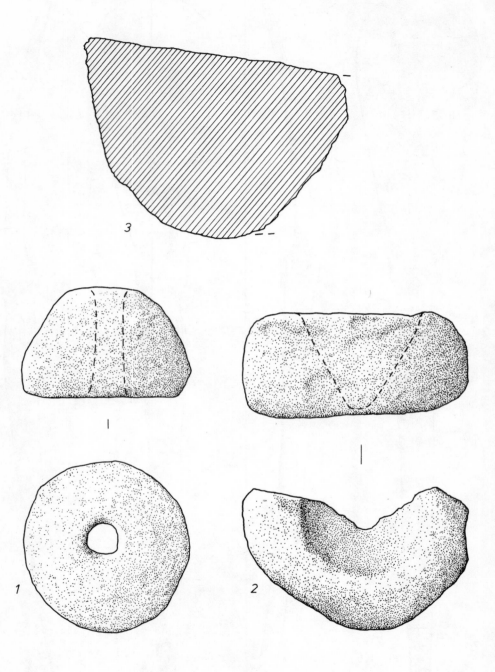

Fig. 105. Westgate Car Park: stone objects (scale: 1: 1/1; 2, 3: ½).

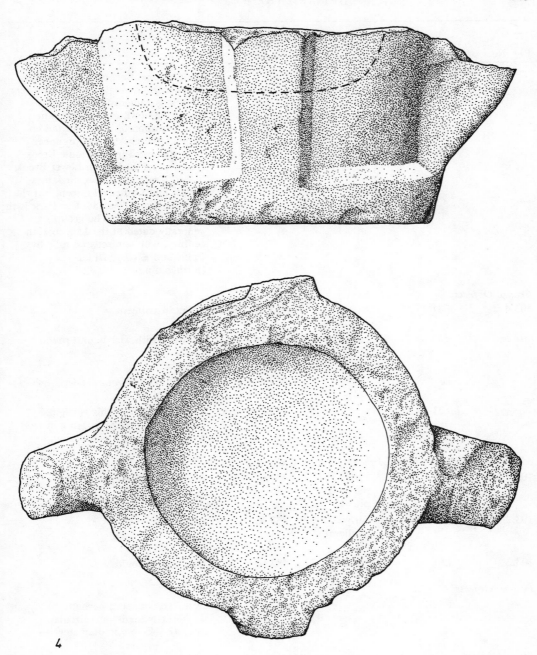

4

Fig. 106. Westgate Car Park: stone mortar from F51 (scale ½).

Fig. No.	Provenance		Museum Accession Number	Description
				complex acanthus on upper surface of bowl and a single acanthus on rear. Handle is zoomorphic with a beast biting the bowl, and a schematic representation of body and tail on handle. Winchester has produced 7 such spoons: 2 from Middle Brook Street and 1 each from Lower Brook Street, Trafalgar Street, St James Villas, and Cathedral Green, but the example from Westgate Car Park is the largest and finest. The group, generally dated to the 11th to 12th century, will be discussed fully by Collis and Kjølbye-Biddle (forthcoming).
Bronze Objects				
103:4	F31-1	first phase Roman bank	483.54	Toilet instrument.
103:5	F33-5	early medieval pit	483.55	Split-pin with wire bound round centre.
—	L2		483.6 483.5	Small piece of bronze sheet. Droplet of bronze.
—	F31-3		483.2	Lump of bronze. This is slight evidence for bronze working in Iron Age or earliest Roman period.
Medieval and Post-Medieval Iron Objects by I. Goodall				
103:1	F38	early medieval pit	483.61	Incomplete U-shaped staple.
103:2	F38	early medieval pit	483.65	Iron nail.
103.3	L8	unstratified	483.60	Iron bullet mould.
Pottery Objects				
—	F32-1		483.63	Iron Age pot sherd perhaps deliberately made into circular disc, 42—45 mm in diameter
Stone Objects				
105:1	F34-3	early medieval pit	483.25	Spindle whorl or weight roughly carved from chalk, and drilled.

Fig. No.	Provenance		Museum Accession Number	Description
105:2	F33-3	early medieval pit	483.24	Stone lamp roughly pecked from piece of sandstone.
105:3	F35	Iron Age pit	483.19	Cross-section of a rotary quern of greensand.
106:4	F51	15th—16th century pit	483.27	Stone mortar.

There are fragments of querns from Iron Age deposits F3 (483.14), F4 (483.15), F22 (483.16), L2 (483.10, 11, 12, 13), from the Roman bank F32-3 (483.17) and F32-4 (483.18), and the late Saxon pit F79 (483.66). Stone pebbles came from F3 (483.23) and L2 (483.21, 22).

Bronze slag was found in the early medieval pits, F33, F38, and F69; iron slag in F31-5 (Roman) and F33, F34, F38, F39, and F69 (early medieval); and crucible fragments in F33, F72, L6, L7, and L10.

EASTON WATER-MAIN TRENCH (SOUTH)
(EWT 55 Site 959)

Between April and October 1955 a new water-main was laid from the village of Easton, three miles northeast of Winchester, to the waterworks in Romsey Road. A trench 0·80—1 m wide and of varying depth was cut for the pipe through the northern and western suburbs. The northernmost observations were made in Edington Road, whence the trench ran along Lank-hills Road, St Paul's Hill, Clifton Terrace, St James' Terrace, and Mews Lane. This list of finds is based upon Mr Cottrill's field notes, and he was able to collect material and make observations with the assistance of the contractors, Bridgewater Bros of Chichester, and the Engineer-in-Charge, Mr G. Hudswell. The finds from the northern suburb are published elsewhere in this volume (p. 155—7) and here we are concerned with Features 4—40 and Layers 4—34.

Summary

The observations made along this length of trench (Fig. 107) are of considerable importance especially for the Iron Age and the Roman periods. In 1955 the line of the Iron Age defences was totally unknown, and the identification of the ditches F4 and F24 gave for the first time the northern and southern limits of an enclosure whose western side it was suggested was formed by the Oram's Arbour earthwork. These lines have since been confirmed by controlled excavation further to the east (Biddle 1964:231, 1969:279) and on Oram's Arbour (Biddle 1966). Equally the negative observations in Mews Lane showed that the Oram's Arbour ditch had changed alignment, and was therefore not part of a dyke cutting off the spur, but part of an enclosure which includes F4 and F24 (Fig. 108).

There was no direct dating evidence from the ditches here, other than the information that the ditch was filling up in the Roman period. Only one Middle Iron Age feature was found, F8, otherwise there are only scraps of pottery in later features. However, the natural subsoil lies directly below the modern road make-up, and presumably archaeological deposits

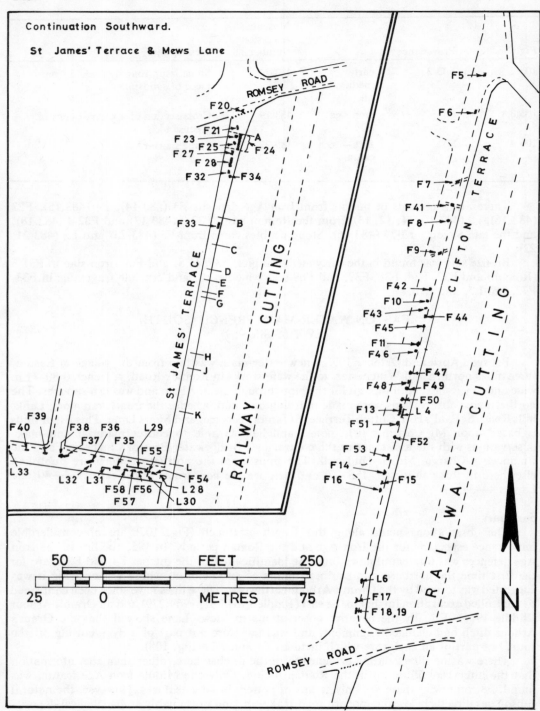

Fig. 107. Easton Water-Main Trench (south): locations of observations.

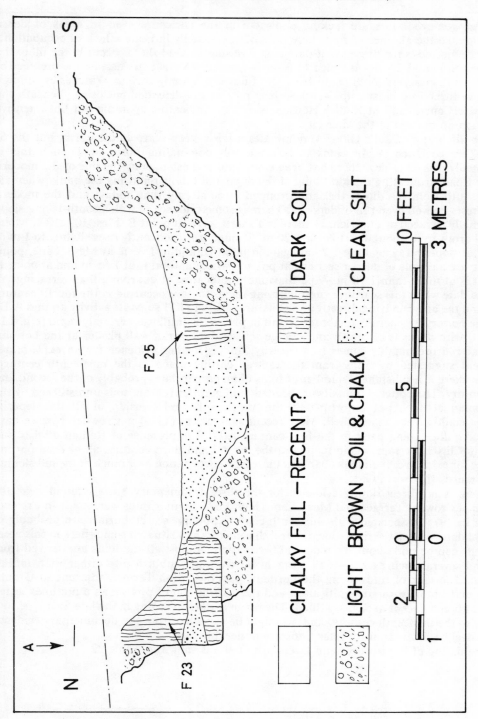

Fig. 108. Easton Water-Main Trench (south): section of the Iron Age ditch F24.

have been removed. Pits are lacking elsewhere in the enclosure even in areas of dense occupation, so the absence of finds here does not necessarily indicate a lack of occupation.

Less expected is the presence of Late Iron Age sherds. Odd sherds occur in the fill of the two ditches F4 and F24, but the pit F11 is fairly certainly of this date, despite the presence of later sherds (contamination?). Late Iron Age finds are notably rare in Winchester, though some have turned up outside the southwestern part of the defended enclosure, beneath the new Assize Courts, and at Radley House (see p. 00), indicating sporadic but not intensive occupation on the site of the later city.

The ditch on St Paul's Hill (F4) dominates a fairly steep scarp to the north, but the St James' Terrace Ditch (F24) seems to be in a less dominating position. Though this is undoubtedly true, it is clear there has been considerable erosion along the line of the modern Romsey Road, truncating the top filling of the ditch and totally removing the bank, whereas, further south from the ditch, the land dropped more steeply than today, and the modern terrace rests on well over 1 m of deposits. There is some evidence that this south-facing slope was partially terraced or quarried, as there is a sharp scarp at point B (Figs. 107, 109), where the level drops from about 0·50 to over 1·20 m. Though it subsequently rises slightly to 1 m at point C, it slopes away again to 1·25 m again at point D, and to 1·35 m at Mews Lane, point L. There are a couple of deeper sections at point H where natural is at 1·55 m and at point K where it is at more than 1·70 m — perhaps more indicative of quarrying than terracing.

The date when this scarping and quarrying seems to have occurred is the fourth century A.D., and the one coin lying directly on the natural chalk in L11 suggests activity around A.D. 350. The pottery is generally unabraded, and in places the infill was certainly rapid (e.g. L13 and L14) with deposits of brown and orange soil, and a layer of wall plaster at the bottom. This material presumably comes from nearby, and is further evidence for an extra-mural settlement suggested by finds from the railway cutting made in the nineteenth century. However there is a substantial number of finds of an earlier date, probably of the second and third century. The pottery is equally unabraded, and may derive from soils undisturbed by the late Roman activity, but unfortunately the stratigraphic relationship of all the deposits observed could not be established. More recent excavations (1974) in Crowder Terrace have produced gullies going back to the first century A.D. The presence of Roman ditches and gullies in Clifton Terrace, again mainly of the second and third century, all give supporting evidence for extensive, though probably not intensive, occupation over much of the hill sloping down towards the North Gate.

There is no direct dating evidence for the three fragmentary burials found near the junction of Crowder Terrace and Mews Lane (F36, F37). Similar finds were made in Crowder Terrace in 1974, associated with thirteenth-century pottery, so the burials are probably of medieval date, during the time when the Jewish cemetery was situated somewhere in this area.

Little can be said about the medieval occupation. Almost all the finds are derived from pits, and several such as F17—F19 seem to be domestic rubbish pits rather than infilled quarries. The lack of finds along the northern part of Clifton Terrace adjacent to Oram's Arbour may not be without significance, and the distribution of pits shows a not unexpected concentration adjacent to Romsey Road. The range in dates, starting in the late Saxon period, runs up to the thirteenth century, and, as might be expected from the documentary evidence for the decline of the suburb, later finds are noticeably rare.

The dating of the features and layers in this site is shown in Table 22.

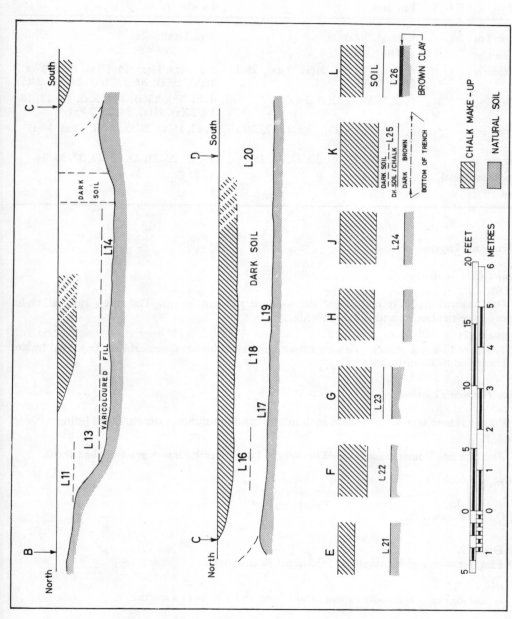

Fig. 109. Easton Water-Main Trench (south): schematic section of deposits in St James' Terrace and Mews Lane.

Table 22. Easton Water-Main Trench (South): age of features and layers (x=later finds also present).

Period	Features	Layers
Saucepan Pot	8, 11(x), 30(x)	7(x), 13(x), 26(x)
Late Iron Age	4, 11(x), 24(x)	
Early Roman	6, 9, 11, 13, 14, 21(x), 24(x), 25(x), 27(x), 28(x)	5(x), 7(x), 13(x), 14, 15(x), 16(x), 17(x), 18(x), 19(x), 20(x), 21(x), 24, 25, 34(x)
Late Roman	5(x), 7, 24(x), 32(x), 34(x)	4, 5, 7(x), 13(x), 14, 15(x), 16, 17, 18, 19, 20(x), 21(x), 24, 25, 34(x)
Early medieval	5, 16, 17, 18, 19, 20, 21, 22, 24(x), 25, 34(x), 39, 40	9, 12, 15(x), 28(x), 29(x), 32(x), 34(x)
Late medieval	23, 24, 27, 28, 29, 30, 32, 34, 35	13, 15, 20, 21, 23, 28, 29, 32, 33, 34
Early post-medieval		7, 27
Modern		6

Features and Layers

St Paul's Hill Features
F4: Ditch 1

The natural chalk is just below the modern road make-up. The ditch runs at right angles to the trench and is 4·20 m wide.

959.4.0/1.
Two Late Iron Age sherds, one with a thick bundle of burnished vertical lines (c.f. Fig. 72:20). Illustrated by Cunliffe (1964:16).

Clifton Terrace Features
F5: Pit 4

Pit in the east section, *c.* 1·40 m in diameter, and of unknown depth. Dark filling.

959.5.0/1.
Rim of a late Roman colour-coated beaker, and a thirteenth-century grass-marked sherd.

F6: Pit 5

959.6.0/1.
One amphora sherd.

F7: Ditch 2

Flat bottomed with a depth of 1·30 m below the surface.

959.7.0/1.
A late Roman colour-coated sherd, also a bone and a piece of a quern.

F8: Pit 6

A shallow excavation in the east side of the trench, 1·40 m wide. The top of the natural chalk is 0·35 m down and the bottom of the pit at 1·08 m.

959.8.0/1.
A friable black burnished Iron Age sherd, presumably of saucepan-pot type, sand tempered.

F9: *Ditch 3*
A V-shaped ditch 1·40 m deep and 1·85 m wide at the surface of the chalk, 0·55 m down.
959.9.0/1.
An early Roman grey ware sherd with burnished lattice, and a fragment of Roman tile.

F10: *Pit 7*
Pit in the east section, 1 m deep, and 0·90 m wide, filled with brown soil and chalk.
959.10.0/1.
One Middle to Late Iron Age sherd, and one early Roman sherd near the top.

F11: *Pit 8*
Pit showing in both sections filled with dark soil. It is 2 m wide in the east section and
0·85 m in the west. It is vertical sided and the flat bottom is 1·03 m down, 0·47 m below
the top of the chalk.
F11-1: From the fill of the pit
959.11.1/1.
Jar (Fig. 110:1). Hard, sand-tempered, grey ware with red-brown exterior, wiped vertically.
Comparable in fabric with sherds from Winnall (Fig. 28:59), Mill Plain, and Airlie Road
Winchester.
Jar (Fig. 110:2). Soft, sandy, black ware with burnished decoration. The sherd has been
deliberately abraded on the upper and lower edges.
There is a second unabraded sherd.
There is a gritty sherd of saucepan-pot type, two early Roman sherds, and a possibly early
medieval sherd.

F11-2: From the dump adjacent to the pit
959.11.2/1.
Bead-rim jar (Fig. 110:3). Hard, sandy, black-brown fabric with red-brown exterior.
Jar base (Fig. 110:4). Hard sandy, black-brown fabric with red-brown exterior.
Jar base (Fig. 110:5). Grey, sandy fabric with black surface and burnished decoration. The
inside of the base is burnished and the underside marked with a burnished X.
There are fragments of a large, coarsely gritted storage jar with horizontal smoothing at the
base, and vertical smoothing on the body.
There are 4—5 other Late Iron Age sherds, but also two Roman sherds.

F13: *Pit 10*
Pit filled with brown soil and chalk, in the west section, 15 cm deep and 2·90 m wide.
959.13.0/1.
Early Roman black-slipped sherd with burnished lattice.

F14: *Pit 11*
Pit in the west side of the trench filled with dark soil and chalk. It is 2·50 m deep, and
deeper than 1·45 m below the surface.
959.14.0/1.
Four early Roman sherds including one from a buff flask.

F15: *Pit 12*
In the west side of the trench, 1·15 m wide and more than 1·50 m deep below the

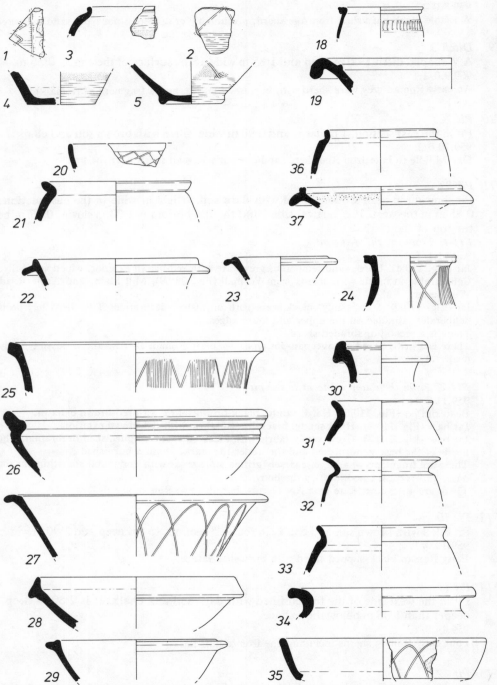

Fig. 110. Easton Water-Main Trench (south): Iron Age pottery from F11 (1—5) and Roman pottery from L8 (18, 19), L9 (20, 21), L18 (36, 37), L13 (22—24), L15 (25—29) and L17 (30—35) (scale ¼).

surface (chalk starts at 0·70 m). Fill of dark soil, oysters, and bone.
959.15.0/1.
Twelve Saxo-Norman cooking-pot sherds, including two rims.

F16: Pit 13

In the west side of the trench, 1·30 m wide and more than 1·70 m deep. Chalk and dark soil infill.

959.16.0/1. From either F15 or F16 (the pottery suggests F15).
One fragment from the upper shoulder of a Saxo-Norman cooking pot (Fig. 111:6) in an oxidized, chalk-tempered fabric which has had the tempering leached out on the inside of the vessel. The outside is smoothed (but not burnished) and decorated with rows of alternating rings and eight-spoked wheel stamps.
Sherd (Fig. 111:7) of Michelmersh ware.
Cooking pots (Fig. 111:8,9) in standard Saxo-Norman gritty fabric.
There are three other gritty Saxo-Norman sherds, and the whole forms a useful tenth- to eleventh-century group.

F17: Pit 14

In the west section more than 0·65 m in diameter and deeper than 2·15 m below the surface (chalk at 0·50 m). Fill of dark soil, oysters, and charcoal. Some slag.
959.17.0/1.
Small globular vessel (Fig. 111:10) with fine, selected, sharp-angled flint inclusions. Completely oxidized and fired quite hard.
Cooking pot (Fig. 111:11), as 8. Saxo-Norman.

F18: Pit 15

Infill to F18, more than 1·90 m deep. No finds. Pit intersecting with F19, seen in both sections. It is 1·60 m wide and 1·45 m deep, and filled with loose soil containing occasional oysters, charcoal, and bone.
959.18.0/1.
A gritty Saxo-Norman sherd. There is also some slag and an iron blade.

F19: Pit 16

Pit similar in fill to F18, more than 1·90 m deep. No finds.

St James' Terrace Features
F20: Pit 17

Pit in the east side of the trench, 1·70 m wide and flat bottomed at 0·85 m (chalk at 0·45 m). Filled with vari-coloured soils and a tip-line of chalk.
959.20.0/1.
Rim and sherd of Saxo-Norman gritty ware.

F21: Pit 18

A shallow pit.
959.21.0/3.
Several oxidized Saxo-Norman sherds including an unusual rim.
There is also an early Roman sherd, and fragments of amphora and samian, and a piece of bronze.

F22: Pit 19

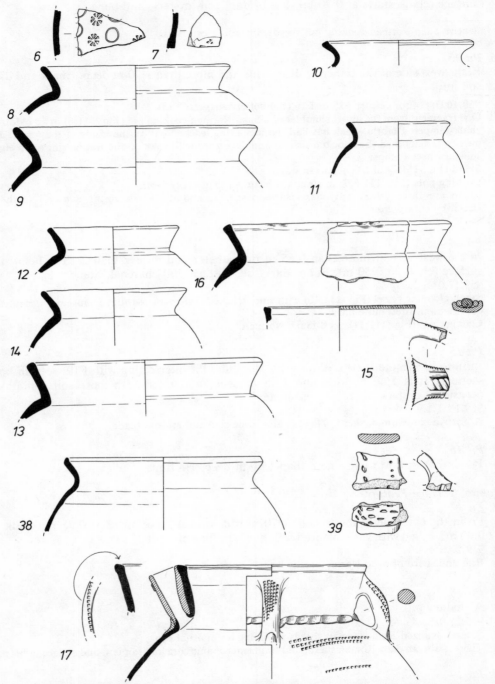

Fig. 111. Easton Water-Main Trench (south): medieval pottery from F16 (6—9), F17 (10, 11), F28 (12—16), L32 (38), L34 (39) and F39 (17) (scale ¼).

959.22.0/1.
Gritty Saxo-Norman wares, presumably eleventh to twelfth century.

F23: Pit 20

Cuts F24, see Fig. 108.
959.23.0/1.
One medieval sherd.

F24: Ditch 4 (Fig. 108)

This is assumed to be the ditch of the Middle Iron Age enclosure, though no material earlier than the Late Iron Age was found. The lowest finds, at 1·20 m depth, are early Roman, as are the majority of the finds, while higher there are late Roman finds, though contaminated by later disturbances. The ground surface has doubtless been heavily scarped on the slope leading down to Romsey Road, and the width of the ditch may originally have been more than the 4 m recorded. The likely depth of the ditch below ground surface would be 3·3 m. The finds are only recorded according to depth and not stratigraphically.

F24-1: At 1·15 m down
959.14.1/1.
Late Roman storage jar, cavetto rim, and piedish.
There is one possible Late Iron Age sherd, and one late medieval sherd.

F24-2: At 1·15 m
959.24.2/1.
One soft Iron Age sherd, and one early Roman sherd.

F24-3: At 1·20 m
959.24.3/1.
Neck of an early Roman buff flagon.

F24-4: At 1·15 m
954.24.4/1.
Fragment of amphora.

F24-5: From south scarp
959.24.5/1.
A Roman black gritty base.

F24-6: From the dump
An early Roman upright-necked jar and a late medieval sherd.

F25: Pit

Cuts F24, see Fig. 108.
959.25.0/1.
A Roman sherd and a Saxo-Norman gritty rim.

F27: Pit 23

Pit filled with dark soil and some chalk. It appears in both sections, 1·70 m wide in the east and 1·45 m in the west, and it is at least 1·45 m deep.
959.27.0/2.
Several cooking pots and glazed jugs, with three handles, one a strap handle of 'Orchard Street type'. Handle of a tripod pitcher. The group is mid to late thirteenth century.
There is a fragment of an early Roman jar and a sherd of samian.

F28: Pit 24

A large pit filled with dark soil and some chalk tips, oyster shell, and bone. In the east section it is 2·85 m wide, and 0·85 in the west. It is at least 1·60 m deep.

F28-1: Definitely from the pit
959.28.1/1.
A base of a gritty Saxo-Norman storage jar, and a Roman sherd.

F28-2: About 1·65 m down
959.28.2/1.
Standard Saxo-Norman cooking pots (Fig. 111:12,13) with collared rims in gritty fabric.

F28-3: Not more than 0·60 m down
959.28.3/1.
A very eroded globular cooking pot (Fig. 111:14) in a soft, chalk-tempered fabric.
Two handles (Fig. 111:15) from a Winchester spouted tripod pitcher in the standard, semi-oxidized fabric with a pale orange-green glaze with a twisted rope handle insert, and notched rouletting on the edges of the handle and the rim. Identical to the vessel found in a cesspit belonging to the New Minster on the Cathedral Car Park site in 1961 (Biddle and Quirk 1962), dated to *c*. A.D. 1110.
Also two Roman sherds, one with burnished lattice.

F28-4: Possibly contaminated by a modern feature
959.28.4/1.
Saxo-Norman cooking pot (Fig. 111:16) in gritty fabric.

F32: Pit

Pit 0·70 m wide and more than 1·50 m deep, filled with brown soil.
959.32.0/1,2.
Medieval cooking pots and glazed jugs, including a rod handle, which suggest a fourteenth- or early fifteenth-century date. There are two fragments of late Roman colour-coated beakers.

F33: Pit or ditch

More than 1·45 m deep and 2·40 m wide.
959.33.0/1.
Four Roman and three early medieval sherds.

F34: Pit

Filled with dark soil with some flints. It appears to be 1·85 m wide in both sections.

F34-1: From the dump nearby
959.34.1/1.
Medieval jugs and cooking pots including a rod handle and a flanged bowl which suggest a late fourteenth-century date. There is also a fragment of a late Roman flanged bowl.

F34-2: Definitely stratified in the pit
959.34.2/1.
Includes an internally glazed sherd and a jug fragment of fourteenth-century date, as well as some early medieval sherds and late Roman internally flanged bowl, a colour-coat flagon, a dish, and a jar.

F35: Pit

At least 1·85 m deep, filled with brown soil.

F35-1: From 1·40 to 1·55 m down

959.35.1/1.
A fragment of tripod pitcher and a grass-marked cooking pot suggest a twelfth-century date.

F35-2: From 1·55 to 1·80 m down
959.35.2/1.
There is a flanged dish not internally glazed, of hard, red, sandy ware, and a strap handle jug. The date should be late thirteenth or early fourteenth century.

Crowder Terrace Features
F36: Burial 1
An extended inhumation of a woman aged 50—60 years, projecting into the north side of the trench, head to the west, in a shallow grave (see p. 262).

F37: Burial 2
Disturbed burial(s) cut by a modern disturbance (F38). Fragments possibly from a man and a woman are present.

Mews Lane Features
F39: Pit (?)
Disturbance 1·55 m down.
959.39.1/1.
The larger part of the rim and shoulder of a Winchester spouted pitcher (Fig. 111:17) and the remains of two handles. This vessel is in the standard reduced interior, oxidized exterior, sandy fabric with a wash of thin, patchy, dark green glaze on the outside and from the inside of the tall collar as far as the return. The tubular spout is held to the body by a thumbed strip at the top which goes round the neck of the pot. Other similar strips descend from the spout and the handles. The handles are rod-sectioned and decorated on the outside with fine square rouletting and also on the top of the rim. Triangular rouletting occurs in rows on the body.

F40: Pit or ditch
The eastern and possibly the western sides of this feature slope inwards. It is filled with brown soil.
959.40.0/1.
Oxidized Saxo-Norman sherds including a cooking-pot rim.

Clifton Terrace Layers
L4:   Layer of clay and charcoal 0·75 m below the surface
959.00.4/1.
Sherds of late Roman cooking pot.

L5:   From the dump near L4
959.00.5/1.
Late Roman flanged dish, amphora, and Antonine samian.

St James' Terrace Layers
L8:   Unstratified, near F24
959.00.8/1.
Beaker (Fig. 110:18). Soft, sandy, light grey fabric with dark grey to black colour-coat, and coarse shallow rouletting on the shoulder.
Mortarium (Fig. 110:19). Harsh, sandy, yellow fabric.
There is a plain sherd of saucepan-pot type and Roman finds of second- to fourth-century date, as well as late and post-medieval sherds.

L9: Unstratified, from several pits near F24—F29
Lies 9—24 m from Romsey Road kerb.
959.00.9/1.
Platter (Fig. 110:20). Fine, light grey fabric with grey slip and burnished lattice. Not as fine as *terra nigra*.
Jar (Fig. 110:21). Hard, light grey fabric with sand temper. Grey slip on the exterior and inside the rim.
There is also a late Roman colour-coated beaker, Saxo-Norman wares, tripod pitcher ware, up to thirteenth-century sherds. One fragment of samian.

L10: Clean brown fill 44·60 m from Romsey road, 0·30 m deep
959.0.10/1.
Roman grey sherd.

L11: Between 44·50 and 48·00 m from Romsey Road, 0·45 m deep
959.00.11/1.
Piedish, two upright-necked rim jars, amphora, and other second- to third-century pottery.

L13: Vari-coloured fill, 0·45—1·15 m, apparently below L11
959.00.13/1—3.
Flanged dish (Fig. 110:22). Dull grey to reddish fabric with some organic and grog temper. Black burnished flange and interior.
Piedish (Fig. 110:23). Hard, dull grey fabric with sand temper. Grey exterior and off-white to brown interior.
Flagon (?) (Fig. 110:24). Hard, light grey fabric with sand temper and burnished decoration.
There is one fragment of saucepan pot rim in hard, dark brown, sand-tempered ware. There are about 60 Roman sherds including one orange and four metallic purple colour-coat beakers, and one red colour-coat; two to three burnished cavetto rims (one with burnished lattice), and an everted-rim cooking pot of late Roman type with heavy grog temper. Generally the finds are similar to Frederick Place F10 (pp. 170—171) and should be early fourth century. However, there are also two medieval sherds, and two of samian.

L14: As L13, 1·15 m and deeper
A layer of plaster was found lying on the chalk at a depth of 1·45 m. At 49·70—55·50 m from Romsey Road.
959.00.14/1.
Grey-ware jar with outcurved rim and a grey storage jar.

L15: In soil between 53·60 and 57·20 m from Romsey Road
959.00.15/5.
Bowl (Fig. 110:25). Hard, light grey ware, sand tempered with rare grits. Burnished rim and decoration.
Internally flanged bowl (Fig. 110:26). Hard, sandy fabric with patchy white slip.
Piedish (Fig. 110:27). Hard, black ware with sand temper and occasional grit. Dark brown to black burnished surface.
Mortarium (Fig. 110:28). Hard, sandy, buff fabric.
Flanged dish (Fig. 110:29). Brown fabric with much grog temper. Black burnished surface.
Some thirty other fragments include six straight-sided dishes, some with external burnished loops; two purple colour-coated beakers; one orange colour-coat base; a rouletted sherd; two cavetto rims; three flanged dishes; two piedishes; a folded beaker in sandy grey ware. There is a large storage jar, coil built, with much coarse grog. It is fingered under the rim and has criss-cross incisions on the rim. This fourth-century group is contaminated by four medieval sherds. There are four Antonine samian sherds.

L16: At 57·20 m from Romsey Road, 0·75 m deep
459.00.16/1.
Shoulder of a cavetto rim jar with burnished lattice, and a straight-sided dish.

L17: Dark soil around 58·90 m, down to chalk at 1 m depth
959.0.17/1.
Flask (Fig. 110:30). Hard, reddish-buff fabric with dull buff surface.
Jar with out-turned rim (Fig. 110:31). Grey fabric with reduced grog temper, darker exterior.
Cavetto rim jar (Fig. 110:32). Fine, grey-brown fabric, darker (slipped?) surface, burnished.
Jar with everted rim (Fig. 110:33). Grit and reduced grog temper. Fabric dull grey to brown, with black, tooled surface.
Storage jar (Fig. 110:34). Hard, grey fabric with sand temper. Dark grey slip.
Straight-sided dish (Fig. 110:35). Hard, dark grey fabric with sand temper. Dull brown surface, burnished internally, and with burnished decoration.
There are about 40 other fragments, some earlier, but mostly late Roman, including the flange of a red colour-coated bowl, three straight-sided dishes, two piedishes, three cavetto rim jars (one in fine ware with burnished lattice, as Fig. 72:30), three metallic purple colour-coated beaker fragments, and one in softer ware. The group is associated with a coin of Constantine II which lay directly on the natural chalk.

L18: Soil infill, around 58·90 to 60·10 m from Romsey Road
959.00.18/3.
Jar (Fig. 110:36). Dull, soft brown fabric with black burnished exterior. A second sherd (burnt?) is orange and sandy.
Mortarium (Fig. 110:37). Hard, orange-buff fabric with white slip.
Among the 25 other sherds there is a vessel similar to vessel 25 in L15, three purple colour-coat vessels (two metallic), one Castor (?) ware sherd with rouletting, a red colour-coated bowl, and two Antonine samian sherds.

L19: Soil fill at 61·00 m from Romsey Road 1·15 m down
959.00.19/1.
Two sherds, one from a late Roman cooking pot.

L20: Soil at 64·90 m from Romsey Road, no depth stated
959.00.20/1.
Ten late Roman sherds including a straight-sided dish, and also a fourteenth-century rod handle, stabbed and slightly grooved.

L21: At 69·50 to 70·50 m from Romsey Road
Soil below make-up, 1·15—1·45 m down.
959.00.21/1—2.
A reed-rim bowl and a flanged bowl, a colour-coat beaker and second-century samian sherds. There is also some fourteenth-century medieval pottery.

L22: Soil at 74·10 to 75·80 m from Romsey Road
959.00.22/1.
Fragments of a buff flask (second century?), and a sherd with a slashed cordon (second/third), as well as a glass fragment.

L23: At 87·10 m from Romsey Road, 1 m down
959.00.23/1.
A tripod-pitcher base, mid to late thirteenth century.

L24: At 104·10 m from Romsey Road, in soil 1·55 m down
959.00.24/1.
Fragment of a late Roman straight-sided dish.

L25: At 119·20 to 120·90 m from Romsey Road, all from a brown soil, 0·45—1·25 m down
959.00.25/1.
Seven sherds including an inturned-rim bowl, two purple colour-coat vessels, beakers (one metallic).

L26: In brown soil 4—20 m from the north corner of Mews Lane
959.00.26/1.
One coarse Iron Age sherd, but the rest is Roman, including a straight-necked jar (c.f. Cunliffe 1964, Fig. 18 no. 20) of late second- or early third-century date, and a first-century samian sherd.

L27: At 2 m north of Mews Lane, just below chalk make-up, at 0·65 m
959.00.27/1.
A group of sixteenth-century sherds.

Mews Lane Layers
L28: Brown soil fill below 1·20 m, 1—2 m from St James' Lane corner
959.00.28/1.
A thirteenth-century group of tripod pitchers and grass-marked cooking pots.

L29: At 3—4 m from St James' Lane corner
959.00.29/1.
Meat dish of late fourteenth-century date with other coarse sherds. Also an Antonine samian sherd.

L30: At 7 m west from St James' Lane corner
Flint, chalk, and light brown soil at 1·30 m depth
There is a late Antonine samian sherd.

L31: Brown soil at 1·45 m, 20 m west of St James' Lane corner
959.00.31/1.
Two sherds of late Roman colour-coat.

L32: At the bottom of dark soil, 0·70 m deep, 28 m from St James' Lane corner
959.00.32/1.
Cooking pot (Fig. 111:38) of late thirteenth- to early fourteenth-century date.

L33: At 8 m west of F40
959.00.33/1.
Standard good quality cooking pot, buff-coloured, sandy fabric, early fourteenth century.

L34: Unstratified finds
959.00.34/1. From Clifton Terrace.
Curfew handle fragment (Fig. 111:39) in fine, sandy, buff-coloured fabric with reduced grey core. Stabbed on the upper surface, and on the junction with the interior of the vessel.
There is a late Roman red colour-coat vessel with circular stamps, an imitation 31, and an Oxfordshire sherd, and seven Roman to medieval sherds.

959.00.34/6. From Clifton Terrace.
There are 35 Roman sherds of second to fourth century date, including a decorated colour-coated flagon, and ten medieval sherds.
959.00.34/7. From Mews Lane.
One Roman and four medieval sherds.

The Finds

The Coin by R. Reece
   From L17 there is a coin of Constantine I of the London mint, dated to A.D. 320—324 (RIC VII London 158).

The Samian by G. Dannell

Provenance	Museum Accession Number	Form	Date A.D.	Kiln	Comment
F21-1	959.21.0/2	31	Antonine	central Gaul	
F27	959.27.0/1	33	Antonine	probably central Gaul	Burnt.
L5	959.00.5/2	Curle 15	Antonine	—	Burnt.
L9	959.00.9/2	31	Late Antonine	central Gaul	
L13	959.00.13/1	31	Antonine	central Gaul	
	959.00.13/2	33	Antonine	central Gaul	Burnt.
L15	959.00.15/1	31R	Antonine	central Gaul	
	959.00.15/2	31	Antonine	central Gaul	
	959.00.15/3	33	Antonine	central Gaul	
	959.00.15/4	Mortarium	Antonine	central Gaul	Well rubbed.
L17	959.00.17/2	31	Antonine	central Gaul	
	959.00.17/3	38	Antonine	central Gaul	
L18	959.00.18/1	31	Antonine	central Gaul	
	959.00.18/2	33	Antonine	central Gaul(?)	Burnt.
L21	959.00.21/1	18/31	Hadrianic/ Antonine	central Gaul	
L26	959.00.26/1	18	1st century	southern Gaul	
L29	959.00.29/1	33	Antonine	central Gaul	
L30	959.00.30/1	31	Antonine	central Gaul	
L34	959.00.34/3	31R	Late Antonine	central Gaul	
	959.00.34/4	45	Late Antonine	central Gaul	

Roman Wall Plaster by J. Liversidge
   The area of L14 produced plaster with red next to black, fine white lines on red or purple, and one piece with a white line separating red from purple. Plain green, cream yellow, and white also occurred (959.7.9).

Miscellaneous Finds
   There is a loop of a medieval bronze strap-end buckle (959.6, Fig. 112:1), from the fourteenth-century pit, F34-2. There is a fragment of bronze sheet (959.5) with two rivet holes and an iron rivet in the early medieval pit, F21, and a piece of base of a Roman glass bottle (959.10) which has been mislaid from L22.

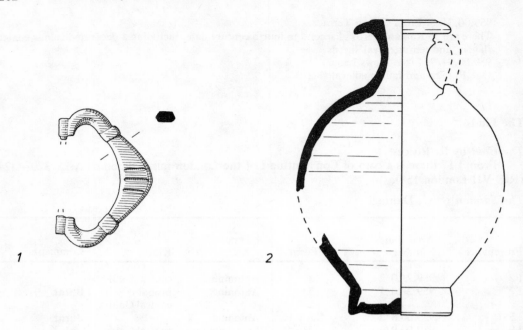

Fig. 112. Easton Water-Main Trench (south): buckle from F34 (scale 1/1); Electricity Cable Trench: pottery from burial F2 (scale ½).

The Burials by C. Wells

Burial 1 (F36). This consists of some extremely fragmented and defective remains of a woman, aged about 50—65. Surviving bones include a few fragments of cranial vault showing the sutures to be almost obliterated. The frontal bone is partly preserved and has a small frontal sinus. Part of the right maxilla shows that two molars were lost ante-mortem. Other fragments include two damaged vertebrae, pieces of pelvis, ribs, clavicles, and scapulae. All long bones are represented but each is much damaged and defective. The left tibia is about 316 mm long, corresponding to a stature of 1532 mm (5 ft ¼ in). A few small bones of hands and feet survive. No significant anomalies or pathologies were detected. Little can be said about these remains.

Burial 2 (F37). This consists of thirteen fragments of cranial vault and four pieces of pelvis. Two of the pelvic fragments duplicate parts of the right innominate. At least two persons are represented here, (a) female (?), (b) male (?), both adult. A fragment of maxilla shows:

$$\underline{? \; 7 \; 6 \; 5 \; 4 \; 0 \; 0 \; 0 \; | \; 0 \; 2 \; 3 \; 0 \; ? \; ? \; ? \; ?}$$

Dental attrition is extremely light, suggesting that this was a young woman. No anomalies or pathology were detected and little can be said about these remains. Both these persons seem to have been lightly built with not very strong muscles.

ELECTRICITY CABLE TRENCH, STATION HILL
(Site 1294)

In 1964 a trench was dug 0·90 m wide to take an electricity cable from the railway bridge at the top of Upper High Street to the top of Station Hill, parallel to the footpath which runs alongside the railway cutting. The site was visited on a number of occasions by F. Cottrill and the writer.

Summary

The major feature noted in this trench was the lip of the Iron Age ditch. Subsequently, in 1975 a length of this ditch was excavated by K. Qualmann, and its nature confirmed. There is also evidence of a single inhumation burial, unfortunately difficult to date, and again the recent excavations have produced late Roman burials (mainly early fourth century) but these were entirely confined to the infill of the ditch, and no other burials were located near the one published here.

Features

F1:   The Iron Age ditch
Only the northern lip of the ditch was noted and the sloping side of it followed to the bottom of the trench 1·85 m below the surface (the level of solid chalk here is 0·45 m below the surface). The infill is of brown soil. There were no finds.

F2:   Roman burial
Sherds and bones were picked up on the dump, and a possible grave pit was noted in both sections, 0·50 m wide and 0·50 m deep. No finds were found *in situ* and the association of the pot with the bones is only assumed. The skeleton is that of a child aged 5—7 years.
1294.2.0/1.
A jug (Fig. 112:2) in orange fabric, slightly coarser than samian, and with a glossy orange slip. It has been variously suggested to be of east Gaulish, North African, or east Mediterranean origin.

F3:   Medieval pit
Assumed to be medieval, but with no finds.

F4:   Medieval pit
Noted in the west section.
1294.4.0/1.
Two sherds of early medieval gritty ware.

The Finds

The Burial by C. Wells
This consists of a few scraps of cranial vault, orbit, and long bone fragments of a child in the 5—7-year range. Nothing useful can be said about these remains.

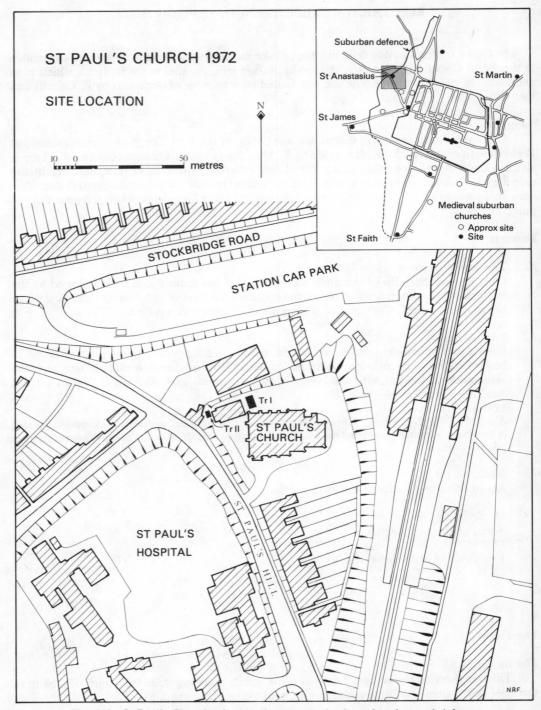

Fig. 113. St Paul's Church: site location plan: suburban churches and defences.

ST PAUL'S CHURCH
(SPC72 Site 1597)
by K. Qualmann

St Paul's Church is situated northwest of the Winchester city centre, on the east side of St Paul's Hill, across the railway cutting from the British Rail station (Fig. 113). Rescue excavation took place from late April to early June 1972, in advance of the construction of an extension to the church hall north of the existing church. The work was directed by the then Winchester Rescue Archaeologist, Peter Wade-Martins, and was jointly funded by the City of Winchester and the Department of the Environment, Ancient Monuments Inspectorate. Excavation was carried out by kind permission of the Rev. Canon C. R. Macbeth and the St Paul's Parochial Church Council.

Three full-time volunteer excavators provided the main labour force, which was supplemented on weekends and in evenings by members of the Winchester Archaeological Rescue Group and the St Paul's Youth Fellowship, the latter organized by the Rev. I. R. Dowse.

The writer is currently the City of Winchester Rescue Archaeologist and is responsible for the post-excavation work and interpretation embodied in this report. He would like to thank all members of the Winchester Research Unit who have helped with its production, especially the Director, Martin Biddle; Assistant Director, Derek Keene; and Research Assistant, Katherine Barclay. Illustrations are by Nigel Fradgley, Nick Griffiths, and the writer.

Human skeletal remains from excavated graves were returned to the church authorities for re-burial; all other finds and site records have been deposited with Winchester City Museum.

Summary with D. Keene

The existing church of St Paul was built in 1870—2 in the parish of Weeke on glebe land representing the site of the medieval church of St Anastasius. Both Milner (1839:207) and Baigent (1865:3, note C) record the discovery of human graves on the site, and in 1870 remains of an earlier building were found by the architect of the new church, John Colson (Hampshire Chronicle, 13.viii.1870). The rescue excavations of 1972 have confirmed that the present churchyard is indeed the site of the medieval church and its graveyard. The observation of at least four human graves on 5 April 1976 disturbed by landscaping at SU 47662990 supports the likely equation of the modern and medieval churchyards (marked X on Fig. 113).

The earliest excavated deposits on the site provide evidence for domestic occupation of possible Saxon date (Phase 1, Figs. 114, 115). The area subsequently came into use as a cemetery (Phase 2), probably representing part of the churchyard of St Anastasius. By the late eleventh century the church had itself been extended or rebuilt over the southern part of the excavated area (Phase 3).

Over the uppermost layers filling a possible ditch (Phase 4), a substantial chalk bank was constructed north of the church after 1100 (Phase 5). The ditch may represent part of an early defensive circuit, but the chalk bank was certainly part of the suburban defences of the medieval western suburb.

Graves were cut within the twelfth-century church (Phase 6) and slight evidence for structural alterations was found.

At least five churches served the western suburb in the twelfth century. Two of these, St James and St Anastasius, were situated near the point where a main road entered the suburban defences. St Faith in the southern suburb and St Martin, Winnall, to the northeast may have occupied comparable sites. It has been suggested (Biddle, ed. 1977:262) that these churches may originally have served small rural settlements once separate from

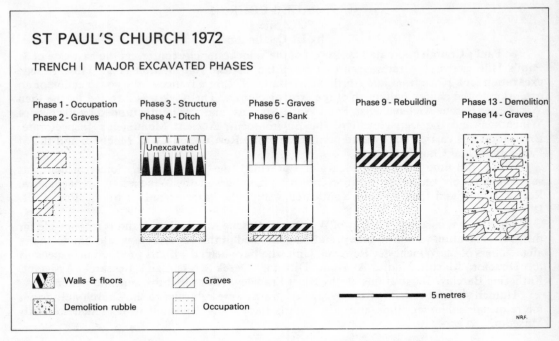

ST PAUL'S CHURCH 1972

TRENCH I   MAJOR EXCAVATED PHASES

Phase 1 - Occupation   Phase 3 - Structure   Phase 5 - Graves   Phase 9 - Rebuilding   Phase 13 - Demolition
Phase 2 - Graves   Phase 4 - Ditch   Phase 6 - Bank   Phase 14 - Graves

Unexcavated

Walls & floors   Graves

Demolition rubble   Occupation

5 metres

NRF.

Fig. 114. St Paul's Church: major excavated phases, shown in plan.

Winchester but later incorporated into the city's suburban area. The existence of a cemetery associated with St Anastasius may also indicate that the church once formed the nucleus of a distinct settlement. In the twelfth century, however, St Anastasius was regarded as a church of the city rather than the surrounding countryside.

At least part of the church structure was demolished early in the thirteenth century. The north wall was rebuilt further to the north (Phase 9), possibly for the insertion of an aisle.

The suburb outside the West Gate suffered rapid decline in the late Middle Ages and was virtually depopulated by the end of the fifteenth century.

St Anastasius underwent periods of disuse and repair, followed by the demolition of the excavated part of the church structure by the mid fourteenth century (Phase 13). Eighteen graves, mostly children, lying in two rows (Phase 14) were found cut into the demolition rubble. No burial in the excavated area took place after about 1400.

Documentary evidence indicates that St Anastasius was in ruins in 1408, although since rectors continued to be appointed into the 1470s, some part of the church structure may well have been repaired in the fifteenth century. On historical grounds one would expect the church and cemetery to have fallen entirely out of use by about 1500.

Any late or post-medieval deposits were removed from the site by levelling (Phase 15) following the construction of St Paul's Church in 1872. Topsoil subsequently brought onto the site for landscaping (Phase 16) has been found to contain bone-working waste and several bone objects, possibly of Roman date.

Excavations

Trench I, measuring 6·2 m by 3·6 m, was excavated near the east end of the church hall (Fig. 113). Investigation was halted at a depth of just over 1 m due to the architect's estimate

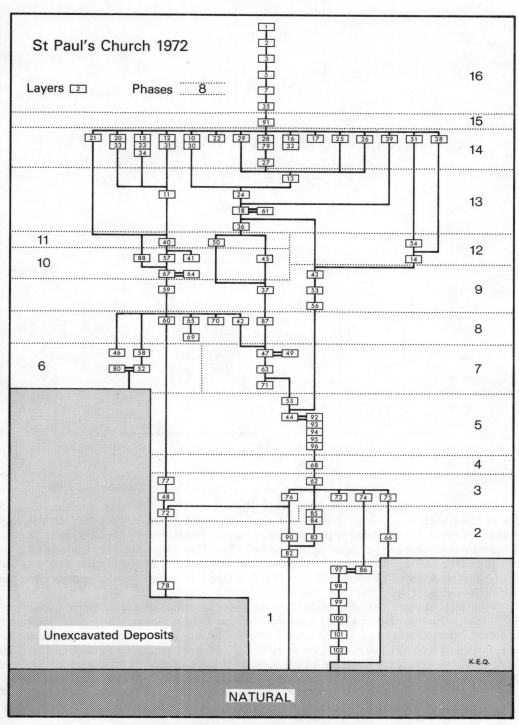

Fig. 115. St Paul's Church: stratigraphic sequence.

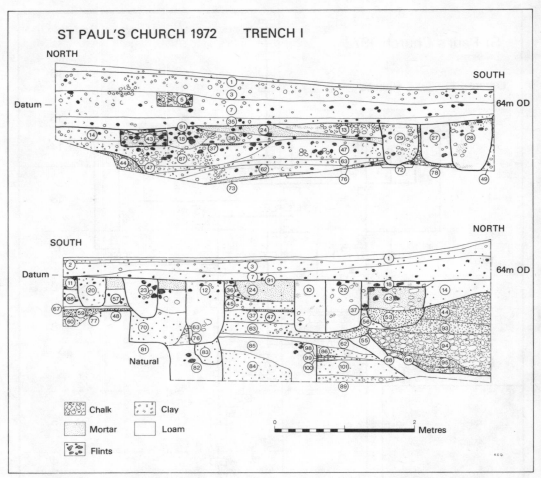

Fig. 116. St Paul's Church: main site sections. Top: east section. Bottom: west section.

of the cost of reinstating any deeper excavation. However, a deeper slot was cut along the west side of the trench to complete a section through the chalk bank of the suburban defences (Phase 5, below). The decayed upper surface of natural chalk was seen at 63·00 m O.D. near the southwest corner of the excavation (Layer 82, Fig. 116).

A smaller cutting, Trench II, was opened at the west end of the church hall, but was abandoned at a depth of about 0·3 m. The five layers recorded were of nineteenth- and twentieth-century date.

Figure 116 shows the stratigraphic relationships of all the layers excavated in Trench I, as stated in the site records. This layer complex has been divided into sixteen phases, separated by dotted lines on Figure 115, and described below. The interpretation of some phases should be regarded as tentative because of the small size of the area excavated. Similarly, the dates ascribed to most of the phases are based largely on the evidence of excavated pottery and should be regarded with caution for the reasons discussed below (p. 272) in the pottery report. The dating used in the following paragraphs is that suggested in the pottery report (Fig. 117).

A deposit of apparent occupation debris and chalk spreads comprises Phase 1. These layers were only seen along the west section and may in fact represent several phases of occupation. Similarly, Phase 2, consisting of four or possibly five graves, was seen only in the deeper slot along the west section of Trench I. Articulated inhumations were apparently noticed during excavation, but the graves were not fully exposed, nor was any significant skeletal material recovered.

Sealing the graves were construction layers related to an east—west wall, possibly of late eleventh-century date, comprising Phase 3. Built of flint and some chalk rubble set in mortar, this wall ran across the width of Trench I near the south section (Layers 48 and 72, Fig. 116).

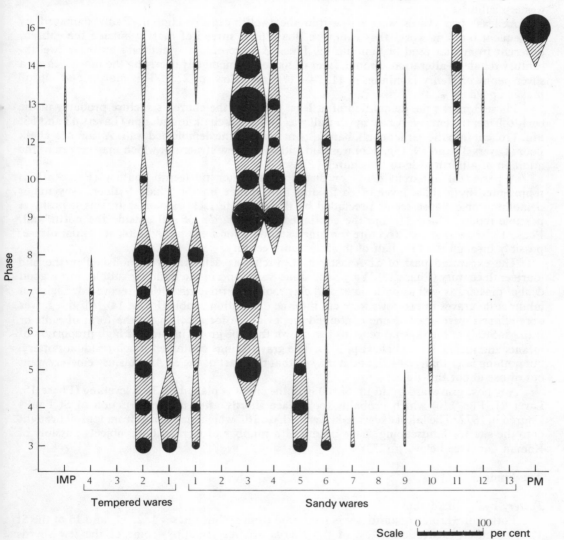

Fig. 117. St Paul's Church: Pottery fabric types by phase: interpretation.
Pots of each type are shown as a percentage of the
total number of pots in each phase.

The inside of the structure lay south of the wall, and therefore largely outside the area of excavation. Evidence for an undated internal alteration (Layer 77, Fig. 116) was found near the west section.

The top of a feature, possibly a ditch, cutting through the mortary layers of Phase 3 was excavated near the north end of Trench I and forms Phase 4 (Layer 68, Fig. 116). A substantial chalk bank (Phase 5) was thrown up over the dark earth which formed the upper filling of this feature. The bank was probably constructed in the twelfth century and, with a ditch which must lie beyond the excavated area to the north, formed the defences of the western suburb.

At least two graves were cut within the twelfth-century church. Badly damaged by subsequent building work, they comprise Phase 6. A spread of mortar outside the church, different from that used in building the Phase 3 structure, may indicate an early twelfth-century repair or alteration. From a layer of topsoil immediately overlying the mortar came a silver penny of Henry I, minted in 1131—4 (?) (see below, p. 273). This mortar and topsoil makes up Phase 7.

Phase 8 marks the demolition of at least a part of the church structure probably in the early thirteenth century. A new north wall was built on a chalk foundation (Layers 43 and 53, Fig. 116) cut into the earlier chalk bank, 3·4 m north of the demolished wall. A rammed chalk floor (Layers 37 and 59, Fig. 116) was laid within the new structure, which may represent the addition of a north aisle to the church (Phase 9).

A period of apparent decay or disuse in the later thirteenth century (Phase 10) is represented by a thick layer of earth and flint rubble on the Phase 9 floor. Any major demolition or collapse seems precluded by the complete lack of mortar in this deposit. A possible repair, Phase 11, and the continued accumulation of soil outside the north wall, Phase 12, show that the structure remained standing for some period after its initial disuse, possibly through the first half of the fourteenth century.

The excavated part of St Anastasius Church was deliberately demolished in the mid fourteenth century (Phase 13). Very little stone was found in the building rubble, but a good deal of plaster, as well as both slates and clay roof- and ridge-tiles, were recovered. Eighteen inhumation graves in two rows were cut into the demolition rubble (Phase 14). All the graves were aligned west—east. None contained any evidence for a coffin, in the form of nails or fittings. Study of the skeletal remains has shown that the group included a high proportion of infants and juveniles (see below, p. 277). The grave fillings contained much residual pottery, but nothing later than c. 1400, and it may be that this part of the St Anastasius cemetery went out of use about this time.

Any post-graveyard build-up of soil over the site was planed off in a levelling (Phase 15; Layer 91, Fig. 116) which probably took place shortly after the construction of St Paul's Church in 1872. The latest excavated layers (Phase 16), which may derive from topsoil brought onto the site for landscaping, have produced a number of worked bone objects possibly of Roman date (see below, p. 273).

The Finds

Pottery by J. Qualmann

Pottery in various quantities was recovered from all but Phases 1, 2, 11, and 15 of the St Paul's Church excavation. Most of the sherds are very scrappy; some of the few sherds indicative of vessel form have been illustrated (Fig. 118). No attempt has therefore been made to form a type-series based on shape. Instead, analysis has proceeded on the basis of fabric, with the presence or absence of glazing being treated as an element of the decoration.

Two sherds of grey ware from Phase 16 and a chip of samian from Phase 3 are the only Roman pottery from the site.

Seventeen post-medieval pottery types have been identified. The group derives entirely from Phase 16 and consists mainly of slip wares, chafing-dishes, and improved cream wares, with some stoneware, tin- and salt-glazed wares, and porcelain. These types have been grouped as 'PM' on Fig. 117, but will not be treated in detail in this report.

Imported pottery. Ten sherds of possible imported pottery have been found and are described below. They are grouped as 'IMP' on Fig. 117. I am grateful for Dr J. G. Hurst's comments on these sherds.

Phase	Museum Accession Number	Description
3	1597.49	Salmon-coloured fabric with small flint inclusions and brush-marked exterior; from the same pot as nos. 1597.48 and 1597.50.
4	1597.52	Early medieval sandy ware; probably not native to the Winchester area.
6	1597.47	Smooth, buff fabric with a partial pale green glazing on the exterior; probably French.
6	1597.48	Part of same pot as no. 1597.49.
9	1597.51	Two sherds of a Spanish water-jug.
12	1597.44	Pale buff fabric with an exterior glaze ranging from pale yellow to orange-brown; probably Rouen ware.
13	1597.45	Eggshell-coloured fabric with some small grits and a thick exterior glaze of pale green with some orange colour.
13	1597.46	Hard white fabric with a deep green, mottled exterior glaze; probably French.
14	1597.50	Part of no. 1597.49.

Local pottery. The remaining pottery, which represents the bulk of that excavated, has been divided into thirteen medieval sandy-ware (MS) fabrics and four medieval tempered (MT) or gritted wares.

Fabric	Description
MS 1	Fine sandy ware, sand 0·1 mm; flint up to 1·1 mm; chalk and grass inclusions; smoothed surface.
MS 2	Sandy ware with sand size varying from 0·1 mm—0·6 mm; uneven sand scatter.
MS 3	Medium-grained sandy ware; sand 0·3 mm; dense even sand scatter; surface not smoothed (Fig. 118:1 from Phase 7; Fig. 118:2 from Phase 9; Fig. 118:3 from Phase 13).
MS 4	Fine sandy ware, sand 0·1 mm—0·2 mm; even sand scatter; easily abraded.
MS 5	Coarse sandy ware, sand 0·3 mm; dense, even sand scatter (Fig. 118:4—5 from Phase 3; Fig. 118:6 from Phase 5).

Fabric	Description
MS 6	Porous sandy ware, sand 0·4 mm; often leached out; flint up to 3 mm and grass inclusions.
MS 7	Sandy ware, sand 0·5 mm; uneven sand scatter; grass-marked exterior surface (Fig. 118:7 from Phase 3).
MS 8	Sandy ware, sand 0·6 mm; even sand scatter.
MS 9	Soft, porous sandy ware, calcite sand 0·5 m; even sand scatter.
MS 10	Hard sandy ware, sand 0·2 mm—0·4 mm; uneven sand scatter (Fig. 118:8 from Phase 6).
MS 11	Very fine, brittle sandy ware; interior and exterior surfaces smoothed.
MS 12	Very soft, porous sandy ware, sand 0·1 mm—0·2 mm; some chalk inclusions up to 1·7 mm.
MS 13	Coarse sandy ware, sand 0·2 mm; flint 0·3 mm; and grass inclusions.
MT 1	Gritted ware, mainly flint with some chalk and iron; grit size varies from 0·2 mm—2 mm.
MT 2	Gritted ware, mainly flint with some chalk and iron; grit size varies from 0·3 mm—4 mm.
MT 3	Coarse gritted ware, mainly flint with some chalk; grit size varies from 0·1 mm—4 mm; uneven grit scatter; grit protrudes from surface.
MT 4	Gritted ware, mainly chalk; grit size varies from 3 mm—4 mm; much of grit leached out.

These fabrics are all known from previous excavations in Winchester, and intensive study of the development of medieval ceramics in the city is in progress (Barclay, forthcoming). The date-range of some of the fabrics recognized in the St Paul's Church material has been firmly established. With this information in mind, the distribution of fabrics by phase was analysed. The number of pots of each fabric was considered as a percentage of the total number of pots in the phase.

This analysis shows thirteenth-century pottery types (MS 4, for example) from the earliest period in which pottery was found, Phase 3. Later thirteenth-century types, such as MS 8, appear in Phase 6, with fourteenth-century material (MS 12) occurring in Phase 12. This would place the first excavated phase of the church, the filling of the Phase 4 ditch, and the construction of the Phase 5 bank in the early thirteenth century. While possible on historical grounds, this chronology is not entirely satisfactory, for most of the later fabric types appear distinctly out of place where they occur in early phases.

Relevant to this problem are repeated references to 'contamination' and 'difficulty in determining feature edges' in the site notebook, especially in relation to the excavation of the latest graves. It seems possible that the later grave-pits may have been incompletely excavated, resulting in the attribution of pottery from these features to earlier phases. This possibility is strengthened by the fact that those deposits most cut by graves have more sherds of later fabric types than those deposits, like the Phase 5 bank, cut only by one or two graves. An attempt has therefore been made to separate the possibly contaminating pottery from that which actually derives from a given deposit. While, in most cases, one or more pottery types appear distinctly as later intrusions in an otherwise earlier group, the following criteria have also been

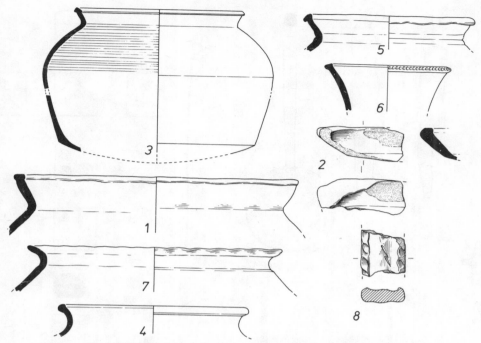

Fig. 118. St Paul's Church: pottery (scale ¼). See page 271—2.

employed: (1) indication of 'contamination' of deposits in the site notebook; (2) sherds of the same pot occurring in a deposit and in a later grave or feature cutting that deposit.

It has been possible in this way to suggest those fabrics which are out of context as recorded during excavation. An illustration, Figure 117, has been constructed to show the results of this interpretation. The chronology suggested by this interpretation of the ceramic evidence has been used in both the summary and excavation sections of this report (pp. 265—270 above), and would seem to tie in well with the historical background cited in the summary.

Silver Coin by C. E. Blunt

A silver penny found in Phase 7, 1597.63, C 1860. Henry I Pellets in quatrefoil penny of the London mint by the moneyer Wulfward.

> Obverse: HENRICUS REX ∴
> Reverse: +WULFWARD: ON: LUND
> Weight: 1·09 g (16·8 gr)
> Die-axis: 90°
> BMC type XIV (North 870)

The coin is exceptional in omitting the obverse initial cross and in reading REX with three pellets after. The type is thought to have been issued from *c.* 1131 to 1134.

Bone Objects and Bone-Working Waste by S. Keene, P. Sheppard, and G. Adams

Since the soil forming this deposit was brought in from an unknown source, in a landscaping exercise carried out in the late nineteenth century, it would seem probable that the objects from it are a haphazard collection covering many periods. It is therefore somewhat

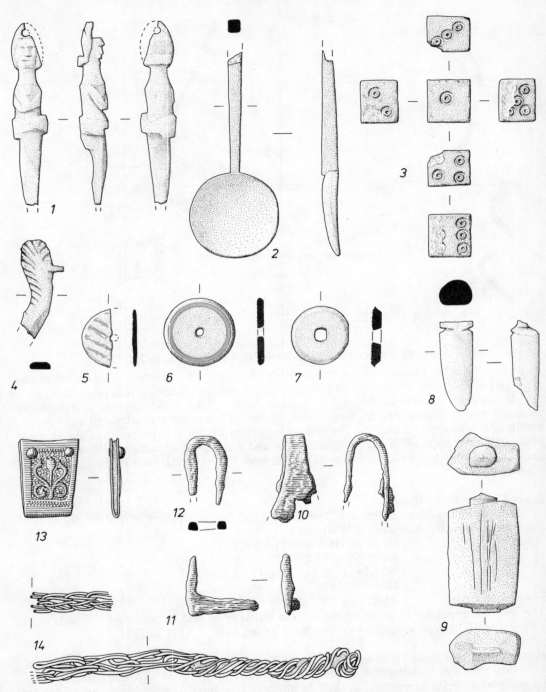

Fig. 119. St Paul's Church: worked bone and metalwork (scale 1/1).

Table 23. Bone objects from Phase 16.

Fig. No.	Museum Accession Number	Description
119:1	1597.18	Figurine, forming the top of a rough peg, possibly an unfinished pin. The female figure has a typically Roman hairstyle. Head and shoulders are shown. A hole runs through the top of the head. The peg is carved in such a way as to make any pin shaft impossibly thin. The piece is probably unfinished, or it might have been discarded because of a mistake made during carving. L 51 mm. Long bone shaft fragment, ox or horse size.
119:2	1597.5	Spoon. Shallow, roughly circular bowl with broken handle. The handle, which has a rectangular section, terminates in a neat point where it joins the back of the bowl. This type of round-bowled spoon is common on Roman sites of 1st- to 4th-century dates. L 56 mm. Ivory.
119:3	1597.4	Die. The '4' side opposes the '3' side, the '5' side opposes the '2' side, the '6' side opposes the '1' side. Sides of 9—12 mm. Ox/horse size bone. Undatable.
119:4	1597.49	Fragment of decorative carving. Flat curved piece broken off a larger object, with oblique cuts giving a fringed or feathered appearance. Could be an animal tail, or a wing. L 28 mm. Unidentifiable bone. Undatable, but perhaps Roman or Anglo-Saxon.
119:5	1597.7	Button. Half of a flat disc with a very small central hole, decorated with five groups of lines, all parallel. D 16 mm; D of hole 0·5 mm. Possibly ox rib.
119:6	1597.8	Button. Surface marks show that this was made by turning. Four parallel scratches may be an attempt at decoration. D 19 mm; D of hole 1·5 mm. Possibly ox rib.
119:7	1597.12	Button. Flat disc with central hole and scribed groove around the extreme outer edge, forming a bevel. D 16 mm; D of hole 3 mm. From large rib.
119:8	1597.44	Bone working waste. Cylindrical piece with rectangular stump. L 25 mm.
119:9	1597.32	Bone working waste. Segment of long bone shaft with medulla visible down one side. Round stub at one end, rectangular at the other. L 33 mm.

surprising that at least some of the bone finds appear to form a coherent group.

Two of the objects are datable on stylistic grounds: the peg or unfinished pin (Fig. 119:1), which has a head in the form of a female figure with a Roman hairstyle; and the small bone spoon (Fig. 119:2), another Roman piece, of a type commonly found on sites dating from the first to the fourth centuries A.D. The die (Fig. 119:3) could be of any period from Roman to late medieval. The decorative fragment (Fig. 119:4) is also undatable, though from its appearance and the technique with which it has been worked it could well be Roman and is probably not later than the Anglo-Saxon period. Discs with central holes (possibly buttons) such as the three in this group (Fig. 119:5—7) do not seem to be particularly common. In the collections of the Winchester Excavations Committee there is only one similar object, from a second-century context.

The bone-working waste falls into three categories:

(1) Sixteen roughly cylindrical or rectangular fragments are from 11 to 51 mm long and from 11 to 22 mm wide with broken stubs at one or both ends, and have been cut from the thickest parts of ox and horse long-bone shafts. Thirteen of these are from ox metacarpal or metatarsal, and two from other long-bone shafts. A similar piece has been cut from a deer antler tip, and a small fragment of the posterior surface of an ox metapodial which includes the nutrient foramen (natural hole in the bone) seems to have been used as a peg hole. All could have been used as support pegs in the carving of small objects.

(2) Four cut pieces from large ribs probably represent bone discarded and wasted in button making; twelve unidentifiable worked fragments and thin slivers of pared bone may represent the residue left after carving the pegged pieces.

(3) Finally, there are the remains of bones which have been sawn. Four fragments of proximal ox metatarsal have been sawn across the shafts at points between 27 mm and 53 mm below the articular surface, and part of an ox distal humerus has been sawn vertically through the capitellum, providing enough thickness of bone for carving a small die.

The objects themselves are described in Table 23. They are fairly commonplace, but the presence of bone-working waste in the deposit gives the assemblage an intriguing aspect. It is possible that the soil came from a limited area, and that the finds are actually part of the debris from a bone workshop. It surely cannot be chance that so many pieces of bone-working waste are present, but are the objects, or some of them, also products of this workshop, or is their presence fortuitous? The small figurine-topped peg would seem to be the most likely workshop product, in view of the rough, unfinished nature of the 'peg', and this would suggest a Roman date for the workshop if, indeed, the finished piece and the waste derive from the same original context.

Metalwork by D. A. Hinton

Fig. No.	Phase	Museum Accession Number	Description
Iron Objects			
—	16	1597.28	Iron buckle; single loop, rectangular with roller bar; for harness or costume.
—	16	1597.33	Part of an iron strip with nail-holes.
—	14	1597.14	Bent iron object, possibly a hook.
119:10	8	1597.66	Iron hinge loop or staple.
119:11	4	1597.67	Iron hook or hinge pivot, for door, etc.
119:12	4	1597.68	Iron hinge loop or staple, for use on door pivot, as last.
Bronze Objects			
—	16	1597.31	Probably part of a rectangular bronze buckle-loop.
119:13	14	1597.39	Strap-end. Strip bent over to form back plate and secured by two dome-headed rivets. Back is undecorated; sub-rectangular front contains panel with symmetrical plant design in relief against

Fig. No.	Phase	Museum Accession Number	Description
			punched background. Bronze gilt. Plant pattern is stylistically close to balanced acanthus leaf designs on such objects as the Southampton mount (Addyman and Hill 1969). Wilson has recently related this to the attenuated tendrils of New Minster Charter (Wilson 1975), and a date in late 10th or early 11th century seems appropriate. An example of the so-called 'Winchester style' adapted to a small, everyday metalwork object.
—	12	1597.12	Part of rectangular bronze strip with rivet-holes along sides.
119:14	4	1597.65	Length of bronze chain, formed by three-loop French knitting, one end tightly twisted, the other broken. Closest parallels are of late medieval date (e.g. the 16th century object in Platt and Coleman-Smith 1975: Fig. 243:179), but the 9th-century silver scourge from Trewhiddle (Wilson and Blunt 1961:92-3) might be comparable.

Osteological Report by G. Adams and P. Sheppard

Both human and animal bones are present in most phases from the St Paul's Church site. The human bones must certainly derive from the use of the site as a burial ground (as identified in Phases 2, 6, and 7), the distribution of human skeletal material in non-cemetery phases indicating disturbance of early graves by building works and later grave digging. The animal bones can all be interpreted as domestic food residue derived either from pre-ecclesiastical use of the site (possibly Phase 1), or resulting from lateral spread from adjacent, re-deposited occupation debris, though this seems less likely. Phase 16 includes a number of fragments of roughly worked animal bone, as well as several bone objects and rough-outs (Fig. 119).

Human bones. No articulated skeletal remains were recovered from Phase 2, the earliest excavated cemetery phase, as investigation of the features interpreted as grave-pits was not completed. Fragments of a single adult were found in fill layers from this period. Similarly, disarticulated bones representing one adult were found in Phase 3, and material from one adult and one infant in Phase 5.

Part of a single adult skeleton (Grave 28, Layers 52 and 80) was recovered from Phase 6, which represents burial within the twelfth century church. Probably male, the skeleton had an almost edentulus mandible, only the right canine and premolar remaining, and worn halfway to the roots. Scattered human bones representing two adults and one juvenile were found in other layers from this phase.

Articulated remains of nineteen individuals were recovered from the major cemetery period (Phase 14). Full details of the skeletal remains have been deposited, with the site records, in Winchester City Museum.

Although this small number of burials cannot be used for statistical purposes, it is of interest to note that two-thirds of the individuals died before the age of twenty-one, the greatest number between the ages of ten and twenty years. Three out of four juveniles had dental caries and dental abscesses were common amongst the adults. Many of the teeth were heavily worn, indicating a rough diet. Statures (estimated on the formula for females given by Trotter and Gleser 1952, and for males on the revised formula by Cullen 1958) varied from approximately 153 cm to 176 cm. Sex determination was possible for ten individuals: six males and two probable males; one female and one probable female.

The disarticulated fragments of human bone identified from all phases represent a minimum of ten further individuals: one infant, three juveniles, and six adults.

Animal bones. The faunal remains consist of a mixture of sheep, cattle, and pig bones from most phases, with a few bird, fish, and small mammal bones. All the bones were in a fragmentary state, very few being measurable. The minimum number of individuals represented (Chaplin 1971) and age-at-death were calculated for each phase. This information has been deposited with the site records. The age groups of the animal bones were classified according to Silver's data (Silver 1969:26), although the actual ages in years have not been given because of the wide variation in maturation dates between improved and unimproved stock. Aging by teeth has not been attempted in this report because so few teeth were found still in the jaw. The state of fusion of the immature bones indicates that most of the animals were killed between the ages of eighteen months and three and a half years, that is, killed in their prime. Lambs were the only very young animals found.

Signs of butchery were found on many of the bones, especially the ribs and vertebrae, the latter frequently being chopped through the long axis of the body. One pig atlas (first cervical vertebra) was chopped transversely, probably to separate the head from the neck. Most of the bones come from the main meat-producing regions of the body, that is, the scapulo-humeral, pelvic-femoral, ribs, and vertebrae.

Sheep provide the greatest number of bones and individuals represented. None of the bones could be attributed to goat. The only complete bones were first phalanges. The bones of possibly one individual from Phase 16 were larger than any others, but this phase also contained bones of the same or smaller size than those from previous phases. The main areas of butchery were situated around the elbow joint, through the median plane of vertebrae, and at the ribs.

Although there were fewer bones of cattle than sheep found in most phases, this is balanced by the probability that the weight of an ox carcase is the equivalent of at least ten sheep carcases, so that no real preference for sheep is shown. A few signs of butchery were found: three scapulae had marks of cutting on the posterior border of the blade; one innominate was chopped through the acetabulum; two metatarsals were chopped above the distal epiphyseal line; several ribs were chopped; and there were some hacked long bone fragments.

Bones of pig were present in small quantities. Very few were measurable and the majority were from juvenile or immature animals. All parts of the body were represented. One scapula was chopped across the neck and three talocalcaneal joints were chopped transversely.

Although remains of birds (identified by J. Coy) were not numerous on this site, domestic fowl bones were found throughout almost all the phases, the upper legs and wings being the most frequent, and both mature and immature individuals being represented. Three proximal humeri showed a wide variation in size. Goose bones were the second most frequent occurrence — at least three individuals were recognized by the same bone (metacarpus) in three different deposits. Wild birds were represented by the humerus of a crow, *Corvus corone* sp., from Phase 3, the metacarpus of a cormorant, *Phalacrocorax carbo,* from Phase 13, and the humerus of a teal, *Anas crecca,* in Phase 9.

The following species of fish (identified by A. Wheeler) were found to be present:
Phase 3:   Plaice, *Pleuronectes platessa.*

Phase 4:   Gadoid, Cod (?), *Gadus morhua.*
Phase 8:   Conger, *Conger conger.*
Phase 12:   Salmon, *Salmo salar.*

Small mammals were represented by only six bones of the following animals:

Phase 6:   One acetabular fragment of the
                  innominate bone, hare, *Lepus* sp.
Phase 14:   One tibia, hare, *Lepus* sp.
Phase 16:   The ulna, femur, tibia and calcaneum
                  of a rabbit, *Oryctolagus cuniculus.*

Assuming that the proportion of meat bearing bones (forelimb: scapula to distal radius; hindlimb: innominate to distal tibia) to waste bones in the abaxial skeleton is 1 to 4, there are 7 times as many meat-bearing as waste bones from Phases 2 to 13, even without taking into account the long-bone fragments which represent shaft fragments of scapula, humerus, and femur. This preponderance of meat-bearing bones from young age ranges of domestic species, together with the ribs and vertebrae, and the fish and bird remains suggests mainly domestic refuse from a varied and good quality diet.

A minimum number of individuals ranging between one and four was recorded for each species in each phase. The total number of bones identified as to species produced almost the same minimum numbers for all phases, except phase 16.

In view of (1) the fragmentary nature of the animal bones, (2) the relatively even distribution through all phases, and (3) the evidence of re-deposited human bone mentioned previously (p. 277), it is concluded that the animal bones represent a residual deposit derived from domestic occupation either earlier than the excavated deposits or possibly lying outside the area of excavation.

BIBLIOGRAPHY

Addyman, P. and Hill, D. (1969) Saxon Southampton: a review of the evidence. *PHFC* **26,** 61—96.

Atkinson, T. (1963) *Elizabethan Winchester.* London.

Baigent, F. W. (1865) *The History and Antiquities of the Parish Church of Wyke near Winchester.* Winchester.

Barclay, K. A. (forthcoming) Ceramics. In *The Crafts and Industries of Medieval Winchester,* ed. M. Biddle. *Winchester Studies* **7.**

Bennet-Clark, M. A. (1954) Excavation at Middle Brook Street, Winchester 1953. *PHFC* **18-3,** 3—12.

Biddle, M. (1964) Excavations at Winchester 1962—3: second interim report. *Ant. J.* **44,** 188—219.

Biddle, M. (1965) Excavations at Winchester 1964: third interim report. *Ant. J.* **45,** 230—264.

Biddle, M. (1966) Excavations at Winchester 1965: fourth interim report. *Ant. J.* **46,** 308—332.

Biddle, M. (1967a) Excavations at Winchester 1966: fifth interim report. *Ant. J.* **47,** 251—279.

Biddle, M. (1967b) Two Flavian burials from Grange Road, Winchester. *Ant. J.* **47,** 224—250.

Biddle, M. (1968) Excavations at Winchester 1967: sixth interim report. *Ant. J.* **48,** 250—284.

Biddle, M. (1969) Excavations at Winchester 1968: seventh interim report. *Ant. J.* **49,** 295—329.

Biddle, M. (1970) Excavations at Winchester 1969: eighth interim report. *Ant. J.* **50,** 277—326.

Biddle, M. (1972) Excavations in Winchester 1970: ninth interim report. *Ant. J.* **52,** 93—131.

Biddle, M. (1973) Winchester: the development of an early capital. In *Vor- und Frühformen der europäischen Stadt im Mittelalter,* ed. H. Jankuhn, W. Schlesinger and H. Stewer, pp 229—261. Göttingen.

Biddle, M. (1975a) Excavations at Winchester 1971: tenth and final interim report. *Ant. J.* **55,** 96—126, 295—337.

Biddle, M. (1975b) Ptolemaic coins from Winchester. *Antiquity* **49,** 213—215.

Biddle, M., ed. (1977) *Winchester in the Early Medieval Ages: an edition and discussion of the Winton Domesday. Winchester Studies* **1.**

Biddle, M. and Barclay, K. (1974) Winchester Ware. In *Medieval Pottery from Excavations,* ed. V. I. Evision, H. Hodges and J. C. Hurst, pp 137—165. London.

Biddle, M. and Collis, J. R. (forthcoming) A new type of ninth and tenth century pottery from Winchester. *Medieval Archaeology.*

Biddle, M. and Hill, D. (1971) Late Saxon planned towns. *Ant. J.* **51,** 70—85.

Biddle, M. and Quirk, R. N. (1962) Excavations near Winchester Cathedral, 1961. *Arch. J.* **119,** 150—194.

Blegen, C. W., ed. (1950) *Troy, Vol. I.* Princeton.

Borg, A. (1967) The development of chevron ornament. *Journal of the British Archaeological Association,* 3rd series, **30,** 122—140.

Brailsford, J. W. (1958) *Guide to the Antiquities of Roman Britain.* British Museum.

Brown, B. J. W., *et al.* (1954) Excavations at Grimstone End, Pakenham. *Proceedings of the Suffolk Institute of Archaeology* **26,** 189—207.

Bushe-Fox, J. P. (1949) *Fourth Report on the Excavations of the Roman Fort at Richborough, Kent. Reports of the Research Committee of the Society of Antiquaries* **16.**

Butcher, S. (1955) Excavations in St George's Street, Winchester 1954. *PHFC* **19-1,** 2—12.

Carson, R. A. G., Hill, P. V. and Kent, J. P. C. (1972) *Late Roman Bronze Coinage A.D. 329—498.* London.

Chaplin, R. (1971) *The Study of Animal Bones from Archaeological Sites.* London.

Charlesworth, D. (1959) Roman glass in northern Britain. *Archaeologia Aeliana,* 4th series, **37,** 54.

Charlesworth, D. (1965) Glass from Pompeii in Alnwick Castle Museum. *Archaeologia Aeliana,* 4th series, **43,** 233—234.

Clarke, D. L. (1970) *Beaker Pottery of Great Britain and Ireland.* London.

Collis, J. R. (1968) Excavations at Owslebury, Hants: an interim report. *Ant. J.* **48,** 18—31.

Collis, J. R. (1970) Excavations at Owslebury, Hants: a second interim report. *Ant. J.* **50,** 246—261.

Collis, J. R. (1971) Functional and theoretical interpretations of British coinage. *World Archaeology* **3,** 71—84.

Collis, J. R. (1974) *Oppida: The Beginnings of Urbanisation in Temperate Europe.* Ph.D. Thesis, Cambridge University.

Collis, J. R. (1975) The coin of Ptolomey V from Winchester. *Antiquity* **49,** 47—48.

Collis, J. R. (1977a) An approach to the Iron Age. In *The Iron Age of Britain: a Review,* ed. J. R. Collis, pp. 1—7.

Collis, J. R. (1977b) Owslebury and the problem of rural settlements. In *Burial in the Roman World,* ed. R. Reece, pp. 26—34.

Collis, J. R. (1977c) The Roman burial from Crab Wood, Winchester. *PHFC,* **33,** 69—72.

Collis, J. R. (forthcoming) Excavations at Silchester, Hants, 1968. *Report submitted to the Department of the Environment, 1976.*

Collis, J. R. and Kjølbye-Biddle, B. (forthcoming) Early medieval bone spoons from Winchester.

Cotton, M. A. and Gathercole, P. W. (1958) *Excavations at Clausentum, Southampton 1951—1954.* London.

Cullen, R. (1958) A re-evaluation of estimation of stature based on measurements of stature taken during life and of long bones after death. *American Journal of Physical Anthropology,* n.s., **16,** 79—123.

Cunliffe, B. (1962) The Winchester city wall. *PHFC* **22-2,** 51—81.

Cunliffe, B. (1964) *Winchester Excavations 1949—1960, Volume I.* Winchester.

Cunliffe, B. (1974) *Iron Age Communities in Britain.* London.

Down, A. and Rule, M. (1971) *Chichester Excavations I.* Chichester.

Dunning, G. C. (1960) Early Norman pottery from recent excavations in Winchester. *PHFC* **21-3,** 134—144.

Frere, S. S. (1972) *Verulamium Excavations Vol. 1. Reports of the Research Committee of the Society of Antiquaries* **28.**

Harden, D. B. (1947) The glass. In *Camulodunum* by C. F. C. Hawkes and M. R. Hull, in *Reports of the Research Committee of the Society of Antiquaries* **14.**

Harden, D. B. (1962) Glass in Roman York. In *Eburacum-Roman York,* Royal Commission on Historical Monuments.

Hawkes, C. F. C. and Hull, M. R. (1947) *Camulodunum. Reports of the Research Committee of the Society of Antiquaries* 14.

Hawkes, C. F. C., Myres, J. N. L. and Stevens, C. E. (1930) St Catharine's Hill, Winchester. *PHFC* 11.

Hawkes, S. C. (1969) Finds from two Middle Bronze Age pits at Winnall, Winchester, Hampshire. *PHFC* 26, 5—18.

Haverfield, F. (1900) Romano-British remains. *Victoria County History of Hampshire* 1, 265—349.

Hedges, J. W. (1973) *Textiles and Textile Production in Prehistoric Britain.* M. A. Thesis, Sheffield University.

Hedges, J. W. (forthcoming) The textiles. In *The Archaeology of York. Vol. 17,* ed. P. V. Addyman. York: York Archaeological Trust.

Heiss, A. (1870) *Description Générale des Monnaies Antiques de l'Espagne.* Paris.

Hermet, F. (1934) *La Graufesenque II.* Paris.

Hoffman, M. (1964) *The Warp-Weighted Loom.* Kragerø, Norway.

Hooley, R. W. (1929) Excavation of an Early Iron Age village on Worthy Down, Winchester. *PHFC* 10, 178—192.

Isings, C. (1957) *Roman Glass from Dated Finds.* Groningen.

Isings, C. (1971) *Roman Glass in Limburg.* Groningen.

Jackson, D. A., *et al.* (1969) The Iron Age and Anglo-Saxon site at Upton, Northants. *Ant. J.* 49, 202—221.

Kenyon, K. (1948) *Excavations at the Jewry Wall Site, Leicester. Reports of the Research Committee of the Society of Antiquaries* 15.

London Museum (1940) *Medieval Catalogue. London Museum Catalogues* 7.

Mattingly, H., *et al.,* eds. (1923—1967) *Roman Imperial Coinage.* Vols. 1—7, 9. London.

May, T. (1930) *Catalogue of the Roman Pottery in the Colchester and Essex Museums.* Cambridge.

Meaney, A. L. and Hawkes, S. C. (1970) *Two Anglo-Saxon Cemeteries at Winnall. Society for Medieval Archaeology,* Monograph series 4.

Milner, J. (1839) *The History and Survey of the Antiquities of Winchester* (3rd edition). Winchester.

Murray Threipland, L. (1966) Excavations at Caerleon 1966 — barracks in the north corner. *Archaeologia Cambrensis* 116, 48.

Ordnance Survey (1962) *Map of Southern Britain in the Iron Age.* Chessington.

Peacock, D. P. S. (1969) A contribution to the study of Glastonbury ware from south-western Britain. *Ant. J.* 49, 41—61.

Platt, C. and Coleman-Smith, R. (1975) *Excavations in Medieval Southampton 1953—1969. Vol. 2, The Finds.* Leicester.

Rogers, G. B. (1974) *Poteries Sigillées de la Gaule Centrale. Gallia* Supplément 28.

Silver, I. A. (1969) The ageing of domestic animals. In *Science in Archaeology,* 2nd edition, ed. D. Brothwell and E. S. Higgs, pp 283—302. London.

Stanfield, J. A. and Simpson, G. (1958) *Central Gaulish Potters.* London.

Stuart, J. D. M. and Birkbeck, J. M. (1936) A Celtic village on Twyford Down. *PHFC* 13, 118—207.

Sumner, H. (1927) *Excavations in New Forest Roman Pottery Sites.* London.

Terrisse, J.-R. (1968) *Les Ceramiques Sigillées Gallo-Romaine des Martres-de-Veyre. Gallia,* Supplément 19.

Trotter, M. and Gleser, G. (1952) Estimation of stature from long bones of American Whites and Negroes. *American Journal of Physical Anthropology,* n.s., **10,** 463—514.

Wacher, J. S. (1962) Cirencester 1961: second interim report. *Ant. J.* **42,** 1—14.

Wacher, J. S. (1974) *The Towns of Roman Britain.* London.

West, S. E. (1969) The Anglo-Saxon village of West Stow. An interim report of the excavations 1965—8. *Medieval Archaeology* **13,** 1—20.

Wheeler, R. E. M. (1928) *London (Roman).* Royal Commission on Historical Monuments.

Wilson, D. M. (1975) Tenth-century metal work. In *Tenth Century Studies,* ed. D. Parsons, pp 200—207. Leicester.

Wilson, D. M. and Blunt, C. E. (1961) The Trewhiddle hoard. *Archaeologia* **98,** 75—122.

Wilson, D. R. (1973) Roman Britain in 1972. I: Sites explored. *Britannia* **4,** 271—323.

Index

Ia. Back Street, St Cross: line of loom-weights F10 *in situ* (PWCM 458).

Ib. Winnall Housing Estate: the Iron Age ditch F17, scale in feet (PWCM 792).

IIa. Water Lane: general view of the site. The Roman tank is in front of the standing figure in the centre of the photograph (PWCM 898).

IIb. Water Lane: Roman stone tank F4 (PWCM 467).

IIIa. 82 Hyde Street: carved stone 720/1 from F5 (Courtauld Institute of Art A74/86, PWCM 5450).

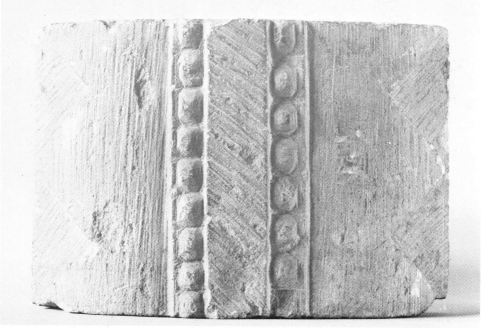

IIIb. 82 Hyde Street: carved stone 720/2 from F5 (Courtauld Institute of Art A74/86, PWCM 5451).

IVa. Easton Water-Main Trench: sarsen, F1, in Edington Road (PWCM 413).

IVb. Westgate Car Park: general view from the south (PWCM 408).